CW00362023

rethinking

social

theory

rethinking
social
theory

Roger Sibeon

SAGE Publications
London • Thousand Oaks • New Delhi

© Roger Sibeon 2004

All rights reserved. No part of this publication may be
reproduced, stored in a retrieval system, transmitted or
utilised in any form or by any means, electronic, mechanical,
photocopying, recording or otherwise,
without permission in writing from the Publishers.

SAGE Publications Ltd
1 Oliver's Yard
55 City Road
London EC1Y 1SP

SAGE Publications Inc
2455 Teller Road
Thousand Oaks, California 91320

SAGE Publications India Pvt Ltd
B-42, Panchsheel Enclave
Post Box 4109
New Delhi 100 017

British Library Cataloguing in Publication data

A catalogue record for this book is available
from the British Library

ISBN 0 7619 5068 0
ISBN 0 7619 5069 9

Library of Congress control number available

Typeset by C&M Digitals (P) Ltd., Chennai, India
Printed and bound in Great Britain by Athenaeum Press, Gateshead

Contents

Preface   vii

Introduction: the Legacy of Four Cardinal Sins   1

1   Metatheoretical Preliminaries   12

2   Agency–Structure and Micro–Macro   34

3   Links Between Theoretical Approaches   60

4   Three Major Contributors to Contemporary
    Sociological Theory: Archer, Mouzelis and Layder   96

5   Social Action, Power and Interests   117

6   Spatial Dimensions of the Social   153

7   Towards an Integrated Metatheoretical
    and Methodological Framework   171

8   Conclusion   195

References   204

Index   222

Preface

Although this is not a text for beginners, it is hoped not only academics but advanced undergraduate and graduate students will wish to engage with the ideas set out in the following pages. Readers will encounter exposition and critique of contemporary theoretical problems and approaches, and be invited to form a personal judgement about the author's proposals for the future development of theoretical sociology. The contents and design of the chapters, and of the notes that follow each chapter, have two principal objectives. With reference to key problems and themes in social theory and, to some extent, in the social sciences generally, the intention is, first, to critically review a range of mainly contemporary theoretical and other materials that are not currently available in one book, and second, to offer a contribution to the development of social theory and to the theoretical development of sociology. With these objectives in mind it is proposed to engage in a critique of four long-standing deficient modes of social scientific thought – reductionism, essentialism, reification and functional teleology – and to develop, in part on the basis of theoretical synthesis allied to sustained critique of these four defective forms of theoretical-methodological reasoning, a set of interrelated concepts that refer, in particular, to agency–structure and social chance, and to time–space and micro–macro. The concepts and supporting ontological arguments are brought together to form an integrated theoretical and methodological framework, elements of which figure in each chapter; an overview of the framework is provided in the final chapter.

Three additional features of the book should be mentioned here. First, although concerned with social theory and in particular, sociological theory, reference will be made throughout to policy-related illustrations and applications of theoretical constructs; this will help clarify what are inevitably rather abstract ideas, and will serve also to make the point that social theory and theoretical sociology are relevant to empirical work, including analyses of governance, politics and public policy in (post)modern society. Second, with reference to the relatively recent movement towards a 'return' to sociological theory (Mouzelis, 1991; McLennan, 1995) in the aftermath of postmodern and other rejections of social science knowledge, it is intended that the book should help stimulate a climate of renewed interest in theoretical sociology while also, as stated earlier, providing a contribution to the development of sociology as an academic discipline. Third, there is no necessary antithesis between, on the one hand, an enthusiasm for sociology and, on the other, recognition of the importance of developments in other social sciences. A theme that permeates most of the chapters is that it is desirable that there should be dialogue between theorists from different disciplines and among interdisciplinary scholars; interdisciplinary work is capable of enhancing social science's explanatory powers while also contributing to the theoretical and methodological development of individual disciplines, including sociology.

Rethinking Social Theory is, then, primarily addressed to scholars and advanced students in social theory and in sociology, though it is anticipated that some of the concepts and concerns discussed in the book will also be of interest to readers whose main disciplines are, for example, political science, policy studies and social geography, as well as those whose social science commitments include interdisciplinary activities.

Introduction

The Legacy of Four Cardinal Sins

Criticisms of sociology's explanatory and emancipatory failures took a fashionable but often theoretically crude turn (Strinati, 1993) in the 1980s when a number of writers – including postmodern critics such as Baudrillard (1983: 4) and others who will be referred to in the following chapter – rejected efforts to further the intellectual development of sociology as an academic discipline; it was argued that any such efforts are misplaced, and to some it seemed that the future of the discipline itself was in doubt. In a paper entitled 'The collapse of British sociology?', Philip Abrams (1981: 53) reported a sense that sociology in Britain was facing 'impending disaster' and that 'we might ... expect to see a withering away of sociology before too long'. Some years previously, Horowitz (1964: 3) had claimed that sociology in the 1940s and 1950s had degenerated into what he described as a cul de sac. In his *The Coming Crisis of Western Sociology* (1971) Gouldner had forecast a distinctly gloomy picture, as did Seidman a quarter of a century later; Seidman argued that sociology, particularly sociological theory, was on the edge of a major crisis (1994: 2). As Bottomore (1984: 12) has observed, the history of sociology is littered with pronouncements that the discipline is 'in crisis' and on the brink of terminal decline. Mostly, these predate the postmodern genre (Smart, 1990: 397). On the whole, such claims tend to be overdone. Undoubtedly, contemporary theoretical sociology has been in the doldrums (see Gibbs, 1989: 11; White, 1992: 3; Holmwood, 1996: 1–3). A factor in this state of affairs was noted by May (1993: 558): 'the modernity/postmodernity debate ... has currently ground to a halt'. But even if May's judgement, a judgement which writers such as, for example, Turner

(1994) have challenged, is accepted as accurate, this does not signal the end of sociology. To the contrary, there are grounds for feeling confident about the future of the discipline. The situation of sociology has changed for the better (Bryant, 1995: 156) since the early 1980s when Abrams had spoken of a 'withering away' of the discipline.[1] At the present time, despite undoubted difficulties, a major drive towards a post-postmodern 'return' to sociological theory and method (McLennan, 1995) seems both feasible and desirable (Archer, 1995; 2000; Mouzelis, 1995; Stones, 1996; Ritzer, 2000; Turner and Rojek, 2001).

Leaving aside for a moment the question of whether the term 'crisis' tends to be overused, it can be argued that many of sociology's undoubted problems of theory and of explanatory failure – as well as problems in general social theory – have been associated with an unfortunate tendency to draw, explicitly or not, upon one or more of four long-standing forms of deficient reasoning that in various ways continue to plague social theory and the social sciences; these four 'cardinal sins'[2] are reductionism, essentialism, reification and functional teleology in the specific terms that they are defined below.[3]

Reductionism

A *reductionist* theory is one that illegitimately attempts to reduce the complexities of social life to a single, unifying principle of explanation or analytical prime mover (Hindess, 1986a; 1988) such as 'the interests of capitalism', 'patriarchy', 'rational choice', 'the risk society', 'trust', 'the information society', 'globalization', or whatever. For example, in accounts of government and the policy process, conventional theories of the state (theories such as pluralism, elitism, corporatism, or Marxism) are reductionist in so far as each of them is predicated on the view that government and public policy can be reduced to a single substantive principle of explanation. A feature of reductionist, general theories of this kind is their ontological inflexibility; each of the theories rests on a priori assumptions about the nature of the state and of society in regard to factors affecting the distribution of power, and in regard to the nature of political and policy dynamics. A more adequate and empirically sensitive form of enquiry would recognize that some policy sectors (education, health, foreign policy, agriculture, trade and industry, social services, and so on) may be pluralist whereas others are dominated by policy networks that have an elitist or corporatist form; moreover, power distributions and policy dynamics within each sector may shift over time, or at any given moment in time they may vary spatially (James, 1997). Thus in the present example we may conclude that rather than employ any of the above reductionist theories of the state, a better understanding of the complexities of politics, power, and public policy is likely to be gained through the use of non-reductionist, ontologically flexible methods of investigation such as, for example, policy network analysis (Rhodes, 1997; Marsh, 1998; Marsh and Smith, 2000) which is a contemporary political science approach that will be referred to in various places throughout the book. Arising from these remarks, three general aspects of anti-reductionism should be clarified at the outset. First, to reject a priori theoretical commitment to analytical prime movers is not to say there are never situations where a very small number of factors (or perhaps only one) may have causal primacy; this, however, should be treated as an empirical question rather than as something that, in advance of empirical enquiry, is theoretically predetermined on the basis of some reductionist social theory. Relatedly, it is not suggested that a substantive theory should, in 'grand theory' fashion,[4] attempt to encompass all the possible factors that may shape the phenomena under investigation; every worthwhile substantive theory is partial in terms of the type and number of phenomena to be explained and the range of explanatory variables addressed (Sibeon, 1999a). Second, there is a difference between non-reductive multi-factorial explanation, and what I term 'compounded reductionism'. The latter involves attempts to combine or synthesize two or more reductionisms (which by definition are mutually exclusive); attempts such as Dominelli's (1997) to combine two or more reductionist theories (of capitalism and of patriarchy, for example), result in theoretical contradiction and explanatory failure (a policy-related discussion of this is found in Sibeon, 1999c). Third, care should be taken to avoid what I term 'deferred reductionism'. This takes an Althusserian-like form where reductionist explanation is not removed from social analysis, but rather, is postponed or deferred until 'the last instance': straightforward or 'obvious' reductionism is replaced by a seemingly non-reductionist and multi-factorial approach that, however, turns out to have a single-order, reductionist theory at its base. An example is Farganis's feminist critique of postmodern theory. Farganis acknowledges that social class, age, ethnicity, and sexuality are important dimensions of social existence, but then goes on to argue that, in the final analysis ('in the last instance'), it will always be the case that gender is the ultimate or primary axis of social life (1994: 15–16). Another example is Harvey's attempt to blend Marxism with postmodernism: despite his postmodern-sounding caveats that refer to contingency and multidimensionality, it is clear that for Harvey the social is animated by a 'prime mover', namely, the mode of production (1989: 107) and what Harvey regards as its 'characteristic' pattern of social relations (1990: 418).

Essentialism

Essentialism is a form of theorizing that in a prioristic fashion presupposes a unity or homogeneity of social phenomena, such as the law or some other social institution, or taxonomic collectivities such as 'women', 'men', 'the working class', 'black people', or 'white people'. While it is inescapable that we have to engage in a certain amount of hypostatization and idealization of phenomena in order to be able to refer to them at all, we should not falsely essentialize them or theoretically ascribe to them more homogeneity than they actually possess. Essentialist reasoning does not regard the degree of homogeneity or heterogeneity of social phenomena as an empirical variable for investigation, but rather, presupposes on theoretical or political grounds[5] a 'necessary' unitaryness of the phenomena in question; see, for instance, Albrow's useful criticisms (1996: 91–2, 94–5) of essentialist notions of 'globalization'. Very often, essentialist thinking is linked to or is a corollary of a reductionist theory (indeed, it tends to be reductionism that underpins or nurtures the other illicit forms of reasoning identified in this introductory chapter); and like reductionism, essentialism sometimes takes a disguised, tacit or 'last instance' form, as when, say, 'the working class' or 'women' are said to be social categories that, though perhaps acknowledged to be in some respects internally divided and cross-related to other categories, should nevertheless be regarded, for theoretical or political reasons, as ultimately possessing a primary, overriding commonality that transcends all other affiliations or category memberships. Against essentialism, it can be argued that where unitaryness is found to be a feature of any social phenomenon, this is a contingent and emergent – and perhaps also a temporary – outcome of social processes, and not a 'necessary effect' of the social totality.

Reification

Reification is the illicit attribution of agency to entities that are not actors or agents. Problems surrounding this invalid theoretical-methodological procedure, and an alternative, non-reified conception of agency, are discussed in Chapters 2 and 5. For the moment it is sufficient to briefly sketch elements of the critique of reification that underpins some of the concepts and propositions developed later in the book. An agent or *actor*, it will be argued in Chapter 5, is an entity that in principle has the means of formulating, taking, and acting upon decisions. This non-reified definition draws upon Harré's (1981) concept of agency and Hindess's (1988: 45) 'minimal concept of actor', a concept which specifies that 'for something to be an actor … it must be capable of reaching decisions and of acting on some of them'. On the basis of this explicitly non-reified definition, there are but two types of actors: individual human actors; and 'social actors' (Hindess, 1986a: 115) or 'supra-individuals' as Harré calls them (1981: 141). The latter are organizations (government departments such as the Home Office, private firms, professional associations, organized pressure groups, and the like); committees, such as the Cabinet or, say, a local residents' committee or tenants' association; and micro-groups, such as a household. Examples of *non-actors*, these being entities that cannot exercise agency – in other words, entities that, in principle, do not have the means of formulating and taking decisions and of acting on at least some of them – are 'society', 'the state', social movements, and taxonomic collectivities such as 'the middle class', 'British people', 'heterosexuals', 'young people', and so on. These entities cannot exhibit agency for the reason that they are not actors; in other words, they are entities that 'have no identifiable means of taking decisions, let alone acting on them' (Hindess, 1988: 105). This non-reified conception of agency signifies, for example, that the notion that, let us say, 'men' are an entity (an actor) that can take action to remedy gender (or any other) inequalities, is a reified, reductionist and essentialist notion that has implications for governance and public policy (Sibeon, 1997; 1999b); that is to say, in so far as agency is a factor in the production or reproduction of social structure (or 'social conditions'; see Chapters 2 and 5), it is, I suggest, incontrovertible that only actors as defined above can be said to have causal responsibility for existing social conditions, including forms of inequality, and only actors are capable of formulating and carrying out actions that reproduce or alter those conditions. As will become evident in the later chapters, reification, like the other three 'cardinal sins' identified in this Introduction, is not confined to any particular paradigm or theory; reification, in the terms that I have defined it, crops up almost everywhere across the theoretical landscape. This is indicated in the following illustrations which are drawn from widely contrasting paradigms and perspectives.

Touraine's early work on a sociology of action and his later writings on modernity contain a number of illuminating theoretical and empirical insights relating to the study of politics and social action. He is described by Delanty as a theorist who is committed to 'the return of agency' (1999: 122) to social theory. Delanty's overall assessment (1999: 122–44) of Touraine, however, seems rather too generous. Touraine's conception of agency and social action is marred by reification. For instance, in his *The Voice and the Eye*, Touraine regards 'society' as an actor (1981: 31, 59), and he claims, too, that social movements are actors (ibid.: 77). He also argues that social classes are actors (ibid.: 32): 'I am unprepared to consider any social category whatever ... as a non-actor. The working-class ... is a historical actor, a suffering, fighting, thinking actor ... always an actor.' A problem here that will be examined more closely in Chapter 5 is that 'society', social movements and social classes cannot legitimately be said to exhibit agency; they are not forms of agency, but rather, elements of social structure (or the 'conditions of action', see Chapters 2 and 5). In his more recent theorizing, Touraine's (1995) conception of agency and social action continues to display the tendency towards reification that featured in his earlier writings. Similarly, some of Habermas's central theoretical concepts exhibit a tendency towards reification: for example, his attribution of agency to social systems is revealed in such statements as 'Social systems regulate their exchanges with their social and natural environments by way of co-ordinated interventions into the external world' (Habermas, 1987: 159–60). There are also strong reifying tendencies in the following: Luhmann's (1982: 265) attribution of agency to what he calls autopoietic social systems; Law's (1991b: 173–4) blend of poststructuralism and translation sociology, which leads him to the view that 'an agent is a structured set of relations'; Foucault's implicit claim that it is discourses, rather than the 'subjects' who employ them, that are agents (see Danaher et al., 2000: 33); and the anti-humanist notion of agency (sometimes described as 'posthuman agency' or 'material agency') in Callon (1986), Latour (1988) and, for example, in Pickering's (2001) use of poststructuralism and actor network theory which he employs in his studies of scientific knowledge and scientific practices. For Pickering and actor network theorists, the material world of nature and physical objects is said to display agency, this being a conception of agency that Jones (1996: 296) rejects – rightly so, in my view – as an 'obscure, hollow metaphysics'.

Functional teleology

Functional teleology is an invalid form of analysis involving attempts to explain the causes of social phenomena in terms of their effects, where 'effects' refers to outcomes or consequences viewed as performances of 'functions'. The point to be made here – always bearing in mind the earlier non-reified definition of actor (or agent) – is that in the absence of a demonstration of intentional and successful planning by actors somewhere, sometime, it is a teleological fallacy to attempt to explain the causes of phenomena in terms of their effects (Betts, 1986: 51). All too often, reductionist theorists – including some who subscribe to varieties of 'critical social theory' – begin with a current social or cultural item (a social practice of some kind or, say, a law, a welfare or health system, or a public policy), then attempt to 'work backwards' and claim, without any demonstration of intentional planning by previous actors, that the item came into being 'because', in the view of the theorist, it accorded with the interests of, say, a taxonomic collectivity such as 'the upper class' or 'white people' or 'men'. Related to this neglect of agency and, as will become clearer in later chapters, to a number of simplistic conceptions of the relation of agency to social structure and to power, interests and social chance, teleology is flawed by a problem of logic in so far as the factors ('causes') that bring a social or cultural item into being must necessarily predate the existence of that item, whereas effects or consequences can, of course, only occur in respect of an item that is already in existence. Although Durkheim in some of his substantive work was guilty of engaging in a certain amount of functional teleology, he was nevertheless aware, in parts of his methodological writings, of the importance of, as he saw it, separating causal explanation from functionalist explanation (Durkheim, 1982: 90, 95). Durkheim argued that it is necessary in sociological enquiry to distinguish between the *causes* of something (the factors which bring a social or cultural item – such as religion or a cultural belief system – into existence in the first place), and the *functions* of something (the functional consequences of that item for the social system, once the item has come into existence). Illegitimate functionalist teleology conflates causal and functionalist explanation and attempts to explain the cause of an item in terms of the item's 'functions', that is, in terms of the item's consequences or effects where these are understood in terms of the item fulfilling a system 'need'.[6] Functionalist teleology occurs when, for instance, particular marriages are explained in terms of a societal or system 'need' for the reproduction of marriage as a social institution; this, however, is rather like claiming that two people got married *in order to* reproduce marriage as an institution (or that they later divorced *in order to* undermine the institution of marriage)!

At various points throughout the book it will be demonstrated that the four 'cardinal sins' – reductionism, essentialism, reification and functional teleology in the terms defined above – have permeated large areas of 'modern' and 'postmodern' social theory and continue to influence sociology and other social sciences. It is important to emphasize quite strongly that these four problematical modes of theoretical and methodological thought are not only a part of the intellectual history of the social sciences: in a variety of guises – and despite, as will be noted in later chapters, some contemporary theorists' partially successful efforts to avoid them – these ways of thinking, quite often in unnoticed ways, continue to influence social theory and method. One of this book's themes is that the future development of social theory and of sociology, as well as progress in developing the explanatory potential of other social sciences, requires that the defective forms of theoretical and methodological reasoning outlined in this Introduction should, given their apparent resilience and continuing influence, be subjected to sustained critique. The form of critical analysis envisioned here is not an exercise that offers no positive alternatives in place of that which is being criticized; critique of the four 'cardinal sins' is employed in this book as the basis for setting out a number of interrelated concepts and postulates that, it is argued, are capable of contributing to the development of sociological theory and method. The intention in what follows is to draw quite extensively on the work of some leading contemporary sociological theorists such as Margaret Archer, Nicos Mouzelis and Derek Layder (though in places it will also be necessary to criticize aspects of the approaches adopted by these writers). It will be shown, also, that there is no reason to remain exclusively within the ambit of the more 'mainstream' theoretical schools; lesser-known writers such as Roberto Unger and his work on 'formative contexts', the conceptualizations associated with, for example, translation sociology/actor network theory, and theory relating to time–space and material diffusion, have much to contribute to the future development of social theory and of sociology and other social science disciplines.

In the first chapter a number of metatheoretical concerns will be examined with particular reference to sociological discourse and its relation to other disciplines and to the wider society, and with reference to postmodern theory, theoretical pluralism, and controversy surrounding the idea of synthesis; it will be argued that metatheory is indispensable to social enquiry and that there are advantages to be gained from an epistemology which specifies that metatheory, substantive theory, methodology and empirical data should be consistent with each other and should regulate each other (Archer, 1995; Layder, 1998a). In Chapter 2 the main topics are agency–structure and micro–macro: it will be argued that these dualisms are perennial but also contemporary problematics in social theory and the social sciences, and that theories which emphasize only one aspect of a dualism, or else which attempt to abandon the idea of dualism altogether, are seriously flawed. Chapter 3 will critically evaluate some major theoretical initiatives that have arisen out of efforts to address the theoretical problems and disputes identified in the preceding chapter, and this is taken further in Chapter 4 with particular reference to the writings of Archer, Mouzelis, and Layder. In Chapter 5 the arguments that were set out earlier in the book are developed in greater depth and with particular emphasis being placed on, first, the dialectics of agency, structure, and social chance, and second, controversies surrounding conceptions of 'power' and 'interests'. Time–space is the focus of attention in Chapter 6. Here, attention shifts to neglected dimensions of social reality that relate to temporality and, in particular, to spatiality; one of the arguments developed in the chapter is that social network analysis and the study of materials and material diffusion processes are significant areas for future development in the social sciences. Chapter 7 draws together the concepts and postulates that figured in the earlier chapters and provides an overview of a multi-level (meta)theoretical and methodological framework that is ontologically flexible and epistemologically pluralist.

Notes

1 Although Bryant (1995: 151–62) is far from complacent about the conceptual and political difficulties that confront sociology, he observes (ibid.: 156): 'British Sociology is … in better shape than seemed possible in the early 1980s'. In America, Ritzer similarly describes (2000: xix) a revival of interest in sociology and, in particular, he refers to the vibrancy of current debates in theoretical sociology. It seems likely that the current renewal of academic interest in sociological theory and theoretical social science will continue into the foreseeable future (Albrow, 1999; Calhoun *et al.*, 2002; Sharrock *et al.*, 2003).

2 This expression, not one of my making, originated at a conference where participants suggested my approach to sociological theory (Sibeon, 1999a) rested partly on identification of four 'cardinal sins' of theoretical-methodological reasoning; the term was subsequently taken up in Thompson's (2000: 38) commentary on my line of argument, and I am content to continue using what seems to be an apt description of four defective forms of reasoning that, either singly or in combination, have in my opinion been major (meta)theoretical sources of explanatory failure in social theory and the social sciences.

3 Not all theorists define each of these constructs in the exact terms set out here (DiMaggio, 1997). For example, the expression *essentialism* is sometimes used in a way that comes close to my definition of reductionism; this is evident in, for instance, Miller's (1993: 695) critique of Durkheim and Montesquieu. For other theorists, such as Mouzelis (1995: 181), essentialism refers to the failure to perceive the socially constructed nature of social phenomena (see also the discussion in Sayer, 1997). *Reification* for some authors, such as Layder (1994: 31–2), refers to a mistaken assumption that society has 'a life of its own' and exists independently of social action, which is not quite the same as regarding reification as the illegitimate attribution of agency to entities that, in principle, have no means of formulating, taking, and acting upon decisions.

4 'Grand theories', such as Parsonian structural-functionalism and Marxism, attempt to explain the historical and present-day totality of social behaviour and social structure. Another way of putting this is to say that grand theories over-generalize: they produce large, sweeping generalizations that bear little relation to concrete empirical happenings in particular times and particular places. Although theoretical generalizations are not illegitimate, indeed, they are unavoidable in social science, one of this book's arguments is that they should be of modest scope,

and provisional. 'Grand' theories, as Mouzelis (1995: 34) observes, 'tend to be either inconclusive (holding only in certain conditions not specified by the theory) or trivial'.

5 Essentialism, in the terms defined here, may be invoked for political rather than purely theoretical or ontological reasons. Sometimes this results in theoretical contradiction: an instance is where essentialist theorizing, by virtue of its essentialism, is acknowledged to have no empirical explanatory value, but is nevertheless said to be justified in terms of a 'theory of practice' that is felt to be necessary to the realization of some political or ethical objective. Within feminism, it has been argued, for example, by Spivak who employs a notion of 'strategic essentialism', that while reductionist and essentialist conceptions of the social category 'women' have no empirical or theoretical legitimacy, feminist use of reductionist and essentialist concepts is nevertheless justified for tactical, political reasons:

> It is not possible ... to ... escape ... essentialism or essentialization ... In ... critical practice, you have to be aware that you are going to essentialize anyway ... strategically you can look at essentializations not as descriptions of the way things are, but as something that one must adopt to produce a critique of things. (Spivak, 1990, cited in Clough, 1994: 116)

The idea of 'strategic essentialism' is, it can be argued, not only analytically redundant but also politically and programmtically self-defeating (Sibeon, 1999c; Thompson, 2000).

6 'Functions' and 'consequences' are not synonymous; the former refers to consequences that are presumed to be the fulfilment of some system need (or 'functional prerequisite'), whereas the latter makes no such presumption. An example of a system need (such needs may be regarded as 'conditions of existence') in the case of, say, factories might be that factories as ongoing social systems require, for their continued survival as systems, a mechanism for recruiting and training new members of staff.

It can be argued, and here I am adapting Mouzelis's defence of Mertonian functionalism (for example, Mouzelis, 1995: 132–3), that despite the controversy surrounding functionalism, it is legitimate to engage in (non-teleological) functionalist investigation of the conditions-of-existence (system needs) of a social system or a social whole, providing the following methodological principles are adhered to. First, a distinction between causal and functionalist explanation should be preserved, the latter being incorporated into analysis when the focus of enquiry is the conditions of existence of social phenomena and their implications for social action. Second, in non-teleological functionalist analyses it is important to distinguish 'necessary conditions' of existence of social phenomena from 'sufficient causes'. For instance, in the above example a recruitment and training mechanism can be thought of as a 'necessary' device that satisfies factories' (systemic) need for some mechanism that is suitable for replacing and training staff. But this explanation refers to factories *in general* and goes only some way towards providing an adequate account of any *particular* recruitment/training mechanism within *a* factory; here, a 'sufficient' explanation would have to relate analysis of general systemic 'needs' to a more detailed, contextual analysis of local factors – including, crucially the operation of agency – that shape recruitment/training mechanisms in specific locations. Third, and this relates closely to the last point, employing both *social integration* and *system integration* modes of analysis, and exploring links between them (see Chapter 3), facilitates investigation of the ways in which the conditions of existence of social phenomena are satisfied (or not, as the case may be), while ensuring that the significance of agency – which tends to be ignored in teleological functionalist theories that emphasize the *consequences* of action while downplaying actors' *reasons* for action – is not lost sight of.

1

Metatheoretical Preliminaries

Without entering into unnecessarily detailed debate of the philosophy of social scientific explanation, the aim of this first chapter is to provisionally outline the part that metatheoretical reflection plays in the social sciences generally and in the construction of the sociological concepts and postulates that figure later in the book. Following a brief statement of the rationale for employing metatheoretical concepts in the social sciences, there is a discussion of the relation of sociological discourse to other discourses and to the wider society. This is followed by a review of controversies surrounding postmodern rejection of theoretical foundations, and an account of theoretical pluralism and cumulative sociology. The chapter ends with an argument in favour of theoretical synthesis as a procedure that is capable of aiding the theoretical and methodological development of sociology as an academic discipline.

Metatheory

One of the first points to make here is that in the social sciences it is appropriate to distinguish between theory (sometimes referred to as substantive theory) consisting of propositions that are intended to furnish information about the social world, and *metatheory*, which is not primarily or directly concerned with specific explanatory problems or with generating new empirical knowledge but with matters of a more general kind relating to ontology, epistemology, and methodology.[1] Metatheory, some aspects of which were touched upon in the Introduction in connection with critique of the four 'cardinal sins', is intended to inform and hopefully improve the construction of substantive theories and the design of empirical studies. Metatheorists are largely concerned with ontological questions, including the following. What, in general terms, is 'society'? What sorts of things exist in the social world? If there are such things as actors or agents, what sort of things are they? Are activities and society indivisible ('two sides of the same coin') and so tightly melded together that (as claimed in doctrines of ontological duality) it is impossible to separate them? Does it make sense to employ a stratified social ontology that refers to micro and macro spheres or 'levels' of society, or is micro–macro – as Foucault, Elias, and Giddens claim – a spurious and misleading distinction? And when we turn to epistemology, it is important to ask: how is reliable knowledge acquired? Is, for example, 'lay' actors' self-experience a better guide to social reality than the supposedly 'objective' perspective of the social analyst? Indeed, a perhaps more fundamental question is whether there is an objective social reality that exists 'out there' independent of our conception of it: maybe there are no 'real' things in the social world, but only words (that is, the names of things)? These kinds of questions, which do not refer directly to specific empirical explanatory problems in the way that substantive theories do, are the stuff of metatheory and of metatheoretical concepts such as 'agency–structure', 'micro–macro' and 'time–space'. Sometimes the expression *sensitizing theory* is used in place of the term metatheory. Sensitizing (or meta-) theory can and should inform the construction of substantive theories, but we have seen that the two types are distinct. In the social sciences substantive theories aim to generate new empirical information about the social world, whereas meta- or sensitizing theories and concepts are concerned with general ontological and epistemological understandings; metatheories and meta-concepts are designed to equip us with a general sense of the kinds of things that exist in the social world, and with ways of thinking about the question of how we might 'know' that world. Of relevance here is Mouzelis's parallel distinction between substantive generalizations and methodological generalizations; in regard to the latter, which are akin to metatheoretical concepts, Mouzelis (1993a: 684) notes that 'their aim is less to tell us things we do not know about the social than to provide us with conceptual tools for asking interesting questions and preparing the ground for the empirical investigation of the social world'. In short, the job of metatheoretical concepts is to generate, at the meta-level, conceptual tools that inform the development of concepts, substantive theories and explanatory schemes, and that underpin the design of empirical studies. This does not mean, as we shall see later, that meta-concepts and metatheories should be regarded as immune from theoretical and empirical sources of revision.

Not all researchers and theorists are happy with the idea of metatheory. Postmodernists tend, mistakenly in my view, to reject metatheory on the grounds that it is a form of 'grand narrative' (Lyotard, 1986) or 'grand theory'. It is true that some meta- or sensitizing theories formulate 'large' generalizations pertaining to common social processes that may be found in a wide variety of social settings. For example, Giddens's (1989: 295) structuration theory, which is one of the better-known examples of metatheory, consists of postulates that 'are intended to apply over the whole range of human social activity, in any and every context of action'. *Meta*theoretical generalizations of this kind, however, are not the same thing as universal ('grand') generalizations associated with reductionist substantive theories such as Marxism, rational choice theory, and radical feminism, theories which are rightly criticized by postmodernists; see, for example, the criticisms by Nicholson and Seidman (1995: 7). In contrast to such theories, Giddens's structuration theory is an example of a sensitizing or metatheory that does not invoke the reductionism associated with 'grand' substantive theories, such as radical feminism which simplistically reduces the complexity of social relations to the notion of patriarchy; structuration theory is ontologically flexible (Cohen, 1987: 279–80, 285, 289, 291), a term that refers to metatheory of a kind which leaves the door open for the development of a wide range of perhaps competing substantive theories, and for relatively open-ended empirical investigation and empirical interpretation that involve no commitment to explanations that rely on generalizations of the kind associated with reductionist substantive theories. Here it is worth noting that Holmwood's criticism of metatheory, which he associates with 'grand theory', is grounded not in postmodernism but in a commitment to a pragmatic sociology that develops theory only in relation to, and as an integral part of, practical empirical research activity (1996: 133). There are three problems associated with Holmwood's rejection (1996: viii, 31–2) of metatheory *per se*. First, what Holmwood does not allow for is that there are helpful as well as inadequate metatheoretical schemes. Those that he criticizes – which build upon versions of Parsonian structural-functionalism, Marxism, and postmodernism – have in common the characteristic that they are prone to one or more of the 'cardinal sins' that were outlined in the Introduction; but as this book is designed to demonstrate, not all metatheory or metatheoretical concepts are of the kind described by Holmwood. Second, in response to Holmwood's (1996: 47–8) justifiable criticism of Jeffrey Alexander's preference for the independence of 'theoretical logic' from empirical sources of revision, there is no reason why immunity from empirically based scrutiny should be sought for metatheory; later in the chapter it will be argued that metatheory, (substantive) theory, and empirical data should regulate or modify each other. Third,

Holmwood does not seem to appreciate that metatheoretical suppositions of one kind or another are *unavoidable* in substantive theory and in empirical explanatory work (see Archer, 1995: 12); far better, then, rather than allow metatheoretical assumptions to influence sociological enquiry in hidden or unacknowledged ways, to make such assumptions explicit and available to the critical scrutiny of others (Ritzer, 1992; 2001). Paradoxically, given Holmwood's (Holmwood and Stewart, 1983) quest to avoid theoretical (as distinct from empirical) contradictions, explicit metatheoretical reflection concerned with social ontology is, as Archer (1998) observed, a way of helping to avoid the tacit importation of theoretical contradictions into substantive explanatory schemes; this will be discussed later in the chapter.

The relation of sociological discourse to other discourses and to the wider society

Postmodern theorists deny that sociological discourse or other disciplinary discourses can have validity (Baudrillard, 1983: 4). It therefore becomes necessary – if one wishes to employ metatheoretical arguments in support of sociological theory as a disciplinary activity, and if, more generally, one wishes to endorse the legitimacy of the idea of disciplinary knowledge – to address the emergence of postmodern theory as a body of thought that challenges the very notion of social science and rejects disciplinary knowledge of the kind associated with, for example, sociology, economics, political science, public administration, and psychology. Within the space available, the intention is to focus only on those aspects of postmodernism that relate to the central concerns of the book as a whole. Reference will be restricted to what might be termed poststructural postmodernism (Baudrillard, 1983; Lyotard, 1986), and for present purposes poststructural and postmodern approaches will be regarded as broadly similar. Hence the discussion that follows is not primarily concerned with those versions of postmodern thought that draw upon Marxism (such as Jameson, 1991, and Harvey, 1989) or versions which argue in non-Marxist terms that we live in a postmodern type of society (see the useful discussion in Lyon, 1994, and Kumar, 1995).

Postmodernism as a *type of theory*, as distinct from the idea of the postmodern as historical periodization and as a *type of society*, rejects the generalizations and nomothetic knowledge that characterize social science, and instead favours small-scale, particularistic or ideographic 'narratives' (Dickens, 1990: 105). Postmodern theorists also adopt a relativism which supposes that all perspectives or theories – such as lay and academic perspectives, religious, political, and professional discourses – have in common the characteristic that they 'produce' the social reality to which they refer, rather than reflect in mirror-image fashion an ontologically prior or pre-existing reality. On this view, the world is *theoretically* constructed and is a product of lay or academic theories; there is no ontologically prior, pre-theoretical, or materially real social world. Unlike structural theorists who argue that pre-existing structure determines thought, postmodernists, poststructuralists, and also ethnomethodologists (Garfinkel, 1967) believe that thought determines or creates (a sense of) 'structure' – social reality is an effect of lay, academic, professional, or political discourses. The assumption here is that there are, so to speak, as many social realities as there are languages and theories, and since there is no pre-discursive or pre-theoretical social reality 'out there' against which we can test the empirical adequacy of our theories, it follows that we cannot say of any theory that it is a 'better' or 'more accurate' representation of reality than any other theory. A related postmodern assumption is that all knowledge, including academic knowledge, is an 'embedded' product of the context of its production (Bauman, 1987: 4). That is to say, postmodernists suppose, in a fashion that is curiously reminiscent of determinist modernist theories, that a person's forms of thought are largely determined by that person's structural location in the social totality (as a man, let us say, or as a woman or a black or white person) and by social, historical circumstances that are particular to a specific time and place. This goes beyond an understanding that social contexts may in various ways and to a varying extent *influence* actors' perception and perspectives, and is a type of hypercontextualism (Alexander, 1992) which assumes that social contexts *determine* actors' forms of thought. Another feature of postmodern theorizing is hostility towards 'western' rationality, the latter being supplanted by the postmodern notion that knowledge is and should be a fragmented pastiche that has no coherence. Vincent (1992: 188), a political scientist, notes that postmodern thinkers 'oppose all closure, totalizing discourse and erasure of difference. They do not believe in truth, rationality, knowledge, subject-centred inquiry or the search for a coherent epistemology ... Contradiction, difference and incoherence are welcomed.' In line with the earlier reference to poststructuralist and postmodern relativism, part of the postmodern argument in favour of contradictory thought is that readers of texts (and observers of social circumstances) are free to construe what they read or see in any way that they like and that any interpretation or reading of a text (or of 'society') is as good as any other. This, incidently, has a potentially awkward implication for postmodernists. Since they accord more importance to readers than to authors, postmodern theorists presumably should not rebut critical modernist readings of postmodern theory nor 'modernist' readings – such as the one offered in this chapter – which, while not unsympathetic to certain nuances of postmodern thought, reject the central tenets of postmodern theorizing.

Against Gellner (1993) who sees almost nothing of value in postmodern thinking, it can be argued that aspects of postmodern theory are relevant to the development of sociological theory (Lemert, 1993) and to methodological concerns relating to the design of empirical studies (Fox, 1991). Poststructuralist and postmodern views of contingency (Bauman, 1992a; Lyon, 1994: 4), locale, and power can legitimately be regarded – subject to the conceptual and methodological departures from postmodernism described in this and later chapters – to have a theoretically sensitizing part to play in the (re)construction of sociological theory 'after postmodernism'. It is worth observing, for example, that Bauman's (1992a: 192–6) depiction of the characteristics of postmodernity (multiple loci of power, contingency and time–space variability, cultural pluralism, flexible and shifting identities, and so on) is in some respects quite close to the anti-reductionist, anti-essentialist and flexible-but-realist social ontology that underlies the approach that I employ in this and later chapters. Putatively non-reductionist postmodern notions of social indeterminacy and time–space variability, providing they are modified in the direction of realist ontology in the terms mentioned earlier, are relevant not only to sociology but also to, for example, political science (Marsh and Stoker, 1995a; Hay, 2002) and to policy analysis (Fox and Miller, 1995; Rhodes, 1997). Postmodern theory, to put this another way, has a certain amount of merit in so far as it attempts to criticize 'modern' theories of the kind that are reductionist and essentialist or which involve functional teleology. In general, however, it seems clear that postmodern thought contains so many deficiencies – including those set out below – that it cannot provide a suitable theoretical or methodological basis for engaging in social analysis.

Without attempting to provide an extended critique, it is possible to briefly identify the main problems of postmodern theory in so far as these relate to the themes of this book. First, postmodern theorists, when they criticize 'modern' theories, tend to equate the latter with problems that are associated with the four problematical forms of theoretical/methodological reasoning that were identified in the Introduction (namely reductionism, essentialism, reification, and functional teleology). To some extent, postmodern critics have here a valid point. However, one of the tasks of this book is to document the proposition that it is possible to develop – in general social theory and in sociology, and other social sciences – forms of reasoning that avoid the four general 'sins' that are associated with many areas of modern theorizing, but while also avoiding the problems that attend relativism, hypercontextualism, and the flawed postmodern doctrine of anti-foundationalism. Second, attention should be drawn to an epistemological contradiction centred upon the previously mentioned distinction between the postmodern as a '*type of society*', and the postmodern as a '*type of theory*'. In the former mode, postmodern writers assert that something called 'postmodern society' is empirically real and exhibits definite structural characteristics (consumerism, extreme cultural pluralism and diversity, social fragmentation, individualism, informationalism, and so on); in the latter mode, however, postmodernists claim that society is never something that is real but is, rather, an effect of discourse. We are simultaneously being told that on the one hand (postmodern) society exists, but that on the other, it doesn't. There is an evident contradiction here (not, of course, that this is a problem for postmodern theorists who, as already noted, welcome incoherence and contradiction); the (meta)theoretical contradiction in question revolves around postmodern attempts to combine realist ontology with idealist epistemology. Third, postmodern theory neglects not only actors' subjectivity, but also intersubjectivity. As Best and Kellner (1991: 61) have observed, postmodern theory underestimates the significance of interpersonal relations and of what Goffman (1983) terms 'the interaction order'. Crucially, interaction and intersubjectivity mediate the relation of agency to structure. This will be discussed in Chapters 2 and 7 with reference to the micro-sphere of social reality. The more general point to be made here is that postmodern thought lacks an adequate theory of agency and of the actor or agent, and subscribes to a flawed conception of agency–structure (see Chapter 2). Postmodern theorists have a tendency to employ deterministic conceptions of the actor, conceptions that, as briefly noted earlier, are curiously reminiscent of the social determinism and reification associated with reductionist modernist paradigms such as Marxism, radical feminism, and Parsonian structural-functionalism. Postmodernists claim that knowledge and theories embody a standpoint that has been determined by the structural location of the theorist in terms of his or her membership of social categories to do with, say, race, gender, or social class, or in terms of the allegedly cognitively determining effect of 'local' circumstances. What we have here is a determinist and reductionist conception of agency in which actors are seen as products or effects of discourses which, it is claimed, are themselves determined by social contexts. Such conceptions – which reveal that postmodern theory no less than some versions of modern theory is implicated in reproduction of the 'cardinal sins' – entail an objectivist conception of agency and structure that sits uncomfortably alongside an opposed, idealist epistemology that, as noted above, is also a part of the postmodern genre. This last point signifies, fourth of all, that postmodern theorists' relativism and their view of the relation of discourses to social contexts, is contradictory. On the one hand, there is a distinct postmodern tendency (as in Seidman, 1994: 325) to claim that society or social contexts determine actors' discourses. This, we have just seen, is analogous to theories of structural predetermination which suppose that actors' forms of thought are largely determined by their structural location(s) (that is, determined by, for example, their membership of various social categories such as 'women', 'white people', 'men', or 'the middle class', as well as by specific ('local') social-historical circumstances). On the other hand, as observed earlier, postmodernists claim that discourses do not refer to any ontologically prior or pre-discursive social reality, for no such reality exists; instead, it is the other way round for postmodernists – discourses 'produce' or construct social reality (that is, discourses produce 'society' or social contexts). Stated in these terms, there is here a patent contradiction: it is argued by postmodernists both that discourses *produce* (or 'determine') social contexts, and that discourses are *determined by* social contexts. For reasons that will be returned to later in the chapter, I believe it is appropriate, at least in regard to this matter (but not necessarily in relation to others) to endorse the position of Berger and Luckmann (1971), White (1992: 305) and Law (1986c: 3–4; 1991a: 18), each of whom regards the relation of discourses to social contexts as dialectical, though sometimes – as in Berger and Luckmann's work – without properly recognizing that the relation is often only *loosely* dialectical. By the latter I mean that there is no automatic or necessary symmetry or 'direct link' between action and structure (see Chapters 3 and 5). Subject to this important proviso, it can be argued that actors' discourses – that is, actors' forms of thought and social practices – both shape and are shaped by the social world(s) of which they are a part: in a loosely dialectical sense that is associated with a stratified ontology as described in Chapter 3, there are grounds for suggesting that actors, employing this term in the strictly non-reified terms outlined in the Introduction, are to some extent both products and creators of society. To say this, in light of the earlier remarks, is to first of all reject the idea of any one-way causal relation in which either discourse *or* context are determinant – rather, and while no necessary 'direct links' are involved, each shapes the other to a greater or lesser degree, this being an empirical question; and second, what is also being rejected here is postmodernists' contradictory endorsement of two opposed and mutually exclusive forms of one-way causal determination.

Implicit in the above arguments concerning discourses in general, is the proposition, which will be examined more closely in the following section, that *sociological* discourse, like others, is in various ways related to – without being wholly constitutive of or wholly determined by – its social context. When discussing the relation of sociology to its social context(s), there is also a need to consider the question of linkages between sociology and other social science disciplines. Although sociology can be regarded as an academic discipline in its own right, there are good reasons for suggesting that cross-disciplinary activity may have beneficial spin-offs for sociology as well as for other social sciences. As suggested by the examples in the following chapters, cross-disciplinary links may enhance the development of sociological theory and, in turn, enable sociological theory to contribute to the development of theory in other social sciences. That is to say, theoretical initiatives directed towards the reconstruction of sociology following 'the postmodern turn' are likely to be enhanced by a process of theoretical (and methodological) renewal that draws upon and contributes to conceptual developments in other social sciences. It should not be overlooked that a confident, outgoing orientation of this kind will not threaten the cognitive and institutional identity of sociology; rather, in the intellectual and academic institutional climate of interdisciplinary collaboration in teaching and research that has come into existence in recent years, it is perhaps the insularity of an exclusively inward-looking disciplinary preoccupation that is more likely to hold back the development of sociology as an academic discipline. And nor, leaving aside interdisciplinary connections, should we lose sight of the significance of the relation of sociology, and of other social science disciplines, to *social theory*.

Social theory, although far from easy to define in any concise way (see Outhwaite, 2000a: 4; 2000b), deals in general categories of thought that refer to the social, these being conceptual categories that tend towards philosophical reasoning but which are broader than those associated with philosophy or with individual social sciences such as anthropology, sociology, or economics. Turner (2000a: xiii) writes: 'Social theory is a diverse and complex collection of perspectives that attempt to understand, to interpret, and to explain social phenomena.' He refers (2000b: 1) to 'the phrase "social theory", rather than a more specific reference to sociological, cultural, or political theory. Social theory encompasses the general concern with the nature of the social in modern society.' Turner's observations serve to illustrate that the dividing line between sociological theory and social theory is a rather blurred one (Antonio, 1998: 63). Nevertheless, there is a distinction to be made in so far as the general categories of thought that comprise social theory (such as Marxism, hermeneutics, cultural analysis, and the relation of subjectivity to social structure) tend, whenever they enter disciplinary discourses, to be employed in differing and specialized ways within each discipline; when economists, psychologists, social geographers, political scientists, policy academics, and sociologists draw upon social theory that refers to, say, the characteristics of the modern state or the nature of human subjectivity, there is a tendency to employ such theory in somewhat different ways that reflect the particularities of each discipline in terms of topics and types of explanatory problems. Thus, social theory is both an important and wide-ranging theoretic field in its own right[2] (which is not to say it is a unitary or integrated field), and also an intellectual resource that is drawn upon and selectively mediated by scholars working within particular disciplines. Conversely, theoretical, methodological, and empirical developments within disciplines are capable of contributing to general social theory. Mutual influence between general social theory and disciplinary theory and method, is, however, not as well developed as it might be. For example, there is not much cross-fertilization of ideas between social theory and current work on postnational governance and public policy (see the discussion in Sibeon, 1999b; 2000) or between general social theory and geographers' theoretical work on time–space (see, for instance, Benko and Strohmayer, 1997). For the purposes of investigating the social it seems to me that general social theory, including the classics (Camic, 1997), is a source of intellectually enrichening insights. Nevertheless, though capable of contributing to disciplinary theoretical renewal, social theory appears to be somewhat isolated from and uninformed by, in particular, the important questions of social ontology that are currently debated within and across a number of social science disciplines; there is, therefore, a case to be made for greater two-way traffic between, on the one hand, developments in general social theory, and on the other, disciplinary and interdisciplinary theoretical innovation.

The question of theoretical foundations

I suggested earlier that while aspects of postmodern thought are a source of potentially useful analytical precepts, the postmodern genre as a whole is seriously flawed. In addition to the earlier criticisms it should be observed that although it is true that there are differences of emphasis among postmodern critics of academic sociology (Martino, 1993: 179), it can in general be said that the strong, distinctive form of postmodern 'anti-foundationalism' is itself a meta-narrative that is foundational; the postmodern theory that there can be no general theory is itself a general theory. Anti-foundationalism also fails to rigorously analyse epistemological incommensurability between the postmodern as periodization and as theory (see the earlier reference to theoretical contradiction as between the postmodern as a 'type of society' and as a 'type of theory'), and is unduly deterministic (Turner, 1990: 248). In place of empirical enquiry involving explicit theoretical criteria and rules of methodological procedure, postmodernists prefer 'pastiche', 'irony', 'parody', theoretical 'mischief', deconstructive 'playfulness', and the like (Featherstone, 1988). Impulses of this kind represent, in my opinion, a somewhat whimsical aestheticism that enjoyed its heyday at the height of the postmodern turn during the late 1980s and early 1990s; they are not impulses that have any useful part to play in the contemporary reconstruction of sociological theory 'after postmodernism'. It is necessary, too, to critically examine postmodern theorists' portrayal of the targets at which their criticisms are aimed. In rejecting sociology, or any other social science discipline that attempts to base its activities on metatheoretical, theoretical and methodological guidelines ('foundations'), postmodernists and others have tended to depict sociology as dogmatic and over-confident. It is, however, doubtful whether the whole of post-war European and American sociology exhibits the degree of superficiality and smug sense of infallibility imputed to it by, for example, Gurnah and Scott (1992: 41, 195). It can just as easily be argued – even if we leave aside the question, raised in the Introduction, of whether the discipline is infused by a peren-nial sense of 'crisis' – that sociology in the modern era is characterized by theoretical pluralism and by epistemological uncertainty and reflexivity, and that these characteristics of the discipline have 'accelerated since the 1950s' (Gibbs, 1989: 11). The history of sociological thought (see the account by Swingewood, 2000) suggests that, on the whole, sociological theory and methodology are permeated as much by intellectual caution and introspection as by smugness or certitude (Calhoun *et al.*, 2002). And of course, Gurnah and Scott's and others' confident assertion that there never can be nor should be any 'foundations' for sociological practice is, as I have already intimated, itself a foundational claim. Nor is Seidman (1992: 48) plausible when he implies that to formulate a sociological perspective based on explicitly articulated theoretical or metatheoretical premises ('foundations') is the same as suggesting that all other, competing sociolog-ical perspectives should be denied the right to exist. Seidman is also uncon-vincing in so far as he begins by arguing that 'foundational rationales ... [for a perspective] ... are never more than local, ethnocentric prejudices' (1992: 60), then goes on, as all postmodernists must, to develop a foundational rationale for his own perspective.[3]

Earlier, it was briefly noted that the postmodern tendency to associate social science disciplines with one or more of the four cardinal sins described in the Introduction, is not entirely misplaced; it was observed in the Introduction that reductionism, essentialism, reification, and functional teleology are quite widespread in social theory and in the social sciences.[4] As observed earlier in the present chapter, however, it is possible to avoid these inadequate forms of 'modern' analysis without having to embrace postmodern hypercontextualism; one of the central themes in the follow-ing chapters is precisely the possibility of developing sociological theory in directions that avoid a crude either-or choice between flawed and ontologically rigid versions of modernist theory, and the no less flawed approach of post-modern theorists. Foundations, which I suggest ought to be regarded as metatheoretical and methodological postulates that serve as provisional and revisable guides to the construction of substantive theories and the design of empirical studies, should, it will be argued in this book, be based on an onto-logically flexible but anti-postmodernist and realist conception of the social.

The approach advocated in this chapter entails a pliable ontology involv-ing a processual conception of the social as potentially indeterminate and variable across time and social space; as just noted, however, the ontology, although flexible in terms that will be returned to shortly, is realist – there is an ontologically prior, albeit heterogeneous and often shifting empirical reality 'out there' – and therefore we are speaking here of a conceptual framework that, while employing what some might regard as a postmodern-type emphasis on time–space variability and contingency, does not endorse the relativism and hypercontextualism of postmodern epistemology. Lyotard's postmodern rejection of 'grand narratives' is, in part, a rejection of reductionist, single-order 'modernist' theories which emphasize, say, capitalism or gender or globalization as universal principles of explanation; it is entirely possible to concur with Lyotard's criticism of such theories and to borrow from postmodernists their sense of conceptual flexibility while at the same time insisting, against postmodernism, upon approaches that are based on ontological and epistemological realism. A pliant but realist ontology recognizes, in other words, that it is possible to conceive of foun-dations in terms of (meta)theoretical postulates pertaining to social processes and mechanisms to do with, for example, such concepts as agency, structure, time–space and social chance, rather than to specific hypostatized empirical structures, events or social patterns. It can be argued, for example, that Giddens's theory of structuration is ontologically flexible (see Cohen, 1987: 279–80, 285, 289). In regard to Giddens's assumptions about large-scale social processes, Cohen (1987: 297) observes: 'Consistent with the ontological flexibility of structuration theory at large, Giddens holds open for substantive enquiry all questions regarding specific systemic patterns as well as the degree to which systems are stable, organized and permeable.' Referring to the concepts employed in structuration theory, Cohen's clarifi-cation of the idea of ontological flexibility at metatheoretical and theoreti-cal levels of analysis, is worth noting:

A primary consideration in the formulation of ontological concepts of this kind must be to allow the widest possible latitude for the diversity and contingencies that may occur in different settings. Therefore, hypostatized accounts of trans-historical determination of circumstances or the universal trajectories of events are neither necessary nor desirable. To the contrary, an acceptable ontology of potentials may be sufficiently flexible to allow for the development of a variety of different substantive theories addressed to the same subject-matter. (1987: 279)

The type of realism referred to by Cohen, and by Stones (1996: 232) who argues for a new and sophisticated realism in sociology, is not at all the same thing as the ill-founded versions of realism found in crude modernist theories of the kind that replicate one or more of the four 'cardinal sins' that, either singly or in combination, continue to directly or else indirectly influence large areas of social theory and social scientific practices.[5]

Postmodern criticisms of foundations also relate to the question raised earlier concerning the relation of sociological discourse to social contexts. Against postmodernism, there is a case for holding to the view that sociology is a discipline in its own right and that as such it can be, and should be, improved and developed (Mouzelis, 1989: 613; 1991: 2–6). This need not conflict with the parallel view that sociology does not stand in grand isolation from 'lay' discourses (Friedrichs, 1972: 298). It can be argued, without sacrificing the notion that the discipline has a cognitive and institutional identity, that the relation of sociological discourse to lay discourses and to social conditions is, as mentioned earlier, a relation that is loosely dialectical; this is described by Giddens as 'the double hermeneutic'. The concepts and theories generated by sociology 'spiral in and out' of social life (Giddens, 1987: 32) although there is no 'necessary match' between changes in lay and social science discourses (Giddens, 1993: 13–14). Whenever social scientists investigate the empirical world, actors' meanings and concepts will tend to wind their way – though some of them may be modified during the process – into social science discourse. For example, sociological studies of juvenile crime draw upon and necessarily refer to (critically or otherwise) the concepts of criminality, responsibility for one's own actions, and so on, that are employed by relevant actors such as young offenders and their peers, probation officers, police officers, and magistrates. The point I am making here is that actors' meanings permeate, and are crucial resources for, social scientific accounts of the empirical world. Conversely, social scientific concepts and research findings (in psychology, economics, sociology, policy studies, and so on) are sometimes diffused to settings outside academia. As Mouzelis (1995: 52) notes, the extent to which particular social science discourses have or do not have an impact upon social contexts is an empirical variable, though this is something that poststructuralists and postmodernists would question (for them, the social world as described by academics is entirely a product of academic discourse). Heuristically speaking, it seems reasonable to suppose that while there is no 'direct link' between academic and lay discourses (changes in the one do not automatically result in matching changes in the other), there tends to be a *loosely dialectical* linkage in so far as each influences the other to a greater or lesser extent, this being a matter for empirical assessment in each instance. More generally, and here I refer to a postulate that will form part of the discussion of agency–structure in Chapter 2, the relation of social science discourse (or indeed, any discourse) to social contexts is such that each is partly shaped by the other but neither fully determines the other; each has relative autonomy (Mouzelis, 1995: 52). For example, to say that social science discourse spirals into and out of the social fabric[6] is not to imply that sociologists by virtue of their having a social location cannot legitimately formulate general social science propositions about the nature of social life (White, 1992: 5, 304): rather, and here I disagree with the relativism of Gurnah and Scott (1992) and Seidman (1992; 1994), the extent to which such propositions embody (or do not, as the case may be) any identifiable cultural, regional, ethnic, political, or gender-related nuances or specificities of time and place, and, where any of these are shown to exist, their implications for social science knowledge, are matters that in each instance merit collaborative academic assessment and reflexive response. Taken together, these considerations suggest that archetypal absolutist and positivist scientism, or the hypercontextualism and relativism of poststructuralism and postmodernism, are not the only epistemological alternatives: relatively impersonal generalized categories of social science knowledge are possible (Alexander, 1992: 323).

In relation to the controversies that surround the idea of theoretical 'foundations', an important epistemological but also partly ontological proposition is that metatheory, substantive theories, and empirical data should, first, be compatible with each other, and, second, should influence each other. Earlier in the chapter, when criticizing Holmwood's rejection of the idea of metatheory, it was noted that there is no compelling reason why, despite Alexander's claim to the contrary, metatheoretical concepts should be regarded as immune from empirical sources of revision. There is a case for suggesting that 'meta' or sensitizing theory – it was observed earlier that in the social sciences metatheory focuses on social ontology, epistemology, and aspects of methodology (Layder, 1998a) – should in principle be regarded as revisable in the light of reflections that accumulate at the point where substantive theory and empirical data intersect; the relation of this intersection to metatheory should be regarded as a dialectical relation. That is, theory–data reciprocity should itself stand in a mutually regulatory relation to metatheory; theory, data, and metatheory should shape each other. Hence the meta-concepts and postulates outlined in this book, though it is argued they have heuristic value for the conduct of empirical enquiry and the development of substantive theories, are provisional and open to revision in the sense just described (Sibeon, 1999a). In some respects this epistemological framework is similar to Archer's (1995), whose morphogenetic social theory is discussed in Chapter 4. Archer makes a distinction between, in her terminology, Social Ontology, Explanatory Methodology, and Practical Social Theory; her argument is, first, that these should be mutually regulative and be consistent with each other (1995: 28), and, second, that an advantage of having an explicit social ontology/metatheory is that – since metatheoretical assumptions of an ontological kind are unavoidable and will inevitably influence substantive theory – explicitness at the level of metatheory will reduce the likelihood of ontological contradictions arising at the level of substantive theories and methodology. However, as Archer rightly observes, having an explicit epistemology that connects and ensures consistency between the various elements referred to above, is not an absolute guarantee against error (ibid.: 5). For example, she notes that what she describes as 'conflationary' conceptual schemes may exhibit consistency between social ontology, explanatory methodology, and practical social theory, yet because they are conflationary (see Chapter 4) such schemes, she argues, can have no explanatory success. In effect, then, the criteria of explicitness, consistency, and mutual regulation in the relation between the elements – ontology, methodology, and substantive theories – that comprise Archer's epistemology are, while 'no guarantee against error' (ibid.: 17), a necessary but not a sufficient condition for explanatory success; the additional ('sufficient') condition for such success is, she argues, her morphogenetic social theory. My own (meta)theoretical framework as set out in the following chapters, has an affinity with Archer's and also with Layder's (1998a; 1998b: 92)[7] whose theory of social domains (see Chapter 4) is in some respects an extension and elaboration (Layder, 1998b: 85) of Archer's 'analytical dualism' which, as we shall see in the next chapter, is opposed to the duality of action and structure that is the hallmark of Giddens's (1984) structuration theory.

Theoretical pluralism, cumulative sociology, and synthesis

Some postmodernists display a tendency to suppose, mistakenly, that their critics wish to instigate single-paradigm disciplinary regimes, or that to advocate a particular style or form of sociological reasoning somehow implies that other approaches or paradigms have no right to exist. In response to postmodern misapprehensions of this kind it is important to spell out that in sociology – as in other disciplines – the vast majority of academics tend to believe there should always be room for opposed paradigms and for competing syntheses and theories. A reason for accommodation of intellectual diversity is that, as well as ethical and political issues to do with freedom of academic expression, recognition of the legitimacy of theoretical pluralism is an appropriate way of acknowledging the probable inevitability of intellectual uncertainties and complex ambiguities surrounding both the contents of social theory and the relation of observers and social investigators to the social world (Alexander, 1987). The postmodern idea that critique of postmodern theorizing is synonymous with an attempt to stifle theoretical discussion is profoundly mistaken and perhaps also slightly odd. Not even Wallace (1992: 64), a keen advocate of conceptual standardization and theoretical consolidation in sociology, would argue for closure of theoretical debate: 'we should be self-consciously and perpetually tentative about any … [perspective] … we reach and therefore permit nonconformity, encourage challenge, and welcome revision'. It is entirely possible, however, to endorse the legitimacy of theoretical pluralism while also arguing that greater attention should in future be given to the development of ontologically flexible metatheoretical and theoretical concepts that are part of a relatively *cumulative* orientation towards the development of sociological theory and the construction of empirical knowledge. That having been said, it is important that, for example, there be room for the intellectual loner whose work falls outside any cumulative tendencies. The so-called intellectual 'maverick' is occasionally a source of highly individualistic innovation. A prime example is Norbert Elias. At the time (the 1930s) that he wrote *The Civilizing Process*, Elias did not engage with the 'leading lights' of sociology, nor with their opponents. As Bauman (1979: 123) observed, 'Elias did not address himself to any of the concerns recognized by contemporary sociologists as theirs … he did not engage, even polemically, any of the dominant writers accepted as leading authorities of the profession. He spoke, therefore, past rather than to the discipline as it was at the time.' Despite this, Elias arguably made a substantial contribution to the development of sociological theory (Mennell, 1992). While acknowledging, however, the importance of accommodating intellectual diversity, it can also be argued that the profileration of approaches in sociology over the last quarter of a century or so, and more recently the unsettling effects of the cultural turn and of postmodern rejection of disciplinary practices, are factors which suggest that at the present time a rather greater emphasis on cumulative sociology is justified. Such an emphasis may nurture sociological reflexivity in so far as a cumulative orientation that works across paradigms and across disciplines is an orientation that, where it is internalized to become a routinely sustained theoretical and methodological procedure, sensitizes the theoretician and the empirical researcher to the dialectics of continuities and discontinuities in the production and accumulation of sociological knowledge. Moreover, as evidenced by, for example, Giddens's theory of structuration, a wide-ranging synthesis and critique of the work of others are by no means incompatible with theoretical innovation; it is not only the academic 'loner', such as Elias, who is capable of creating new intellectual pathways. Importantly, a cumulative orientation can engender a reflexive process of learning from previous mistakes. The existence of highly specialized sub-disciplinary academic networks that have little contact with other networks (see Webster, 1993) and the generally non-cumulative style of theory development and knowledge construction in sociology and social theory are, I suggest, part of the explanation of why it is that sociologists too often re-employ variants of unhelpful concepts – including those that involve combinations of reductionism, essentialism, reification, and functional teleology – that replicate or compound previous explanatory failures. Illustrations are contemporary feminist uses of a confused postulate that is known as 'strategic essentialism' (Charles, 1994: 582–3; Spivak, 1990);[8] neo-Marxist employment of the problematical concept 'structural contradictions' as a way of referring to allegedly *empirical* (or 'real') contradictions which, upon closer inspection, turn out to be *theoretical* contradictions and therefore instances of explanatory failure (see the useful discussion in Holmwood and Stewart, 1983: 235); and the reificationist tendencies of writers as diverse as Touraine (1981: 31–2, 59), Eyerman and Jamison (1991: 80), Clegg (1989: 188, 200), and actor network theorists such as Callon (1986: 204; 1991: 140, 142) and Law (1991b: 172–3) who persist in attributing agency to phenomena (such as social movements, physical objects, written materials, diseases, and networks of social relations) that it would be better to regard not as agency but as part of the conditions-of-action, or 'structure' (see Chapters 2 and 5). In light of the above and the earlier references to the 'cardinal sins', there is justification for increased emphasis upon a relatively cumulative sociological orientation in which the development of concepts builds upon critique and draws upon the work of, in particular, those theorists and researchers who attempt – even if not always successfully – to develop conceptual schemes that go beyond the four deficient forms of theoretical and methodological reasoning that were identified in the Introduction.

Implicit in the arguments set out above is the desirability of theoretical and metatheoretical *synthesis* as a way of combining what appear to be the useful elements of theories and conceptual frameworks drawn from a range of, in some cases, mutually opposed schools of thought. Here it is worth emphasizing that theoretical synthesis does not always involve attempts to combine theories that are either wholly alike, or wholly unalike. A multidimensional comparison of a number of theories may reveal that in their original form (that is, prior to any attempts to re-work them) they are already similar in some dimensions (for example, methodology, field of study, or unit of analysis) but dissimilar in other dimensions, such as epistemology or substantive world-view (Glucksmann, 1974: 231–2). For instance, what Law refers to as recursive historical contingency is, as he notes (1994: 97), a method of enquiry associated with symbolic inter-actionism, with Elias's figurational sociology, and with Giddens's theory of structuration. An aspect of synthesis that was touched upon earlier is reflected in Giddens's observation that synthesis implies some degree of closure of the diversity of standpoints within an academic discipline, but that this is not the same as supposing that synthesis rests on simplistic 'cumulative and uncontested' models of the generation of sociological knowledge (1987: 31). There is room in sociology for special theories and theoretical pluralism, *and* for cumulative and synthetic orientations (Bryant and Jary, 1991: 30). In fact, however, there is considerable opposition to the idea of synthesis; part of the reason for this was broached in the earlier discussion of postmodern thought. Postmodernists' rejection of theoretical synthesis and conceptual integration is part and parcel of their hostility towards foundational perspectives and cumulative social science. However, although postmodernists are 'for' theoretical fragmentation, the idea of theoretical consolidation via synthesis is, ironically enough, compatible with the postmodern notion that the boundaries between theories should be subverted or dissolved (Kellner, 1990: 277): there is, as the following chapters will endeavour to show, something to be gained by engaging in a process of synthesis that involves 'intertradition boundary work' (Alexander and Colomy, 1992: 41). Not, of course, that all objections against the idea of synthesis are postmodern. Traditional objections take the form that opposing paradigms are incommensurable (for example, Jackson and Carter, 1991) and that it is logically impossible to combine – in a single scheme – mutually exclusive concepts (Holmwood, 1996: 36, 39). The post-modern and other objections are flawed. The grounds for this judgement derive partly from the previously described idea of ontological flexibility; partly from related arguments concerning an avoidance of essentialism and reductionism; and to some extent from the previously mentioned procedure which Glucksmann (1974) refers to as a multi-dimensional comparison of theories. There may also be variation in the extent to which concepts are tied to their theoretical origins – that is, variation in the range of meanings that can meaningfully be ascribed to a particular concept, and the degree to which concepts can be modified or re-worked – and it would be simplistic to claim that the truth of this matter lies either with Durkheim or with Garfinkel (Wallace, 1992: 62–3). In other words, it is not necessary to sup-pose that all concepts are wholly context (or 'paradigm') dependent; for example, the concept of fortuity or *social chance* (this being a significant concept in some of the approaches described in later chapters) has evolved in a variety of sociological paradigms (Smith, 1993). Therefore, in response to traditional objections of the kind voiced by Hamilton (1974: 150) in his criticism of the idea of synthesis, all that need be said here is that there are, as illustrated in the following chapters, good reasons for suggesting that synthesis and theoretical integration – within, but also, wherever appropriate, across social science disciplines – is perfectly legitimate providing the integration, where it combines otherwise unaligned or mutually exclusive concepts, does not contradict itself through failure to re-work the cluster of imported conceptualizations so as to make them compatible.

Summary

•

Meta-concepts and metatheory, sometimes referred to as sensitizing theory, are unavoidable in social analysis. The meta-concepts – such as agency, structure, micro and macro – referred to in this and later chapters are developed in conjunction with a critique of the four 'cardinal sins' of (meta)theoretical and methodological reasoning (namely reductionism, essentialism, reification, and functional teleology).

•

Postmodern theory, though one or two elements of postmodern thought can usefully be incorporated into social analysis, is an inadequate metatheoretical framework: postmodern theory entails idealism and hypercontextualism, is determinist, and has a confused notion of the relation of discourses to their social contexts.

•

Discourses, whether academic, political, cultural, professional or other discourses, spiral into and out of social contexts, but they have varying degrees of independence and there is no 'necessary match' here: the relation between discourses and context(s) is generally loosely dialectical – discourse and context may to some extent influence each other, but change in the one does not result in automatic or matching change in the other.

•

There are grounds for suggesting that social analysis should be based on a flexible, realist social ontology that in some sense is minimal: by 'minimal' is meant that it is not metatheory or social ontology, nor indeed substantive theory but empirical enquiry that should do the bulk of the work in revealing the characteristics and significance of any particular empirical phenomena. Overblown and inflexible ontologies tend to lead to premature (meta)theoretical and ontological closure. There is a case, also, for suggesting that four important elements – metatheory, substantive theory, methodology, and empirical materials – should (a) be consistent with each other, and (b) should regulate each other. This means that metatheoretical (including ontological) concepts should be regarded as open to theoretical and empirical sources of revision.

•

The argument of this book is that there is much to gain from a cumulative, synthetic orientation that involves both disciplinary and interdisciplinary activities.

Notes

1 In discussions of methodology and philosophy of social scientific explanation, it is appropriate to retain an analytical distinction between ontology and epistemology. However, it should be borne in mind that we are speaking here of a matter of emphasis and focus: there is some blurring of the distinction in so far as, for example, realist epistemological propositions concerning the question of how we might acquire reliable knowledge about the empirical world are not unconnected to ontological conceptions of, in general terms, the kinds of things that constitute social reality. In short, our conception of what and how we can know about any particular things is conditioned by our conception of the general nature of things.

2 The difficulty, as evidenced in the literature, of clearly demarcating 'social' from 'sociological' theory, is not central to this chapter, though it is something that is worth noting. For Delanty (2000: 22) the 'defining characteristics of modern social theory' are 'three problems; the socialization of the individual (or social subjectivity), the rationality of knowledge, and the legitimation of power'. Delanty, though his introductory account of the foundations of social theory is scholarly and generally insightful, seems convinced (ibid.: 23) in his claim that there is an important distinction to be made between sociological theory and social theory, yet his claim relies on the vague assertion that the former is in some unspecified way 'more narrowly defined' than the latter (ibid.: 43). These observations are less a criticism of Delanty than a reflection of the absence of unambiguous conceptual schemes for addressing both the question of the distinction to be made between sociological theory and social theory and the question of the relation of the one to the other (see Sica, 1998; Antonio, 1998: 63).

3 Interestingly, Seidman's (1992) rationale for postmodern thought is in some sense an inverted form of Spivak's feminist 'strategic essentialism' (see Introduction, note 5). Seidman does not argue for strategic essentialism but for a putative strategic

anti-essentialism that is also anti-foundational. He states (1992: 60) that instead of epistemological and ontological (that is, metatheoretical) debate of, for example, agency–structure and idealism–materialism, all such matters should be decided not by theoretical or metatheoretical reasoning and/or by methodological considerations but by selecting a conceptual 'solution' that has the most favourable 'moral-political consequences'; unfortunately, we are not told how this rather vacuous criterion of conceptual-cum-political adequacy might be operationalized.

My own view is that Seidman's and others' postmodern prescription for turning the whole of sociology into a series of 'local', particularistic, and *discontinuous* discourses geared in some unspecified way to the achievement of (which?) moral-political objectives, should, as Krokidas put it, be avoided as 'a particularly bad piece of metatheoretical advice' (1993: 534).

4 It is worth recalling here that, as briefly noted in the Introduction, the four illicit modes of theoretical reasoning described earlier, while perhaps most visible in certain types of 'modernist' theorizing (such as Marxism, radical feminism, rational choice theory, structuralism, and teleological functionalism), are not absent from poststructuralist/postmodern approaches such as Foucault's which in places slides towards reification and essentialism (see Chapter 3).

5 For reasons that are examined later in the book and which are implicit in this chapter's discussion of a flexible but realist social ontology, the frequently employed distinction between *modernist* theories (by which postmodernists generally mean reductionist, essentialist, and teleological theorizing), and *postmodern* theories which refuse to countenance realist ontologies, is not an altogether satisfactory distinction. The distinction implies an oversimplified either-or choice of metatheoretical orientations.

Also, the 'type of society' version of postmodernism tends to assume that modern and postmodern societies are two readily identifiable and distinct structural types that are almost entirely unalike. In fact, the dividing line between modern/postmodern societies is far more blurred than most postmodern theorists recognize, and postmodernists generally fail to recognize that there are empirical discontinuities *and* continuities as between the so-called 'traditional', 'modern', and 'postmodern' types of society (on this, see Smart, 1991: 20, and Rose, 1988: 362).

6 In her study of social stratification and forms of inequality, Bradley (1996) to some extent mirrors the arguments set out here concerning the loosely dialectical relation of discourses to their social contexts, whereby discourses spiral into and out of the social fabric (though I would want to emphasize more explicitly than Bradley the more general metatheoretical postulate that discourses may be modified (a) as they travel across time–space, and (b) as they are mediated at differing levels – micro, mezo, and macro – of social process: see Chapters 6 and 7). Combining modernist realism with a postmodern-type flexible ontology, she observes that for post-structuralists and postmodernists, 'class' and 'women' are purely mental or linguistic constructions with no real empirical referents. Hence, she argues, postmodernists signally fail to address 'real' social differentiation and social inequalities. For Bradley, social categories such as 'men', 'class', or 'race' and ethnicity may indeed be fluid and mutable, but the constructs ('men' and so forth) that refer to those categories have some basis in 'lived experiences' (material reality); the constructs, when employed in social scientific, cultural, political, professional or other discourses are perhaps not a perfect match with, but are at least partly or loosely grounded in, material reality (Bradley, 1996: 3, 6–7, 9–10, 202–3). In turn, the discursive constructs that refer to these social categories tend in one form or another to 'feed back'

to material reality and modify social categories and contexts (1996: 8) The general question of the relation of discourses to social contexts is taken up in Chapter 3.

7 However, what I call metatheory is referred to by Layder (1998a: 94) as 'general theory'; he fears that the term 'meta'-theory implies a body of theorizing that is cut off from empirical concerns, and that use of the term therefore lends ammunition to empiricists and others who reject general, abstract 'sensitizing' theory of the kind that both Layder and I regard as having an indispensable part to play in sociological practice. While I am sympathetic to Layder's concerns, my inclination, along with Ritzer's (1992), is to retain what is, after all, a fairly well-established terminology: the word 'meta', it seems to me, is as good a term as any for denoting a distinction between general sensitizing (or meta-) theory, and substantive theories.

8 See Introduction, note 5.

2

Agency–structure and Micro–macro

In the following pages, which provide part of the theoretical background to themes and topics that will take centre-stage in later chapters, the intention is to provide a synopsis and critique of various theorists' attempts to handle two highly significant but controversial metatheoretical formulations – widely referred to as *agency–structure* and *micro–macro* – that in my approach are grounded in the previously described idea of a flexible but realist social ontology allied to concept development that builds upon a critique of the four 'cardinal sins'. Conceptual controversies and ambiguities surrounding agency–structure and micro–macro are perennial but also contemporary features of general social theory, and of theoretical and methodological debate in virtually all of the social science disciplines (Ritzer, 1990). This chapter has two main aims. They are, first, to establish in general terms the importance of agency–structure and micro–macro as concepts that refer to differing dimensions of social reality, and second, to review conceptual problems and disputes surrounding contemporary debate of these concepts and, on the basis of critique, to offer a personal view of how the concepts should be employed. The chapter begins by examining some of the ways in which the concepts have been used in classical theory, and more particularly, in modern social theory. With reference to the work of major contemporary sociological theorists such as Giddens, Archer, and Mouzelis, the later section of the chapter addresses problems of definition and interpretation, as well as differences of theoretical approach that continue to shape debate of these contested concepts.

Agency—structure and micro—macro in
classical and contemporary theory

Mouzelis argues that 'the present debate on the links between micro and macro sociology, as well as the older, related debate on methodological individualism versus holism, *have led precisely nowhere*' (1993a: 680, my italics). He perhaps slightly overstates the case. Nevertheless, progress in resolving the difficulties to which Mouzelis refers, has undoubtedly been slow and fragmented. Theoretical, methodological, and empirical advances have tended to be scattered across various social science disciplines and across specialized areas of social theory, and at the present time there is, bearing in mind the discussion in the preceding chapter, a good case for a rather more cumulative and synthetic approach to conceptual and methodological problems surrounding agency—structure and micro—macro. It should be observed, first of all, that there is a certain amount of concept standardization in the ways that the terms 'agency', 'structure', 'micro' and 'macro' are used, but also some definitional variation and not a little ambiguity; therefore, in addressing instances of theoretical disagreement concerning these concepts it is not always easy to distinguish between substantive differences of perspective among opposing theorists, and exchanges that seemingly reflect terminological confusion and misunderstanding of others' theoretical position. Part of the concern of this chapter will be to map variations in uses of these terms, as well as tracing important differences of perspective. I will also indicate, in the next section, my conception of how these concepts should be employed, taking into account – here as elsewhere throughout the book – the earlier arguments for concept development that builds upon critique of the four problematical modes of reasoning that were defined and discussed in the Introduction.

In social theory and in social science disciplines, *agency* tends to be associated with human creativity and social action, *structure* with patterned relations, with constraints upon action, and with macro-social phenomena; *micro* is for the most part employed as a term that denotes settings of face-to-face interaction (situations of 'co-presence', as Giddens calls them), while *macro* is frequently used to refer to 'society' and social institutions. Quite often, agency is linked to micro, with structure (or 'social structure') being more commonly associated with macro-social phenomena. Later, it will be argued that some of these conceptualizations are highly problematical, and should therefore be resisted. Nevertheless, it is important to recognize that they enjoy quite wide support and there is a general (though not universal) tendency among social theorists to accord considerable importance to distinctions between agency and structure, and micro and macro.

It is the view of some contemporary theorists that agency–structure (Archer, 1988: ix–x) and micro–macro (Knorr-Cetina, 1981: 2; Munch and Smelser, 1987; Ritzer, 1990) are *the* core underlying problematics of social theory and sociology; this is not a view with which I have any major disagreement, though I would add that 'social chance' and 'time–space' are also significant, and that all of these metatheoretical concepts (meta-concepts, for short) are too often employed in a tacit fashion that fails to *explicitly* address the part that they play in the development of substantive concepts and theories and in the design of empirical studies.

The major classical theorists – there is space here to refer only very briefly to Marx, Durkheim, and Weber – each in their own way tackled the problematics with which this chapter is concerned. Though Marx often referred to agency, subjectivity, and individual consciousness, it is very clear, taking into account his work as a whole, including changes in emphasis as between the 'early' and 'late' Marx (for example, Marx, 1954; 1957; 1964; 1973; 1984), that he gave analytical primacy to social structure and to 'objective' social reality. In terms of micro–macro, the bulk of his work was concerned with macro-structural phenomena. In opposition to Hegel's idealism, Marx argued that it is not ideas that shape society; rather, material existence largely determines ideas. Concepts such as ideology, class interests, structural contradictions, and false consciousness are employed by Marx in ways that make some allowance for agency and subjectivity but which tend to prioritize the macro-structural elements of society, particularly economic institutions. Structuralist Marxism associated with, in particular, the writings of Althusser (1965; 1971) and Poulantzas (1973) is an attempt to remove economism, social determinism, and reductionism from 'orthodox' Marxism. However, it can be argued that the central structuralist Marxist concepts of 'relative autonomy' and 'determination in the last instance' fail to displace economic reductionism and determinism from Marxist and neo-Marxist theorizing (see the excellent discussion of this point in Hindess, 1981; 1983a: 39–42).

Like Marx, Durkheim focused mainly upon 'objective' and macro dimensions of the social. Durkheim's later work (1965; 1982) had a considerable influence on twentieth-century structuralist thought. His emphasis (Durkheim, 1951; 1964) on macro-social phenomena led him to insist that 'social facts' – a concept used by Durkheim to signify, for example, religion, the division of labour, the 'collective conscience' or central value system of a society, and social institutions such as property and marriage – should be explained in terms of *other* social facts; this was a fairly significant step in the history of sociological thought, since it explicitly codified and elaborated the idea that explanatory problems encountered at one level of reality (Durkheim's main interest being the social, the level at which social facts have their existence) cannot legitimately be reduced to phenomena which occur at *other* levels of reality (such as the psychological, or the biological). Like physical facts in nature, social facts in Durkheimian terms have distinct empirical properties of their own; for example, it is often possible to discern patterned regularities and also causal relations between social facts. As just noted, a defining characteristic of social facts is that they are not reducible to – that is, cannot be explained in terms of – phenomena that exist at other levels of reality. For example, in Durkheim's (1964) theory of social development it is argued that the transition from traditional to modern society resulted from population growth and an increase in 'dynamic density' (the 'extent of interaction' or number of social relationships per person) leading to increased competition for land and other resources, and to the emergence of a specialized division of labour as a response to increased competition; here, social change occurs for *social* reasons that cannot legitimately be reduced to the level of individual motives. That is to say, individuals as they went about their lives did not set out to produce a new type of society with a high level of occupational and social specialization. In Durkheim's theoretical scheme, 'jumping' levels of analysis, and in particular, attempting to explain the social level of reality in terms of the psychological level consisting of individual motives and individual attributes, is rejected as an illicit methodological procedure. This relates, of course, to the argument that society has emergent properties that are 'more than', and therefore cannot be explained in terms of, the interactions and actions of individuals; because social facts are 'emergent' (a concept that will be examined more closely in Chapter 3) they must, as noted earlier, be explained at the level of reality – the social – at which they occur, that is, in terms of *other* social facts. It was this strongly anti-individualist reasoning that underscored Durkheim's (1951) classic study of suicide rates. For Durkheim, social facts, including the social facts that shape suicide rates, are macro-phenomena that are relatively continuous – they precede any particular individual, and will continue to exist long after particular individuals have departed the social scene. Although a Durkheimian focus on macro-structure and 'objective' social reality usefully addresses aspects of the social that some later theorists such as symbolic interactionists and phenomenologists tended to neglect, the approach is vulnerable to the criticism that it fails to properly take account of the significance of agency and of the micro-social; this is something that will be returned to later.

We have noted that Marx and Durkheim tended to downplay agency and to place too much emphasis upon social structure and upon the idea of an 'objective' macro-social order that largely determines social action. When compared with Marx and with Durkheim, Weber (1932; 1947; 1949; 1978) in some respects had what might be called a more 'balanced' view of agency and structure.[1] He recognized the importance of macro-structural processes, such as the rise of capitalism as a social and economic system, but his conception of macro-structure was non-reductionist in so far as he remained empirically open to the possibility that social phenomena may have multiple, interlocking causes; this relates to Weber's understanding – which contrasts with Marx's rather deterministic conception of historical development – of the part that unplanned 'conjunctions' (by which Weber meant unintended and causally unrelated combinations of social phenomena) may play in shaping the course of social life (Turner, 1992a; Kalberg, 1994a). Weber also gave more emphasis than either Marx or Durkheim to actors' meanings, understandings, and motives. His work influenced the development of interpretative sociology, even though he himself was, as Campbell (1998) observed, more individualist than, for example, interpretative theorists and researchers who, in the years after Weber's death became associated with the symbolic interactionist tradition. Weber was more complex and arguably more sophisticated than Marx and Durkheim in his treatment of agency–structure and micro–macro: he attempted, with some success, to avoid the extremes, as he saw them, of positivism and idealism, and he also tried to give due theoretical and methodological weight to individuals and social action while attempting to develop a non-reductive conception of the macro-social. However, it also has to be said, with reference to the concerns of this chapter, that there was a certain amount of ambiguity in his reasoning (Kalberg, 1994b: 13–14, 31). Weber's work undoubtedly had a micro and agency dimension; indeed, his methodological prescriptions advocated an individualist and micro-orientated 'bottom-up' approach to the study of social structure. But in his empirical studies, such as *The Protestant Ethic and the Spirit of Capitalism* (1932), he emphasized macro-structure and did so in somewhat 'top-down', macro-to-micro fashion; large-scale patterns of meanings and social institutions (to do with, for example, Calvinist religion and the 'spirit of capitalism') were regarded by Weber as forces that powerfully shaped the forms of thought and behaviour of individuals. The existence, however, of certain tensions and ambiguities in Weber's work does not obscure the importance of his contribution to the development of sociological thought; for example, his work is relevant to recent theorizing on the relation of agency and structure to 'social chance' (see Chapter 5).

When we turn to modern social theory we find there are approaches – some that draw quite explicitly on classical theory – which emphasize structure in ways that neglect agency and which accord analytical primacy to the macro-social. One such approach – some others are discussed below – is *structuralism*. Structuralist theory entails an analytical movement from subject (or actor) to structure: people are viewed as products of structure and as 'decentred' from their own meanings, and for structuralists it is structure, not agency, that is the main focus of analysis. Theoretical movement from action to structure rests on a claim that structure is self-regulatory, systemically self-sustaining, and synchronic: 'At the heart of the idea of structuralism is the idea of system: a complete, self-regulating entity that adapts to new conditions by transforming its features whilst retaining its systemic structure' (Scholes, 1974: 10). It is evident that this statement entails reification (here I am using the definition of reification set out in the Introduction). Reification together with determinism based on a reductionist notion of language and action is a feature of the sub-field of structuralism that became known as structuralist linguistics (Saussure, 1974; Lévi-Strauss, 1963; 1974): in this objectivist, autonomizing conception of language, 'it is not we who think and then use words but our language that thinks for us' (Sharp, 1980: 99). The deterministic supposition that language (or *langue* in Saussurian terms) is an autonomous entity existing independently of its situated practice by individuals or groups is part of the structuralist proposition that human actors are unknowingly 'inserted' into language (Barthes, 1967). Relatedly, in structuralist linguistics there is no correspondence between a word and the object to which the word refers; rather, the meaning of a word (or sound-image) is determined by its relation to other words and to concepts of objects (but not, as just noted, to objects in the real world).

Not only structuralism, but also *poststructuralism* (for example, Lacan, 1977; Foucault, 1970; 1972; 1980a) is implicated in a form of social determinism that neglects agency. The structuralist link between words/sound-images (the signifier) and the concept of an object (the signified) is broken by poststructuralist theorists, for whom meanings are constantly shifting and arbitrary. Structuralists propose, first of all, that neither signifier nor signified represent or are linked to anything 'real', but second, that there is a more or less stable link between signifier and signified. Poststructuralism rejects the second proposition. Texts and, by implication, society are open to multiple 'readings' (an emphasis on the reader) and any interpretation or reading is never 'finished' or 'final' but is and should be subject to endless challenges and re-interpretations (Derrida, 1982). Nothing is really real and therefore analysis has to centre on discourses and the processes involved in textual constructions of a putative 'reality'. For example, the poststructuralist concept of *intertextuality* refers to the interplay of texts, which results in texts modifying each other when they are read and re-read (re-interpreted) and therefore texts – and any account or 'discourse' that purports to refer to a 'real' empirical world – are indeterminate and subject to continuous re-interpretation and reformulation; and nor, as intimated earlier, is there a conventional or 'correspondence theory' criterion for arbitrating among interpretations or discourses, since for poststructuralist theorists there is no real world 'out there' against which competing discourses or representations can be empirically tested. As briefly noted in the Introduction, in poststructuralist and postmodern theory it is not only that discourse reigns supreme; a deterministic conception of agency is also involved in so far as, despite an ostensible emphasis on authors and 'readings', the author or actor is 'decentred' and viewed as an effect or product of discourse(s). *Discourse theory*, and here I have in mind Laclau and Mouffe's (1985; 1987) influential work, borrows in part from Saussure's structuralist linguistics. However, unlike structuralist linguistics, discourse theory also draws upon poststructural and postmodern theory and it is argued that discourses (and societies) are never 'closed' – there are no 'fixed' or stable meanings – but rather, they exist in a state of endless reformulation and flux. Incorporated within discourse theory, then, are the following poststructuralist propositions: there is no pre-discursive social reality and therefore no benchmark against which we can empirically test the veracity of competing discourses or representations of 'reality' (rather, what counts as 'truth' is, as, for example, Foucault insisted, a matter of politics, power and rights to define the world); any discourses which attempt to convey a sense of 'the real world' are arbitrary, and endlessly reformulable; and actors' forms of thought and actions are effects or products of discourses. Discourse theory raises interesting questions about 'the social construction of reality' and about the part that politics plays in exchanges between competing discursive attempts to define the world (Derrida, 1996; Laclau, 1990: 31–3). However, my own sympathies lie with the view that discourse theory can legitimately be criticized for its brand of social determinism and neglect of agency, and for its refusal to take seriously the idea that there exists an ontologically complex and more or less indeterminate but nevertheless real empirical world that is at least partly independent of discursive activities.

The following are examples of other deterministic approaches that elevate one or another conception of structure above agency. It was observed earlier that structuralist Marxism is a theoretical perspective that is flawed by a commitment to social determinism and a neglect of agency. The 'last instance' reductionism of revised Marxism is revealed in, for instance, Leonard's Marxist theory of social work; he argues that 'ideology' rests ultimately on 'economic imperatives' (1984: 49) and, in effect, his argument is that the empirical complexities of social life are reducible to the thesis that 'economic production is determinant "in the last instance"' (1984: 104). Habermas's (1986; 1987; 1989) theoretical scheme is another example of over-emphasis on macro-structural phenomena and a neglect of agency.

Habermas attempts, in theoretical terms that are ultimately contradictory, to combine voluntaristic action theory with a deterministic systems theory; it is true that, in principle, non-contradictory theoretical syntheses of action and structure are possible (see Chapter 1), but such a synthesis is not achieved by Habermas. Systems are imbued with agency in his theoretical scheme (1987: 159–60), and thereby reified. A further complication – relating to the system/social integration distinction which will be discussed in Chapter 3 – is Habermas's contradictory tendency to largely ignore agency in the study of what he calls 'System' (polity and economy). In his theoretical framework, System is inspected only in system-integration terms, whereas, he argues, the 'Lifeworld' (taken-for-granted meanings employed in everyday life among family, friends and associates) should be viewed in social-integration terms: this neglect by Habermas of agency and actor–actor relations in politics, bureaucracies, and markets, and conversely, the neglect of systemic, role-patterned, and institutional aspects of the lifeworld, limits the usefulnessness of his approach to agency–structure (see the useful discussion in Mouzelis, 1997). This is not to deny that there is much that is of value in Habermas's extensive writings; rather, it is to challenge and criticize his handling of agency–structure. Much the same can be said of Bourdieu (1977; 1984; 1990; 1998), who is widely regarded as another major theorist of agency–structure. Bourdieu, for all his references to the importance of agency, is ultimately committed to a deterministic view of agency; his version of what he calls 'constructivist structuralism' is much closer to structuralism than to constructivism. For example, Bourdieu (1984: 110) believes actors' dispositions are largely determined by the social positions they occupy and by their 'habitus' (this is defined by Bourdieu as tacit knowledge, derived from life experience, which actors habitually draw upon).

Having briefly identified a number of classical and contemporary macro-structural perspectives that tend to downplay the micro-social order and to neglect subjectivity, agency, and intersubjectivity, it is important to note that adoption of a macro-social approach does not necessarily mean that agency will be neglected or viewed in purely deterministic terms. As will become clearer later, a macro-social orientation need not rely upon theories of structural predetermination. For example, Roberto Unger's (1987a; 1987b; 1987c; 1997) theoretical work, which has been largely overlooked by European and American theorists, is indubitably of macro scope, but Unger recognizes that contingency and indeterminacy play a large part in human affairs (see the discussion of Unger's work in Chapter 7). A closely related point is that the macro-social order, though likely to have some influence upon social life at 'lower' – that is, mezo or micro – levels of social process, may shape social conditions not only in the direction of systemic stability and predictability, but also in the direction of unpredictability, indeterminacy, and social flux. The point being made here is that although seemingly paradoxical in light of the connotations of constraint and prede-termination that have tended, erroneously, to be seen as the hallmark of the concept 'structure', structural conditioning may sometimes take the form of the creation of tendencies that stimulate social indeterminacy and unpredictability. An illustration is to be found in the policy process associ-ated with the European Union (EU). In political science and policy analy-sis literature – including writing on governance (Rhodes, 1997; Burns, 1999; Kooiman, 1999) – there is for the most part an understanding that the macro-dimension of politico-administrative systems influences the policy process and to a greater or lesser extent shapes interaction among political and policy actors. In the case of the EU, which may be regarded as a macro-postnational system of governance (Cram, 1997), it is often argued (for example, Kassim, 1994; Richardson, 1996; Cram *et al.*, 1999) that the architecture of the European Union – including the complex formal and also informal relations between its main organizational and institutional components; dispersed loci of power and shifting, highly variable sources of influence; and the EU's multi-level governance processes within and across nation–states – makes for a Euro policy process that, far from being corpo-ratist or hierarchical, is highly fluid, unstable, and variable: this is quite often reflected in shifting, unpredictable patterns of interaction among political and policy actors at the micro and mezo levels of the EU policy process (see the empirical material in Bulmer, 1993, and Judge *et al.*, 1994). Macro-shaping of social conditions may, then, be in the direction of the routinization of social action – or, as in the example of the European Union policy process, in the direction of social flux and indeterminacy (George and Bache, 2001). This is one reason – there are others, which are discussed in the following section – for challenging the tendency of some theorists to assume, often in a tacit kind of way, that the idea of macro-structure must necessarily imply constraints upon agency, institutionalization of behaviour, and predictability of social outcomes.

Empirical investigation of situations of co-presence – which is where a large part of our lived experience occurs – is a vital part of the study of social life. As Layder (1997: 1) observes: 'Much of everyday social life is conducted at … [the] … face-to-face level in which participants formulate their conduct in the light of the behaviour and intentions of the others pre-sent.' Even in what Albrow refers to as 'the global age', where the signifi-cance of relations associated with place, community, and family is often said to be in decline, face-to-face relations 'still matter' (Albrow, 1996: 138, 167). If we wish to avoid what Mouzelis (1991: 138) calls 'downwards reductionism' (or 'downwards conflation' in Archer's (1995: 7) terms), which rests on the assumption that micro-phenomena have no dynamics of their own and can be explained in terms of macro-phenomena, it is necessary to incorporate micro-situational theory and methodology into sociology's *modus operandi*. Macro-structural theories – including variants of structuralism, Parsonian structural-functionalism, and Marxism – which portray actors' forms of thought and practices as direct or indirect expressions of a determinate macro-system or macro-discourse, are rejected by micro-situational researchers associated with the symbolic interactionist approach, an approach that focuses upon actors' creativity and capacity for modifying existing meanings and also upon the emergence of 'new' meanings and intentions that come into being *during* the actual process of face-to-face interaction.[2] The intellectual roots of symbolic interactionism – and here I am not concerned with differences of emphasis among its proponents (see Meltzer *et al.*, 1975) – lie in the writings of Weber, Georg Simmel, Robert Park, William Isaac Thomas, Charles Horton Cooley, John Dewey, and George Herbert Mead (see Rose, 1972). Interpretative sociology as represented by, for example, Cooley (1902), Mead (1967) and Blumer (1969) stands in sharp contrast to, say, structuralism, Marxism and Parsonian sociology, and gives emphasis to subjective experience and, in particular, the intersubjective 'negotiation' of experiences and meanings in situations of co-presence. In regard to agency–structure and micro–macro, it should be noted that postmodern and poststructuralist thought and discourse theory fail to recognize the significance of intersubjectivity and the interaction order. Although modern macro-structural theory and postmodern theory are in some respects diametrically opposed, what they tend to share in common is a determinist image of social action (Turner, 1990: 248). Poststructuralist and postmodern theorists fail to perceive the analytical significance of a non-deterministic conception of the micro-social sphere (Best and Kellner, 1991: 66); for example, postmodern theory (together with structuralism and discourse theory) neglects interaction and intersubjectivity as a crucial mediating factor that may result in 'local' modifications or perhaps local transformations of the contents and meaning of macro 'discourses'. As already noted, in the symbolic interactionist tradition the typical unit of analysis is situations of co-presence, and investigation focuses on local handling of trans-situational meanings and also the emergence – during the process of interaction – of wholly or partially new meanings and motives: writers within this tradition emphasize that even (macro-) institutionalized meanings and understandings that stretch widely across time and space can be re-assembled, re-negotiated, and 'mixed' in novel ways in local (micro-) settings. Unlike, say, structuralist linguistics or discourse theory, a micro-situational approach to the study of words, language, and cognition rests on the methodological rubric, 'Don't ask for the meaning: ask for the use' (Ryle and Findlay, 1972: 7), which in turn is derived from a theoretical postulate which suggests that practice and speech in micro-settings are not 'signifiers' of macro-structures (Heller, 1986: 155–7). In micro-social studies informed by symbolic interactionism, emphasis is placed on *inter*subjectivity and *inter*action (Simmel, 1971: 23); the approach is therefore distinguishable not only from methodological collectivism but also from methodological individualism.[3] Micro-social analysis, it is worth noting, is of considerable value in the field of policy studies (Haimes, 1993). For example, Jewson and Mason's (1986) study of equal opportunities policies in a manufacturing firm and in a local authority drew attention to the importance of adopting a micro-empirical focus as a means of gaining an understanding of participants' meanings and motives; by concentrating their enquiry on the *in situ* employment of meanings and the negotiation of, and sometimes the re-formulation of meanings during ongoing social interaction in organizational contexts, Jewson and Mason were able to empirically document actors' struggles and confusions surrounding 'liberal' versus 'radical' conceptions of equal opportunities policies and practices. Also, and while care must be exercised whenever attempts are made to extrapolate from individual case studies, it would appear that Jewson and Mason's micro-situational study throws light on general problems and ambiguities surrounding equal opportunities policies, problems that are not entirely 'local' or situationally specific and which in some form are likely to be encountered wherever such policies are practised (see Bagilhole, 1997). It is not only in sociology that there has been some renewal of interest in micro-studies. In political science, Marsh and Stoker (1995b: 292–4) argue that future work within their discipline should pay explicit attention to micro-processes, and that greater attention should also be given by political scientists to the problem of finding a satisfactory method of integrating micro-, mezo- and macro-levels of analysis (see Chapters 3 and 7). However, it is important to observe that in terms of finding a satisfactory way of addressing agency–structure and micro–macro, there are limits to what can be achieved by micro-situational analysis. Symbolic interactionism, and also phenomenology (Schutz, 1962; 1972) are not well equipped, theoretically or methodologically, to undertake investigation of macro-phenomena; this limitation is discussed in some detail in Chapter 7, which pulls together key methodological aspects of the arguments set out in the earlier chapters. As well, it will be observed in the next chapter that some writers have argued that symbolic interactionists' emphasis on *inter*subjectivity and *inter*action has resulted in neglect of a 'Weberian' recognition of the importance of the individual and of subjectivity (for example, Campbell, 1998: Layder, 1997). For the present, however, it remains to identify a number of central themes and controversies arising from the various points made above; to do this it is intended to refer in the following section to three major sociological theorists (namely Archer, Giddens, and Mouzelis) whose work throws up a number of rather complicated conceptual twists and turns relating to contemporary debate of agency–structure and micro–macro.

Themes and controversies

In order to adequately address contemporary themes and controversies that relate to the preceding discussion, it is necessary, first of all, to recognize the existence of miscommunication among theorists. It was briefly observed earlier that a certain amount of ambiguity and also variation in meaning are features of the debate surrounding agency–structure and micro–macro. Caution is therefore required in mapping differing uses of these concepts. Misinterpretations occur quite often. An instance is Mouzelis's (1991: 35) criticism that Giddens's theory of structuration ignores what Mouzelis calls 'macro action' (a term Mouzelis uses to denote action that has far-reaching consequences affecting many people; he particularly has in mind decisions made by people in positions of authority such as government ministers or the heads of large firms, as well as decisions made by meetings or committees whose members have a high level of formal authority, such as a meeting of heads of state). This criticism, which is repeated in Mouzelis (1993a: 682), seems to rest, as Giddens (1993: 7) himself observes in a response to Mouzelis's critique, on a misunderstanding of how the theory of structuration relates to what Mouzelis (but not Giddens; see later) terms the 'micro–macro' distinction: nowhere, despite Mouzelis's claim to the contrary, does Giddens deny the existence of what Mouzelis rather confusingly calls 'macro action'. Another example of misinterpretation over the debate of agency–structure and micro–macro is McLennan's (1995: 121) erroneous claim – made in a paper that in other respects is scholarly and insightful – that Mouzelis (1991) criticizes Giddens on the grounds that Giddens associates micro with voluntarism and with agency, and macro with structure viewed as constraint upon agency. In point of fact, Giddens (1984: 139; 1993: 7) rejects the conflations micro-agency and macro-structure (as does Mouzelis, 1991: 32); it is also the case that Mouzelis (1991: 32) recognizes that Giddens opposes these conflations, and here McLennan seems to have misinterpreted the theoretical positions of both Giddens and Mouzelis. It is true, as I shall observe in Chapter 3, that Mouzelis (1989; 1991; 1993b; 1995; 1997) formulates reasons for being critical of some aspects of Giddens's conceptual framework, but these are not the reasons adduced by McLennan.

Leaving aside the above examples of conceptual confusions that arise from contemporary theorists' misapprehension of others' terminologies and differing ways of handling agency–structure and micro–macro, there are divergences that rest less on misunderstandings than on real differences of approach at the level of social ontology. One of these differences concerns the unusual and, in my opinion, the inadequate conception of micro–macro that is to be found in Archer's morphogenetic social theory (as with the work of many of the theorists criticized in this and other chapters, what follows is not intended to be a wholesale condemnation of Archer's theoretical scheme: there is much that is invaluable in her framework, as indicated in Chapter 4). Most theorists employ the term 'micro' to refer to social phenomena or units of analysis – situations of face-to-face interaction, or co-presence – that in terms of 'size' are small-scale, as distinct from macro-phenomena that (as in the case of social institutions) are large-scale in the sense that they extend widely across time and social space. In contrast, Archer (1995: 8–9, 12) argues that micro–macro should not refer to differences in the absolute 'size' of social phenomena, but rather, to *relative* differences in size and to a relational conception of scale associated with the concept of 'emergence'. It is perhaps unusual, given the sheer significance of Archer's critique of social theory and her 'anti-conflationary' theoretical sociology, that her view of this matter has hardly been noticed (indeed, and as King (1999: 199) observes, her theoretical framework as a whole has, until very recently, received surprisingly little attention from social theorists and sociologists). The immediate point of interest here is Archer's insistence that a given unit of analysis may be 'micro' in relation to one stratum of society, and 'macro' in relation to another: 'what justifies the differentiation of strata and thus use of the terms "micro" and "macro" to characterize their relationship is the existence of emergent properties pertaining to the latter but not to the former, even if they were elaborated from it' (Archer, 1995: 9). Thus, in Archer's terms, a dyad may be regarded as micro, but if that dyad formed part of a slightly larger social grouping (a committee or a household, say), then the latter, in relation to the dyad, would be investigated as a 'macro' phenomena. Archer's own illustration of this principle, a principle which in my opinion misappropriates the otherwise important notions of relationalism and emergence, is as follows: the 'societal properties of Britain' (1995: 10) may be 'macro' when viewed in terms of a study that is focused on Britain, but 'micro' when Britain is looked at in the context of Europe. Archer's unusual conception of micro–macro – though I have no quarrel with the general idea of 'emergence', to which she refers[4] – should be resisted, in favour of a more conventional definition. It is obviously true that the size of social phenomena and of social wholes (a family, a small group, an organization, a community or whatever) is in some sense relative rather than absolute, but in social enquiry this can be perfectly adequately catered for without having to incur the potential confusion of a switch to a new conceptual terminology in which, say, France is for some purposes described as a micro-entity, and a small group of friends described as a macro-entity. A reason for Archer's wish to abandon conventional distinctions between micro and macro, is her contention that 'micro–macro' and 'agency–structure' are simply different 'versions of *exactly the same debate*' (Archer, 1995: 7, my italics). Here I disagree with Archer, for reasons that are set out at the end of this chapter, where it will be observed that micro is not at all the same thing as agency, and macro is not the same thing as structure. Like Giddens and Mouzelis, whose work was briefly mentioned earlier, I believe (though not for the same reasons as Giddens or Mouzelis) that it is appropriate to avoid the conflations micro–agency and macro–structure. Given the conceptual variations that exist among major sociological theorists concerned with these matters, these being a potentially confusing series of variations that have received remarkably little attention in the literature, it will be necessary for me to return to these matters later: for instance, Giddens's reasons for avoiding theoretical conflation of micro with agency and macro with structure are not coterminous with Mouzelis's. Also, my own conception of agency–structure and micro–macro in some respects departs from Giddens (who elides the distinction between micro and macro and conflates agency with structure) and from Mouzelis (whose interesting recasting of structuration theory is not, however, completely satisfactory; see Chapter 4). It should be observed that another of Archer's motives for proposing her unusual notion of micro–macro is her assumption (1995: 10–11) that those who employ the term 'micro' to refer to small-scale phenomena, such as situations of co-presence, tend to regard the micro-social sphere of interpersonal relations as insulated from the macro-social sphere. This is a curious and unwarranted assumption on Archer's part. Numerous researchers and theorists who employ the micro–macro distinction to indicate differences in the properties and scale of social phenomena insist on precisely the idea of links between micro and macro (for example, Knorr-Cetina and Cicourel, 1981; Munch and Smelser, 1987; Ritzer, 1992) even though they might disagree about the nature of the links; many, if not most, theorists are strongly opposed to the notion of what Archer (1995: 10) critically refers to as an '"isolated" micro world'. Many aspects of Archer's morphogenetic social theory may be regarded as a significant contribution to theoretical sociology (see Chapter 4). However, for the reasons to which I have just referred, we should reject Archer's notion of micro–macro. The micro–macro distinction, providing it is employed differently than in Archer's work and used in ways that avoid the four sins of theoretical and methodological reasoning referred to earlier, is a useful conceptual tool for marking out variation in the properties and temporal and spatial scale of social pheno-mena, for denoting corresponding differences in the nature and size of the units of analysis employed in social enquiry, and for exploring links between those units of analysis.

Archer (1988; 1995; 1998) is centrally involved in the contemporary debate of 'dualism versus duality', a debate which centres mainly though not exclusively upon critique of Giddens's theory of structuration (Giddens, 1981; 1982; 1984; 1991b; 1993). Dualism and duality relate in various ways to this chapter's focus upon agency–structure and micro–macro; what follows is a preliminary theoretical sketch, leaving further treatment of dualism–duality until the next chapter. Giddens (1984: 139–44), who subscribes to what might be termed a 'flat' rather than 'hierarchical' social ontology, collapses the distinction between micro and macro, as do some other theorists such as Elias, Foucault, Callon, and Latour, and poststructuralist and postmodern theorists. Giddens believes tensions between micro-theorists and macro-theorists arise out of 'a phoney war' (1984: 139) and that micro–macro is a false and unhelpful dualism (1993: 4) that polarizes social scientists into proponents of two opposing approaches; he also is of the view that the distinction helps perpetuate a mistaken tendency on the part of some theorists to equate micro with agency, and macro with structural constraint upon agency (1984: 139; 1993: 7). Another factor in Giddens's unwillingness to employ these terms is that the micro–macro distinction is a dualism that has tended to empha-size the difference between small groups and larger social phenomena. Archer, as noted earlier, makes a similar critical observation, but she rejects Giddens's elision and substitutes her idiosyncratic version of micro–macro dualism – whereas for Giddens (1979: 204–5), a more important distinction is between face-to-face interaction in situations of co-presence, and inter-relations with others who are physically (spatially) absent, and often tem-porally absent as well (this relates to Giddens's questionable re-shaping of Lockwood's (1964) distinction between social-integration and system-integration modes of analysis; see the discussion of this in the following chapter). Giddens argues that just as micro–macro is a false dualism, so too is agency–structure. This is dealt with more fully in Chapter 3, with refer-ence not only to Giddens but to other theorists. Briefly put, Giddens favours the idea of a *duality* – not a *dualism* – of action and structure. In structuration theory the 'duality of structure' is a concept which insists that agency (or action) and structure are not separate domains, but instead are 'two sides of the same coin': the notion of duality specifies that structure is not external to or apart from action – unless structure is currently being practised (or instantiated) by people, it has no current existence (other than as 'memory traces' in people's minds). On those occasions when structure is not being put into practice by people (that is, not being instantiated), it has only a 'virtual' existence; structure is 'all in the mind' unless and until it is instantiated. In other words, action and structure are a duality, not a dualism; they are not different kinds of social things, but two aspects of the same thing and are, so to speak, inseparably rolled together into one. This concept of a duality of structure and action is, as we shall see in Chapter 3, a reason for Giddens's (1984: 2) emphasis on 'social practices'. In Chapter 4 it will be observed that Archer is highly critical of what she calls 'central conflationism' (here she mainly has in mind Giddens's conflation of agency and structure), as is Layder and Mouzelis, although, as we shall see, Mouzelis tries to accommodate both duality and dualism in his theoretical approach. Giddens's 'methodological bracketing' connotes a methodological procedure that rests on his distinction between what he terms 'institutional analysis', a form of analysis which refers to the study of large-scale, historical processes and which 'places in suspension the skills and awareness of actors' (Giddens, 1984: 375), and 'strategic conduct analysis' which Giddens (ibid.: 373) defines as 'social analysis which places in suspension institutions as socially reproduced, concentrating upon … actors'. Giddens argues that for the purposes of practical empirical analysis it is necessary to employ this distinction and, in effect, to concentrate any particular piece of analysis on either agency *or* structure. His argument, in effect, is that even though in reality action and structure are not ontologically separate or different things, it is in (research) practice necessary to treat them as distinct, separable phenomena. A number of critics, including Layder (1984: 215; 1998b: 101) have suggested that although at the *ontological* level Giddens argues for a duality in which agency/action and structure are inextricably combined and therefore cannot be separated or treated theoretically as an ontological dualism, his practical strategy of *methodological* bracketing involves a separation of action and structure which, in effect, smuggles back in to his framework the ontological dualism that he is trying to avoid. Layder is right. For reasons that are implicit in the preceding pages and which will be returned to in the following chapter, it can, I suggest, be reasonably argued that the dualisms of agency—structure and of micro—macro are indispensable in social analysis; we should, as Layder (1994) aptly puts it, seek to build bridges between agency and structure (and between micro and macro) rather than theoretically collapse these distinctions by compressing the elements so tightly together that they cannot be separated. It follows that as well as my being critical of Giddens's insistence upon a 'duality' of action and structure, I am unconvinced by the rejection of dualism in Law's (1994) 'sociology of ordering' (which is a synthesis of structuralism, poststructuralism, actor network theory, and, to a much lesser extent, symbolic interactionism). Although Law's Foucauldian focus on social networks and recursion is not without some merit (see Chapter 6), I cannot go along with his attempt to dissolve the micro–macro distinction (for details, see Law 1994: 11, 18, 138) nor his attempted dissolution of the agency–structure distinction (1994: 158–60, 103, 138). Law's supposition that maintaining the agency–structure distinction is synonymous with essentialist and reductionist reasoning is profoundly mistaken, as should be clear from the preceding chapter. Law draws upon structuralist and post-structuralist 'decentring of the subject' (1994: 24) and, borrowing from Foucault, he regards agents as effects of discourse (ibid.: 113): since there is no 'knowing subject' (ibid.: 113), there can be no dualism of agency and structure. Stated in more general terms, Law wrongly assumes that the agency–structure distinction is redundant by virtue of agency being variable, contingent, and relational; against Law, however, it can be argued that agency is, indeed, often contingent and relational but that this is no reason for collapsing the distinction between structure and agency (this is taken up in some detail in the next chapter).

There is another complication arising from divergence in contemporary sociological theorists' handling of the micro–macro distinction. Mouzelis (1995: 123) observes that a reason for Giddens's rejection of the micro–macro distinction is Giddens's belief that social scientists tend to erroneously link micro with agency, and macro with structure. But such links are not necessary nor endorsed by all social scientists and therefore, Mouzelis argues, it is a pity that Giddens rejects the micro–macro distinction, thereby abandoning an invaluable analytical tool. Giddens tries to replace micro–macro with his own conception of the social-integration/ system-integration distinction: for Giddens, a social integration form of analysis focuses on the study of 'co-presence' relations (that is, face-to-face interaction in local settings or in small groups) and system integration is a form of analysis concerned with relationships across time and space. Mouzelis (1995: 124; 1997) suggests this leads Giddens to wrongly regard face-to-face relations as micro-phenomena whereas – as noted earlier, with reference to Mouzelis's (1991: 83, 109; 1995: 124) concept of 'macro action' – face-to-face relations between powerful actors (such as a meeting of heads of state or of the chief executives of large corporations) should in Mouzelis's view be classified as macro-phenomena in so far as the decisions taken at such meetings may, unlike decisions taken by 'weak' actors such as shopfloor workers in a factory, have repercussions that stretch widely across time–space and that may affect the lives of literally millions of people. One of Mouzelis's (1991: 83) examples is the meeting between Churchill, Roosevelt, and Stalin at Yalta in 1945, an encounter that 'led to crucial decisions which ... shaped the map of post-war Europe and radically affected millions of lives'. Although there are grounds for agreeing with both Giddens's and Mouzelis's refusal to link micro with agency and macro with structure, and with Mouzelis's rebuttal of Giddens's modification of Lockwood's (1964) social/system integration distinction, there nevertheless is a case for challenging Mouzelis's criticism that Giddens errs in linking micro with co-presence; as briefly observed earlier, it is better to remain with the conventional understanding that face-to-face interactions are micro-phenomena. For Mouzelis, as we have seen, co-presence is not the defining feature of micro-interaction, since such interaction in those cases where the participants are powerful tends to result in decisions with far-reaching ('macro') consequences that extend widely across time and space. Mouzelis's arguments are unconvincing. At least in regard to the matter under discussion here, it is better to remain with social scientific convention and to define *all* situations of co-presence – irrespective of the power of the participants – as micro-social phenomena; also, micro-social phenomena should be regarded as relatively autonomous of, though not completely detached from or unaffected by, macro-social phenomena, these being empirical questions. If we were to apply Mouzelis's terms to, say, governance in the European Union, his conception of 'macro action' (or 'macro-events') would apply to, for example, interactions in the Council of Ministers or in the European Commission. Mouzelis's formulation is prob-lematical, for the following reasons. First, the emergent micro-situational properties of a face-to-face situation (a committee, that meets regularly, say, or else an ad hoc meeting) may significantly influence the course of inter-action and thereby shape the decisions taken (for empirical examples in the foreign policy field, see Russett and Starr, 1996: 242–3). In his general theoretical framework Mouzelis recognizes the interactional-situational dimension of social action but for some reason – despite a brief, unexpli-cated reference to 'macro actors' having forms of power that may not be 'positional' (Mouzelis, 1991: 144) – this is not related by him to his for-mulation of 'macro-events' and 'macro action'. In Mouzelis's references to powerful actors involved in what he terms 'macro events', an overriding emphasis is given to positional power (for example, 1991: 91; 1995: 24) (see the discussion of power in Chapter 5). It is as if Mouzelis believes that personal interaction and power dynamics in relations among top dogs can in principle have no significant emergent micro-processual or relational dimensions that affect decision-making. Second, as Giddens notes, Mouzelis wrongly downplays the extent to which 'macro action' involves far more than an initiating decision made by a few powerful leaders; social action and processes leading up to and during decision-making, and afterwards in the implementation phase, are often embedded in systems of power that entail a very large number of 'routinized circumstances of co-present interaction'

(Giddens, 1993: 7). In respect of these factors, Mouzelis's insistently hierarchical concept of 'macro action', is an oversimplification. Third, events which Mouzelis (1991: 90–1) describes as 'micro-events', where decisions are taken by weak or so-called 'micro actors' (1991: 144; 1995: 27, 120), may, depending on the circumstances and the operation of social chance and unintended consequences, turn out to have far-reaching ('macro') outcomes; for example, the seeds of radical political transformation may, in principle at least, be found in encounters among 'ordinary' people. And more mundanely, it often happens that decisions taken by, say, a group of shopfloor workers in a factory may turn out to have quite far-reaching consequences extending far beyond their own workplace. In terms of the operation of power and in terms of causes and effects, the social fabric is rather more empirically complex and more heterogeneous and unpredictable than Mouzelis implies. Fourth, some meetings of committees with a 'top dog' membership may be routine, with no significant decision taken; in what sense, in terms of Mouzelis's own formulation, can such meetings be described as 'macro events' that are energized by 'macro actors'? Fifth, and closely related to the first point above, Mouzelis's examples of 'macro events' and his references to 'macro actors' (powerful actors, in his scheme) rest on a largely systemic, role/positional conception of power. He gives insufficient attention to relational and broadly Foucauldian dimensions of power; his writing contains many examples of a tendency to adopt, in regard to the matters under discussion here, a mechanical and overly systemic view of power (for example, Mouzelis, 1991: 75, 83, 90–1, 168). Finally, and again related to an earlier point, a fairly commonplace observation among policy analysts and political scientists concerned with governance and public policy (for example, Parsons, 1995; Rhodes, 1997; Dye, 1998) is that in the field of politics and policy 'big' decisions are often not implemented in the way intended by the policy-makers, and sometimes decisions taken by top dogs have only minor consequences. In some instances there may be technical implementation difficulties, or successful resistance by implementation agents such as administrators or professionals; and contingent events can throw a public policy off course in innumerable ways (Richardson, 1996; James, 1997). Moreover, and while the ideas of 'postmodern public administration' (Fox and Miller, 1995) and recent Dutch scholarship on governance (Kickert and van Vught, 1995; Kickert et al., 1997a, 1997b; Kooiman, 1999) sometimes involve an over-reaction against the traditional concept of hierarchical government (for a review and critique, see Sibeon, 2000), the fact remains that traditional mechanisms of hierarchical, 'top-down' government are in some policy sectors declining in significance in the face of newer, non-hierarchical mechanisms of societal 'steering' and 'co-governance' (Pierre and Peters, 2000; Kooiman, 2003). All in all, and despite there being much that is invaluable in Mouzelis's overall theoretical framework, his specific proposals concerning what he describes as macro-action, macro-events, and macro-actors are – like Archer's and Giddens's dissimilar though no less problematical conceptions of micro–macro – open to criticism and they should not, in my opinion, be incorporated into current efforts to reconstruct sociological theory 'after postmodernism'.

The preceding discussion has entailed exposition and clarification of theoretical themes together with critique and, where appropriate, the discussion moved beyond critique in order to enable me to outline some of my own proposals for the development of sociological theory and metatheory; now I should like to draw together the earlier references to agency–structure and micro–macro so as to summarize my own approach to these important meta-concepts. Reification, it was argued in the Introduction, is one of four long-standing 'cardinal sins' that continue to influence many areas of social theory and methodology. My conception of agency was sketched in the Introduction with reference to a non-reified concept of actors (or agents) as entities that, in principle, are capable of formulating and taking decisions and of acting on at least some of them; this non-reified definition of agency will be developed at greater length in Chapter 5. It is a parsimonious definition that rests on a *minimal* concept of actor (Hindess, 1988: 45) which does not insist upon any other restrictions on what may count as an actor (such as, on the one hand, the criterion of a 'postmodern subject' who is 'fraught with cognitive confusion, emotional malaise, and ontological insecurity' (Smith, P., 2001: 25), or on the other, so-called modernist criteria of subjectivity such as 'rational' thought, a unitary self-identity, the holding of logically consistent attitudes, or having a 'coherent' or integrated set of objectives). However, my explicitly anti-reified conception of agency *does* insist upon the 'minimal' concept of actor in the form just stated. This tightly drawn conception of agency, though in some sense minimal, is actually 'stricter' and more focused than in the work of most social theorists or theoretical sociologists, such as Habermas, Bourdieu, Giddens, Archer, Mouzelis, or Layder; there is among social theorists an unfortunate tendency to treat agency as a received notion, and to attribute agency to entities – social classes and other taxonomic collectivities, social movements, social networks, and the like – that, on the basis of the above definition, cannot conceivably be regarded as actors or agents but should, rather, be thought of as elements of structure. In my approach (for example, Sibeon, 1999a; 2000) the concept structure (or 'social structure') refers, as I shall clarify shortly, to temporally enduring or temporally and spatially extensive social conditions that to a greater or lesser extent influence actors' forms of thought, decisions and actions, and which, depending on the circumstances, facilitate or constrain actors' capacities to achieve their objectives. Structure refers to the 'conditions of action' (Betts, 1986: 41) or, put more simply, 'social conditions' (Hindess, 1986a: 120-1). The conditions-of-action/social conditions ('structure') are, in effect, the circumstances in which actors (as defined above) operate, including the resources that actors may draw upon. On this intentionally broad and 'minimal' definition, which will be amplified in Chapter 5, structure refers to a variety of phenomena that include discourses; institutions; social practices; individual and social actors (from the standpoint of any particular actor there is agency-in-structure, that is to say, structure includes other actors and their motives, capabilities, actions and the intended and unintended outcomes of their actions; conversely, there is structure-in-agency, in the sense that actors' form of thought, decisions, and actions are to a greater or lesser extent influenced by structure); social systems or networks (these are defined below); and power distributions, with power viewed as multi-dimensional and as a partly systemic, partly relational phenomena. Social conditions ('structure') are very often fluid; should some conditions become stabilized across large extensions of time–space, this is not a necessary effect of the social totality but a contingent outcome of interaction between agency, structure and social chance. It is also worth re-emphasizing with reference to the four forms of deficient reasoning described in the Introduction, that social conditions ('social structure') are not a unitary phenomenon that can be said to have a single 'cause'; to insist otherwise in advance of empirical enquiry, is to engage in essentialist and reductionist theorizing.

Micro–macro as defined in my theoretical framework – and here, as stated earlier, I in some respects part company with a number of major contemporary sociological theorists including Giddens, Archer, and Mouzelis – refers to differences in the units of and scale of analyses concerned with the investigation of varying extensions of time–space. Micro-analysis, which like macro-analysis can refer to institutional and/or figurational dynamics (Mouzelis, 1991; 1995) (this relates to the discussion of system and social integration in Chapter 3) involves investigation of meanings, positions/roles, and actor–actor relations in small-scale settings of face-to-face inter-action (situations of co-presence); macro-analysis is the study of large time–space extensions of actors, social conditions and 'materials' (this term is defined in Chapter 6), including large social systems and networks. Social systems and social networks, which can be studied at macro- but also micro-levels of analysis, are in my theoretical scheme regarded as the same type of phenomena; they refer to more or less patterned relations between actors, and between social institutions and positions/roles. In later chapters, and particularly in Chapter 7, it will be argued that micro and macro are distinct and relatively autonomous levels of social process. On this last point I am largely in agreement with sociological theorists such as Layder (1994; 1997) and Mouzelis (1991; 1995); since there is no 'upwards' or 'downwards' determination of social life,[5] events at one level do not determine events at another, although there may be contingently produced and contingently sustained empirical connections between levels.

Finally, it is necessary to clarify a central theoretical rubric that will underpin some of the discussion in the next chapter; this concerns the previously mentioned contention that there are no good reasons for equating micro with agency, and macro with structure. The conflations 'micro-agency' and 'macro-structure' should be rejected, for the following reasons. First, 'micro-agency' is a false conflation for the reason that some social actors (for example, large organizational actors such as central government departments, the European Union, or corporations such as General Motors) are not micro-entities; and, second, structure (social conditions/the conditions-of-action) may be said to exist at macro *or* micro levels of social process or, always providing the relative autonomy of these levels is recognized, at both levels simultaneously. A defining characteristic of macro-conditions (macro-structure) is that – as contingently reproduced outcomes – they have become extensive across time–space; the question of *which* conditions have become temporally and spatially extensive, bearing in mind that that which is 'macro' is not given by nature or by the social totality, is something that has to be empirically determined on each occasion that the question arises. Social conditions ('social structure') may, then, be macro-phenomena; that is, they may be conditions that stretch widely across time–space. As briefly observed earlier, however, social conditions ('structure') may also be micro-phenomena; these, viewed in terms of the matters under discussion in this chapter, are of two main types. First, some micro-conditions are to a greater or lesser extent local expressions of macro-phenomena that extend widely across time–space; for example, at least some elements of the interaction that takes place between a schoolteacher and his or her pupils in a classroom are reflections of macro-social institutions and role scripts to do with education. Second, however, some micro-conditions ('structure') such as a uniquely local but temporally reproduced set of power relationships, may be confined to a specific micro-setting and have no significant connections to any other micro-setting or to the macro-social order. If they are temporally relatively enduring rather than episodic, any such purely local and unique features of a micro-setting, even though they are not spatially extensive, should for analytical purposes be regarded as elements of structure: certainly for the actors located in the setting, and indeed for other actors who have dealings with that setting, enduring setting-specific properties of interaction are no less a part of the conditions-of-action ('structure') than those features of the setting that are local ramifications of the macro-social order. In these terms, social structure may be defined as a contingently reproduced set of social conditions at the macro- and/or micro-levels of social process; that is, 'structure' refers to contingently sustained social conditions that extend across relatively large stretches of time and/or social space. There are, then, very good reasons for suggesting that it is important to avoid the quite widespread tendency to tacitly conflate agency with micro, and structure with macro.

Summary

●

Agency–structure and micro–macro are major meta-concepts that refer to highly significant dimensions of social reality; however, debate of these meta-concepts is characterized by conceptual controversies and ambiguities. The classical theorists engaged with agency–structure and micro–macro and in doing so raised ontological issues that have continuing relevance: for example, Marx and Durkheim tended to neglect agency in favour of an emphasis on the idea of an 'objective' macro-social order; Weber attempted, with a certain amount of success, to encompass subjective and objective dimensions of the social and to develop a 'balanced' conception of agency and structure.

●

Structuralism, poststructuralism, and discourse theory are examples of deterministic approaches that in a priori fashion elevate one or another conception of structure above agency; this tendency is also evident in the writings of, for example, Habermas and Bourdieu. It should be noticed that the idea of macro-structure can refer to relatively indeterminate social conditions, and need not necessarily imply constraints upon agency, institutionalization of behaviour, and predictability of social outcomes.

●

Micro-social perspectives such as symbolic interactionism are a necessary part of social analysis, though such perspectives are neither theoretically or methodologically equipped for macro-level analysis concerned with large extensions of time–space; hence the importance of finding a satisfactory way of integrating micro, mezo and macro levels of analysis.

●

Miscommunication and conceptual inconclusiveness, as well as plain disagreement are features of recent debates of agency–structure and micro–macro.

The intricate web of conceptual ambiguity and controversy that characterizes contemporary debate of these key meta-concepts has been insufficiently documented, this being something that is addressed in this book. For instance, major sociological theorists such as Mouzelis and Archer employ idiosyncratic definitions of micro–macro, and some theorists – including Giddens, Elias, Foucault, poststructuralists and postmodernists, and actor-network theorists – employ a 'flat' rather than hierarchical (or 'depth') social ontology and thereby efface a distinction between micro and macro.

•

Drawing upon critique of the four 'cardinal sins' and employing the flexible social ontology referred to in Chapter 1, agency is defined in terms of an explicitly anti-reificationist and minimal concept of actor; social structure is defined, in similarly 'minimal' fashion, as 'social conditions' (or the 'conditions-of-action'); and micro–macro refers to the units and scale of analyses concerned with the investigation of varying temporal and spatial extensions of the social. In particular, it was emphasized that social structure is not a unitary phenomenon with a single cause; social structure is a contingently reproduced set of social conditions, not a necessary effect of the social totality or something that is historically predetermined.

•

Finally, it was observed that levels of social process (micro, mezo and macro) are relatively autonomous and that 'upward' and 'downward' conflation are forms of analysis that should be avoided: and that agency is not synonymous with micro (for the reason that some actors – such as the European Union – are not micro-entities) and that social structure is not synonymous with macro (structure may be macro; or it can be micro, either in the form of local ramifications of the macro-social order, or in the form of relatively enduring but uniquely 'local' conditions-of-action).

Notes

1 This to some extent relates to the commentary on epistemology, ontology, and realism in the concluding chapter.

2 Symbolic interactionist research focuses attention on co-presence. A fuller account of the notion of 'types' of social interaction, though there is not the space to develop this here, would relate co-present encounters to a typology of communications among physically separated actors. Here there are a number of established analytical avenues that merit closer attention than has been accorded to them by

contemporary theorists and methodologists. One such avenue is Schutz's (1972) phenomenological sociology, including his distinction between the *Umwelt*, which refers to face-to-face relations, and the *Mitwelt* which refers to the realm of social reality that consists of relations with, in particular, people who are spatially distant from us. The *Mitwelt* includes, for example, a friend whom one saw most days but who has now moved to another part of the country and with whom one now has only infrequent contact; the *Mitwelt* also includes, at a 'deeper' level of anonymity than in the example just given, countless people whom we have never met but with whom we are somehow connected, such as the mail-sorter who helps ensure our letters are delivered to us, and the official who handles our social security records. Contemporary factors relating to *Umwelt* and *Mitwelt* relations include, for example, cheap and rapid transportation and the increased physical mobility of people. Also relevant is the increasing use of electronic communication, including cyber-space interaction, which introduces dynamics of interaction that in some ways differ from those that occur in face-to-face interactional contexts (see Fox and Roberts, 1999). Other underexplored theoretical perspectives that are of potential relevance here are network analysis, and Elias's (1978, 1991) conceptual scheme relating to 'figurations'. Also, Layder's (1997) theory of social domains is to some extent attuned, in a fashion that is sensitive to the idea of time–space, to the existence of variable degrees of 'personalization' in social relations.

3 Methodological individualism, as in rational choice approaches, is an 'upward conflationist' (Archer, 1995) form of reductionism that illegitimately attempts to reduce the complexities of social life to a single explanatory principle which specifies that the social fabric is the aggregated outcome of the decisions and actions of countless human individuals (see the illuminating critique in Hindess, 1988). Four problems associated with methodological individualism are, first, micro-interaction and intersubjectivity, which are either completely ignored or else downplayed in 'rational choice' and other theories based on methodological individualism; second, there are important actors other than human individuals (see Chapter 5); third, methodological individualism fails to grasp the significance of the emergent properties of social systems and of society, the latter being 'more than' the sum of its parts (individuals) (see the discussion of 'emergence' in Chapter 3); fourth, and related to the previous points, actors operate within conditions of action ('structure') which are themselves not reducible to the actions of individuals (nor, indeed, to any other single principle of explanation). Aggregated outcomes of individual actions are not unimportant (consider 'global warming', for example), but there are no good reasons for reducing *the whole* of social scientific explanation to the actions of individuals; methodological individualism, in short, is a reductionism that has no useful part to play in social analysis. Conversely, methodological collectivism is an opposed but equally illegitimate form of reductionism that – as in Marxism, teleological functionalism, structuralism, some versions of cultural studies, and radical feminism – attempts to explain agency as a necessary effect of the social totality or of discrete structural mechanisms ('capitalism', 'patriarchy', 'system needs', and the like) that are said to be directly or indirectly causally determining. With regard to methodological individualism and methodological collectivism, we should reject both of these mutually exclusive and general forms of reductionism, on the grounds that society is not reducible to any single general principle of 'micro' or 'macro' explanation. Nor should attempts be made to combine both of these reductionisms in a

single explanatory scheme; when this is attempted, the inevitable result, as in Dominelli's (1997) purportedly 'anti-sexist' and 'anti-racist' normative theory of social work, is theoretical contradiction and explanatory failure (see Sibeon, 1999c).

4 Archer's (1995: 173–4) particular understanding of emergence is, however, somewhat restrictive: see the discussion of emergence in Chapter 3.

5 See note 3 on methodological individualism and methodological collectivism.

3

Links between Theoretical Approaches

In order to flesh out the earlier arguments for a synthetic orientation towards sociological theory's underlying ontological concerns – prominent among which, as we have seen, are agency–structure and micro–macro – this chapter examines selected aspects of the work of leading social theorists and establishes links between their work and the concepts and controversies identified earlier. The chapter opens with a short overview of the work of four major social theorists, each of whom have important and interesting things to say about structure and action and the micro–macro distinction; the theorists that I have selected are Peter Berger, Norbert Elias, Michel Foucault, and also Anthony Giddens. There then follows a section that focuses upon interrelated meta-concepts and ontological themes that, it is argued, are of considerable importance to theory construction as well as to methodology and the conduct of empirical enquiry. These are: (a) the concept of 'emergence'; (b) the social integration and system integration distinction; (c) the question of the relation of discourses to their spatio-temporal contexts; (d) structural (or systemic) contradictions; and (e) the concept of recursion (or 'path dependency').

Agency–structure and micro–macro in the work of four major theorists

Peter Berger – a dialectical approach

Some years ago in an important volume on theoretical sociology (Knorr-Cetina and Cicourel, 1981) an American writer, Karin Knorr-Cetina (1981: 41) referred to 'a widening gap between micro- and macro-social theories and methodologies'. In Britain, Outhwaite (1983: 17) suggested that opposition between micro-social and macro-social perspectives was 'the most important opposition in contemporary social theory'. Throughout the 1980s, particularly in the United States (for example, Alexander *et al.*, 1987; Ritzer, 1990) there were innumerable attempts to address what Knorr-Certina (1981: 2) had called 'the micro–macro problem'. It was against this background that Wuthnow *et al.* (1984: 21) in adopting the term 'Bergerian sociology' reflected a renewal of interest (see also Hunter and Ainlay, 1986) in Peter Berger's earlier sociological attempts to construct a theoretical integration of micro- and macro-sociologies (Berger, 1966; Berger and Luckmann, 1971). Berger's thinking concerning what he regards as a dialectical link between micro and macro is exemplified in Berger and Luckmann's (1971) *The Social Construction of Reality*. In what follows it is mainly Berger and Luckmann's book that I shall refer to.

Bergerian sociology is a large-scale synthesis that draws upon Marx, Durkheim, Weber, Mead, and in particular, the sociologically oriented phenomenology of Schutz (1972) whose own approach had been influenced by Weber. Berger's central argument is that human subjectivity is – during the course of social interaction – externalized and objectified, and in turn, objectified social reality acts back upon and shapes subjectivity. The general form of Berger's theory of micro–macro is indicated in the following observation (Berger and Berger, 1978: 18–19):

> The micro-world and what goes on within it only makes full sense if it is understood against the background of the macro-world that envelopes it; conversely, the macro-world has little reality ... unless it is repeatedly represented in the face-to-face encounters of the micro-world.

There is a two-way relation between micro and macro. Actors' meanings and interaction in micro settings, when repeated and objectivated across time and space (this entails what Berger calls 'habitualization' or institutionalization) in effect 'become' the macro-social world via a process that Berger describes as the social construction of reality; however, once it has been constructed 'from the bottom upwards' in the way just indicated, the macro-social order (defined as temporally and spatially extensive institutionalized meanings and practices) enters back into the micro-sphere and shapes the consciousness and actions of individuals. This dialectical process is expressed in three of Berger's (1969: 3–4) key concepts: people's meanings, intentions and actions construct a social world ('*externalization*'), which over time becomes institutionalized (the process of '*objectivation*'); and the objectified social world is then mentally absorbed or re-appropriated by individuals ('*internalization*'). As Berger and Luckmann (1971: 79) put it: 'Society is a human product. Society is an objective reality. Man (*sic*) is a social product.' At the heart of Berger's theory, then, are the notions that the relation between actors (the producers of the social world) and the social world (the product of actors) is a dialectical one in which the product ('society') continuously acts back upon its producers, and that society has no meaningful existence apart from its regularized re-enactment in countless micro-settings. There is considerably more to Bergerian sociology than I have the space to discuss here; however, the above account is sufficient to highlight those aspects of Berger's schema that relate to this chapter's concerns.

Berger's theoretical reflections have an importance that should not be under-estimated. For example, Turner (1992b) observes that Giddens's (1991b) theory of self and the pluralization of meanings is, to some extent, an investigation of ground that had been explored twenty years earlier by Berger and Luckmann. In much of his work, Berger, with some success, tries to avoid simplistic assumptions which specify that societies are characterized by unity or coherence, and he also avoids the equally simplistic notion that societies are chaotic, entirely indeterminate and in a state of constant flux (Berger and Luckmann, 1971: 80–1). There can be little doubt that Bergerian sociology is an instructive and worthwhile attempt to integrate subjective and objective domains of social reality and to link micro-social and macro-social spheres (Hunter and Ainlay, 1986). The importance of Berger's work, especially when compared to Durkheimian, Marxist and Parsonian theorizing, lies in the significant (meta)theoretical questions that are raised by its phenomenologically-oriented focus on the subjective dimension of social life and the nature of consciousness, and the relation of subjectivity to culture.

However, Berger, who, as we have seen, set out to provide an account of both the subjective and objective dimensions of society and of links between them, over-emphasized the subjective at the expense of the objective.[1] He often writes as if objectivated social reality has no relatively independent existence *apart from* the subjectivities of the individuals involved in its creation or maintenance. It is claimed that we 'reify' institutions (for Berger, reification means forgetting that society is 'person-made') if we 'bestow on them an ontological status independent of human activity' (Berger and Luckmann, 1971: 107). Berger frequently refers (for example, ibid.: 35) not to an objective social reality that has *real* existence, but to actors' 'sense of' or 'experience of' an objective social world that, he suggests, actors tend to falsely reify; individuals attribute a Durkheimian 'thing-like' facticity to an institutionalized macro-social order that they take for granted as normal, inevitable and 'given', but which, according to Berger, is actually a social order comprised of externalized, ongoing subjectivity that is only precariously sustained. Berger, who is keen to avoid what he regards as reification and to avoid Parsonian functionalism, supposes that, in effect, people and society (or social contexts) are 'the same thing' and possess the same or similar properties. This leads Archer (1995: 13, 63) to suggest that Berger and Luckmann's social constructionism is an idealist version of the 'central conflationism' that, she argues, mars Giddens's structuration theory. Wuthnow *et al.* (1984: 243–6) take the view that there is a theoretical contradiction or at least an ambivalence in Berger's theorizing, since he appears to be arguing simultaneously for two opposed theoretical principles relating to the duality–dualism debate (this debate, which will be returned to later, was introduced in Chapter 2 with reference to structuration theory). On the one hand, Berger appears to be saying that people and society are in some sense the same kind of thing: structure is objectified subjectivity, and therefore structure *embodies* subjectivity. I concur with Wuthnow *et al.* that this type of theoretical argument – which implies that if we begin with social institutions we can 'work backwards' to uncover individual subjectivities/intentions that created or recreated the institutions – features quite strongly in Berger's work. This limits the usefulness of Berger's theoretical framework. Collapsing the distinction between subjectivity/ action and structure makes it difficult to account for unintended and perhaps unwanted cultural objects and structures; we are prevented from studying cultural objects and the 'parts' of social systems, and relations between them, in their own right, independently of the subjective intentions of those involved in creating or maintaining them. On the other hand, as Wuthnow *et al.* rightly observe, Berger in another phase of his analysis seems to be contradictorily arguing that, after all, 'people' and 'society' *are* different types of phenomena. That is, Berger contends that externalization and objectivation mean that cultural objects such as social institutions (including myths and legitimations which justify the social order) often *do* differ from the subjective intentions of individuals. In this connection, Mouzelis (1991: 78) is of the opinion that, unlike Giddens, Berger and Luckmann do not conflate subject and object, but rather, postulate a dialectical link between the two; for Mouzelis, Berger's theory should be regarded as a theory that subscribes to the notion of a subject–object dualism at the paradigmatic level (see Chapter 4). Mouzelis's observation centres on those strands in Bergerian sociology which – employing the concepts of externalization and objectivation – seem to accord to social institutions a certain amount of autonomy from subjectivity. My own interpretation of Berger's dialectic of subjective and objective dimensions of social reality is in some respects congruent with Wuthnow *et al.'s* observation that Berger and Luckmann attempt to follow two mutually exclusive theoretical strategies. Contradictorily, Berger and Luckmann collapse the distinction between subjectivity/action and structure while simultaneously arguing for the relative autonomy of structure from subjectivity; the former implies a *duality* of action and structure (or in other words, of subject–object), the latter a *dualism* in which action and structure are seen as dialectically connected but nevertheless as distinct and separable phenomena.[2] This theoretical contradiction appears to be related to Berger and Luckmann's desire to find a solution to the problem of how, on the one hand, to avoid Durkheimian and Parsonian social determinism and methodological collectivism, while, on the other, avoiding methodological individualism: the Bergerian solution to this problem is, as described earlier, to theoretically construct a *dialectical* relation between subjectivity/action and social institutions/'society'. The problem with this 'solution', however, is that in trying to avoid both methodological collectivism and methodological individualism – two opposed forms of reduction that Archer (see Chapter 4) refers to as 'downward conflation' and 'upward conflation' – Berger and Luckmann came up with a theoretical scheme that reproduces *both* of these deficient conceptions of the relation of subjectivity/action to structure. This critical interpretation is supported by Bhaskar (1979) who suggests Berger and Luckmann adopt both of the opposed approaches that they criticized. On the one hand, Berger and Luckmann's concepts of externalization and objectivation imply that society has no emergent properties and is the aggregated outcome of individual subjectivities and actions; on the other, the proposition that objectivated social reality is internalized by individuals (as part of a people–society dialectic that reproduces society) entails a deterministic conception of agency that smacks of downwards conflation. It is Berger and Luckmann's particular prescription for avoiding upwards and downwards conflation that leads them to reproduce these antithetical conflations and to attempt, in contradictory fashion, to combine both of them in a single, synthetic framework. Like each of the other theorists discussed in this chapter, Berger offers thought-provoking formulations that enrich our appreciation of the complexities that surround agency–structure and micro–macro but ultimately we must conclude that his contribution to the development of sociological theory is less than satisfactory.

Norbert Elias: figurational (or 'process') sociology

Elias is perhaps best known for his classic treatise *The Civilizing Process*, first published in 1939. His 'figurational sociology', or process sociology as he came to call it in his later work (1978; 1991), contains a number of important concepts and theoretical insights as well as a rich body of empirical material (Dunning and Rojek, 1992; Mennell, 1992). As will be noted shortly, his work relates closely to agency–structure and micro–macro.

Although it will be suggested later that his approach is deficient in certain respects, there are a number of conceptually important elements in Elias's framework: these include his processual image of the social world; his largely relational view of power; and his theoretical and methodological emphasis on social networks ('figurations') and interdependencies. The concept 'figurations' refers to interrelations – whether co-operative or con-flictual – between interdependent individuals; the concept refers equally to small-scale networks (such as small groups, or, say, households) and to figurations of much larger scale, including whole societies (Elias, 1978: 131). A crucial aspect of figurations, in the terms that Elias views them, is that social analysts should avoid an atomistic notion of individuals as isolated beings or as 'self-contained' entities that are somehow detached from the social fabric; the focus of enquiry in figurational sociology is *interdependencies* between people, interdependencies that shape individuals' forms of thought and actions. There is, as Law (1994: 113) observes, some similarity between aspects of Eliasian sociology and actor network theory; while the points of similarity between these otherwise dissimilar approaches should not be exaggerated, what Elias and actor network theorists have in common is their rejection of methodological individualism and methodological col-lectivism, and their emphasis on social networks and interdependencies. Elias's focus on interdependencies among individuals is bound up with his mainly relational notion of power. His conception of power is one with which I have some sympathy (see Chapter 5). Elias regards power (*contra* Foucault's version of relationism) as a 'capacity' that individuals can possess and exercise, but power nonetheless is largely relational and may fluctuate – it is not something that is structurally predetermined or necessarily vested for long periods in any particular individuals, social groups or strata; there is, in other words, no single or invariant locus of power in society but, rather, shifting patterns of power within social networks/figurations. Relatedly, and somewhat like the view of power associated with Giddens's concept of a 'dialectic of control' (see later), interdependencies for Elias sig-nify that rather than power being something that is divided between domi-nant individuals, on the one hand, and 'the powerless', on the other, people tend for the most part to have at least some control over each other, arising from the interdependencies associated with the '*interweaving* of countless individual interests and intentions' (Elias, 1994: 389, my italics). For exam-ple, even ostensibly all-powerful individuals such as absolute monarchs or dictatorial rulers are in some degree dependent upon administrative staff (Elias, 1978: 65–9).

Of relevance to the notion of 'interweaving', the concept *emergence* will be examined later in the chapter and for the moment it should be noted that Elias's concept of figurations and therefore – in Elias's terms – of the social fabric in general, entails a commitment to a notion of emergence (though not in the objectivist, dualistic sense discussed later). The social fabric is the unintended outcome of interwoven activities, and is emergent in so far as it is 'more than' the sum of individuals' activities (Elias, 1994: 444):

> This basic tissue resulting from many single plans and actions of men (*sic*) can give rise to changes and patterns that no individual person has planned or created. From this interdependence of people arises an order *sui generis,* an order more compelling and stronger than the will and reason of the individual people composing it. It is this order of human impulses and strivings, this social order which determines the course of historical change.

Thus, and here we glimpse a difference between Elias and part of Berger and Luckmann's theoretical scheme, society is not a reflection of subjectivity or of people's intentions. In Elias's terms, society is an outcome that is planned and intended by no particular individuals even though it results from individuals' intentional actions: and in turn, the emergent, unintended social contexts that are produced by intentional actions condition future intentions and actions. Structure or social context is, in other words, both an unintended outcome of actions and something that shapes intentional actions. Employing this conception of the social order, Elias rejects reductionist theories which claim to have discovered 'first causes' or single causes of social phenomena: the social is the ever-changing outcome of a complex, unintended interweaving of intentional actions. Hence for Elias, society is never a state, a condition, or a static formation, but rather a continuous figurational process.

An aspect of his processual conception of the social is his rejection of a dichotomous distinction between individual and society (Elias, 1978; 1983; 1991). The distinction, argues Elias, is an entirely false one. Society in general as well as smaller-scale social contexts are figurations of interdependent people (ibid.: 113), and to support the notion of an individual–society dichotomy is, according to Elias, to reify society and to endorse atomistic psychology. Individuals and ('figurational') society are inextricably interwoven, and figurations, though emergent in the sense described above, have no separate ontological existence apart from the networks of interdependent, interrelated individuals who constitute them; on the one hand, individuals are not isolated entities acted upon by an autonomous social fabric that exists apart from people, and, on the other, the social fabric ('society') has no existence independent of individuals' activities. This theoretical principle is developed empirically by Elias in *The Civilizing Process* (1994) and *The Court Society* (1983) where empirical materials are deployed in support of the idea that subjectivity and psychological mindsets are shaped by and shape figurations (Elias, 1994: 446).

In some, though not all, respects I concur with Elias's general notion of contingency and his processual conception of the social: this relates to the discussion of the dialectics of agency, structure, and social chance in Chapter 5. More specifically, although certain elements of his framework are questionable, there is heuristic value in his proposition that individual mindsets and behaviour shape and are shaped by unintentionally produced and unintentionally re-produced social contexts. It is also worth noting that policy network analysis – which has become a centrepiece of theory and methodology in the disciplines of political science and public administration/ public policy – makes use of conceptual tools (to do with resource inter-dependencies and relational, shifting configurations of power and social action) that, though the parallel remains unexplored in the literature, bear some resemblance to the analytical methods employed in Elias's process sociology (see the data on governance processes and the conceptual frames developed for the purposes of policy analysis in, for example, Pierre and Peters, 2000; Stoker, 2000a; 2000b; Hay, 2002).

However, there are some aspects of Elias's theoretical framework that are open to criticism. First, there is a certain amount of unresolved inconsistency between, on the one hand, Elias's postmodern-like emphasis on inde-terminacy and the open-endedness of social change (not, I hasten to add, that postmodernists are the only theorists to acknowledge indeterminate and processual aspects of social life), and on the other, his modernist-sounding thesis that there is an overall direction ('the civilizing process') to history. True, the civilizing process – a long-term historical trend towards a refine-ment of social manners – is not claimed by Elias to be monocausal, nor inevitable: nor does Elias claim the civilizing process is entirely unilinear or without variations, breaks or even temporary 'reversals' in the overall direc-tion of change. Nevertheless, his theory speaks – in a rather universalizing manner – of a quite specific, directional process of historical development and to some extent there is a tension between Elias's processual metatheo-retical position and his substantive theory of 'civilizing' social development. This is not to say Elias's process sociology as a whole has no value. Nor is it suggested here that his theory of 'the civilizing process' is incapable of being refined and improved, rather than abandoned. Indeed, the theory is in some respects a significant improvement on reductionist and teleological modernist theories of social change (Sztompka, 1993: 206–7), and is an improvement upon postmodern accounts which, it was argued in Chapter 1, are inherently flawed. As it stands, however, *The Civilizing Process* has a universalizing 'grand theory' feel to it. There is some justification, there-fore, for taking the view that the theory of the 'civilizing process' could, in principle at least, become a better theory if its propositions were related more closely to subtheories referring to specific spatio-temporal conditions under which its propositions do or do not hold true (see Mouzelis, 1995: 71–4).

Second, there is a tension between Elias's sense of emergence, referred to earlier, and other aspects of his handling of agency–structure. As already observed, for Elias the social fabric consists of figurations, which are networks of interrelated, interdependent people: social structure and social systems are said to be figurational, that is, they are 'people who are constantly moving and constantly relating to other people' (Elias, 1978: 113). Figurations, though unintended and in some sense emergent outcomes of the interweaving of myriad intentions and actions rather than embodiments of individuals' subjectivity, are seen as having no existence independent of individuals and their activities, and therefore, argues Elias, individual–society is a false dichotomy: people and (figurational) society are inextricably interwoven. The claim being made here by Elias is fundamental to his theoretical position and to any critique of it: Individuals are not 'isolated' beings but rather should be thought of as interrelated in figurations that shape (and are shaped by) individuals' forms of thought and actions, and to make a theoretical separation between individuals and society is, for Elias, to endorse both an atomistic psychology and a reified notion of society (Layder, 1986). Now it can certainly be argued that the proposition that activities reproduce or alter (and are influenced by) social contexts and social systems is not itself erroneous, but it is a proposition that is sometimes deployed in ways that wrongly imply that there is a '*direct* link' between individuals and society (Layder, 1997: 91) or between action/activities and structure. Layder (ibid.: 228) is critical of those theorists (such as Berger and Luckmann, Elias, and Giddens) who *compress action and structure into an indivisible amalgam and who claim every encounter or activity simultaneously 'creates' and re-creates society*. Rather than examine here some important general issues that implicitly are raised by this criticism of Elias, it will be better to focus upon them as and when they arise in later parts of the chapter and in the next chapter.

Third, a related criticism of Elias that also links into the later discussion, is Mouzelis's (1995: 76–80) observation that social structure has a figurational/syntagmatic element (actual social practices and relations between people), the investigation of which calls for a social-integration form of analysis focused on the study of actor–actor relations; and an institutional/paradigmatic element (the mental and, for Mouzelis and for Giddens, the 'virtual' aspect of society, comprised of roles/positions, values, rules, and social institutions) that should be studied in terms of a system-integration form of analysis that focuses not upon actor–actor relations but upon part–part relations (the relations between the 'parts' of social systems, for example, role–role relations or links between systems of rules). The criticism developed by Mouzelis is that while some theorists, such as Talcott Parsons (1966; 1967; 1971) over-emphasize the institutional dimension of society and neglect the figurational, Elias's over-emphasis on the figurational dimension causes him to largely ignore the institutional and its relation to the figurational. Mouzelis (1995: 80) goes on to say:

> Of course, the ways in which figurations and institutional structures are linked to each other constitutes one of the most interesting problems in sociological theory. I am not sure where its solution lies, but I am quite certain that no progress towards it will be made so long as we conflate, or refuse to distinguish between … figuration … [and] institutional structures.

Mouzelis's observation raises important and controversial ontological themes that go well beyond Elias and which will be returned to in the following chapter.

Michel Foucault: discourse reigns supreme

Foucault's writings are remarkably wide-ranging (for example, 1970; 1972; 1980a; 1980b; 1982). Here it is intended to refer only to those aspects of his work that relate to agency–structure and micro–macro and to the related conceptual themes identified earlier. Foucault's conception of the topic of 'power', which is, of course, one of his central concerns, will be discussed in Chapter 5 as part of a critical review of theories of power. The following sketch refers to selected aspects of Foucault's work and will set the scene for a critique which in large part will be critical of Foucault's overall approach. In speaking, though, of his 'overall approach' it is necessary to note that there are some differences between Foucault's early structuralist emphasis on the 'archaeology' of knowledge (a search for deep, hidden codes that determine discursive practices) and, in his later work, a post-structuralist focus on 'genealogy'. The scale of this transition in Foucault's work is sometimes exaggerated (see Dean, 1994). It is true that the early and later phases of Foucault's writings are in some respects dissimilar – for example, in comparison with the early Foucault his more recent work gives more emphasis to the relation of power to knowledge, to the contingent aspects of social life, and to the idea of self and agency – but throughout his work there are also continuities, to do with, for example, his scepticism towards representation theories of social reality, and it remains the case that the concept 'discourse' in one way or another figures in all his writings.

Foucault rejects 'totalizing' (or 'grand') theory, and instead expresses an interest in small-scale (or 'local') narratives. This epistemological standpoint runs alongside an ontological conception of modern society as highly differentiated and fragmented: contradictorily, however, Foucault also argues, in grand theory fashion, that each historical period is characterized by a single *episteme* (a world-view or mind-set which defines what is thinkable and knowable). The episteme, though it may subsume conflicting view-points, is ultimately a relatively unitary practico-cognitive structure (Foucault, 1970: 168). The concept *discourse* for Foucault refers to specific discourses and discursive practices (a psychiatric discourse, for example, or a discourse of criminal justice, or more generalized discourses such as nationalism or sexism). Viewed in terms of the approach adopted in this book, attractive features of Foucault's concepts of episteme (or 'regime of truth') and discourse are his insistence that these are not simply expressions of 'objective' interests (the so-called 'real' interests of, for example, taxonomic collectivities such as classes or gender categories), and his idea that historically there is no predetermined transition or unilinear development from one episteme to another. Relatedly, Foucault argues that discursive practices should not be seen as the intentional effect of the will of any single actor (such as 'the state'); this, incidentally, resonates with the ideas of Elias and with, for example, the position taken by Archer whose morphogenic social theory is discussed in the next chapter. Another Foucauldian concept, that of *discipline*, refers to the notion that as a consequence of surveillance of the population by professionals, administrators and others, and as an effect of processes not unlike those which many sociologists call socialization and internalization, individuals engage in self-control and act responsibly as subjects whose subjectivities are constructed for them by the episteme and by the discourses associated with a particular epoch. Subject to the criticisms of Foucault set out later and in Chapter 5, the Foucauldian concept of 'discipline', suitably modified to avoid the four 'cardinal sins' described in the Introduction, is acceptable but also, let it be noted, unexceptional; individual actors' forms of thought and practices are, as so-called 'conventional' or non-Foucauldian social scientists have long been aware, influenced by social contexts and by patterned systems of thought and social practices ('discourses').

Foucault's views on *power* will be discussed in Chapter 5, but here it is worth mentioning – leaving aside the criticisms concerning, in particular, failure to adequately grasp systemic dimensions of power and its 'storage' in, for example, social institutions, roles, and patterned sets of rules – that Foucauldian emphasis on strategic, relational, and non-unitary aspects of power, is, I suggest, an invaluable counter to the rather mechanical conceptions of power and social action found in modernist structural theories associated with, for example, Marxism and structural-functionalism. Related to this are Foucault's (1991) ideas on governmentality, a line of reasoning that, I have suggested elsewhere (Sibeon, 1997: 114–19), is a source of conceptual insights that, with some revision, can usefully be incorporated into studies of governance and the policy process.

However, there are certain inadequacies in Foucault's theoretical position, a number of which relate not only to the concerns of this chapter but to the book's overall approach to questions of social ontology. First, despite Foucault's rejection of 'totalizing' (or 'grand') theory, critics have observed that in some parts of his work his conception of society is overly holistic and unitary. It can be argued, with reference to the four 'cardinal sins', that some of his ideas have essentialist undertones. In his early, 'structuralist' period Foucault (1970) did not adopt Lévi-Strauss's idea of universal unconscious structures (this was one reason why in interviews Foucault frequently said that he was 'not a structuralist'). Instead, Foucault argued that unconscious codes and rules underpin a specific episteme (and its associated discourses); an episteme is relatively unitary, and is not universal but is, rather, characteristic of a particular society and epoch. It has been suggested, however, that Foucault's supposition that each society has a current episteme or regime of truth (its 'general politics of truth') is too holistic (White, 1992: 227–8). Usually there exist numerous conflicting and interacting 'politics of truth' within a society; for Padgett and Ansell (1989: 33), a problem with Foucault's theorizing is that it fails to acknowledge discontinuities between macro-cognitive and micro-behavioural spheres of the social, resulting in an approach that 'rips individuals out of their (often contradictory) multiple network contexts and obscures … heterogeneity and complexity'. Supporters of Foucault would no doubt argue, and not without a certain amount of justification, that the above criticism has rather less force when it is applied to Foucault's (1980b) 'genealogical' thesis which argues that history is discontinuous (there is no 'necessary', 'logical', or evolutionary progression from one episteme to another) and that since there is no immanent direction to history, the meanings associated with a particular era are contingent outcomes of events and struggles. What we have here, however, is one of the tensions and ambiguities that are to be found in Foucault's work; some strands of his writing veer towards holism and essentialism, whereas elements of his critique of modernist theorizing imply diversity, heterogeneity, and a fragmentation of the social. It is also worth noting that in his governmentality writings (1991), which preoccupied Foucault in the years immediately preceding his death in 1984, we find criticism of essentialist theories which suppose that governance discourses (and policy programmes) necessarily 'hang together' or form a unity: however, O'Mally *et al.* (1997: 513, 515) in their much-quoted paper on governmentality correctly observe that while Foucault refers to heterogeneity and diversity *between* government programmes, he fails to acknowledge heterogeneity *within* programmes.

Second, the tendency in poststructural and postmodern theory – including Foucauldian writing – to collapse distinctions between agency and structure and between micro and macro, results in what Archer calls 'central conflation'. Like Elias and Giddens, Foucault compacts agency and structure together, instead of treating them as a dualism comprised of separable, ontologically distinct and relatively autonomous dimensions of the social. Analytical and methodological problems associated with duality and central conflation are re-examined in the next chapter, and for the moment it is sufficient to observe that while the motive behind Foucault's attempt to 'transcend' dualism is in some ways laudable (the intention in much of his work is to avoid, as he sees it, the 'extremes' of humanism and structuralism), one of the problems of duality theorizing is that formally eliding dualistic distinctions does not remove the possibility that one or other of agency and structure is – even if not overtly – in fact given analytical primacy. In Foucault's theoretical scheme, structure is elevated to prominence, resulting in a flawed and lopsided form of analysis that tends to neglect the part that agency plays in social life.

Third, and this criticism follows closely on the heels of the previous remarks, Foucault's theorizing implies a notion of agency that rests on an unfortunate combination of reification and social determinism. In his earlier, structuralist phase, Foucault 'decentred the subject' and in his later, poststructuralist phase it is – despite numerous references to the self – still discourses that dominate action; the claim is made that subjectivity is an effect of discourses. Indeed, it seems that Foucault presumes discourses are themselves actors or agents. The problem here is that there is a crucial sense in which discourses – patterned ways of thinking and of behaving – are a form of material that must be mobilized by *actors* (as defined in the Introduction) before the discourse(s) can be said to have any social consequences or effects. Discourses influence (though do not determine) actors, and are a part of structure (defined in Chapter 5 as relatively enduring 'conditions-of-action') but discourses as such are not actors, a point that is lost upon poststructuralists who, as we have seen, refuse to distinguish between agency and structure and therefore do not regard them as relatively autonomous phenomena. It is true that Foucault's later work attempted to 'bring in' agency, but this was done in a way which over-emphasized individuality and – in common with poststructural and postmodern theory in general – failed to provide a theory of intersubjectivity (Best and Kellner, 1991: 66); what this highlights is that Foucault not only downplays the significance of subjectivity and of agency and its relative autonomy from structure, but also fails to appreciate the significance of intersubjective/ micro-interactional dimensions of agency and social action, and of power.

Finally, Foucault's theorizing displays strong elements of another of the 'cardinal sins', namely functional teleology. The logic of Foucault's position asserts that society has a need for docile, obedient, and self-controlling subjects and that disciplinary technologies arise in response to that need. However, this tacit assertion by Foucault is made without reference to the part that agency plays in the constitution of social life, and without reference to the contexts of agency (political, organizational, occupational, administrative, professional, religious, familial, and so on) and their influence upon the exercise of agency. There is in Foucault's work a failure to acknowledge the significance of links between agency and social settings (for example, organizational and inter-organizational contexts of action) and a general neglect of subjectivity (other than as 'an effect of discourse') and of intersubjectivity, all of which are crucial factors in the creation, application, and transformation or reproduction of discursive practices; the existence and form of the latter tend to be 'explained' by Foucault in terms of their satisfying the functional needs of 'disciplinary society'. As observed earlier,[3] it is legitimate to enquire into the functional needs (or 'conditions of existence') of social phenomena – including social wholes, whether a small group, an organization, or a nation–state – but such enquiry is incomplete and cannot fully explain the form taken by phenomena (such as a 'discourse') that may have been shown empirically to contribute to the maintenance of social wholes. A fuller, more rounded explanation of the phenomenon in question has to also make reference to agency and the contexts of action; failure to incorporate a non-reified concept of agency into social analysis as part of a dual system- and social-integration approach, results in illegitimate teleological forms of explanation such as one finds in the work of Foucault.

Anthony Giddens: duality versus dualism

In regard to Giddens's theorization of the 'duality versus dualism' debate and the relation of his theorizing to the concerns of this chapter, all that is necessary here, bearing in mind the brief discussion of structuration theory in Chapter 2, is to provide a critique of his concept of 'the duality of structure'. First, however, let us recall what is entailed in Giddens's commitment to a duality of action and structure.

Giddens's concept of duality is central to his theory of structuration, a theory which attempts to avoid voluntarism on the one hand (an approach that he associates with, for example, ethnomethodology and phenomenology), and determinism on the other, which Giddens associates with structuralism and functionalism: he draws upon some of these and other theoretical schools, and combines them in a synthesis that departs from conventional sociological conceptions of social structure. Giddens employs the term structure to refer not to particular social forms such as groups, organizations or collectivities (1982: 121), but to 'generative rules and resources' (ibid.: 127). Social groups, families, committees, organizations, and so on are not structures; they are *systems* that 'have' structures or structural properties. Structure consists of rules, defined as 'social conventions and knowledge of the context of their application' (Giddens, 1981: 170), and resources, which are 'capabilities of making things happen' (ibid.). Rules include, for example, unwritten norms as well as written regulations. Resources are of two main types: 'allocative resources' such as land and raw materials, and 'authoritative resources' consisting of non-material resources such as status or hierarchical position. According to Giddens's concept of the 'dialectic of control' (1984: 16, 374), structure generates behaviour, but does not wholly determine it: although power is rarely equally distributed, everyone – including subordinates – almost always possesses at least some power and most individuals are able to exercise an element of choice arising from the relational dynamics of power (prisoners sometimes go on hunger strike, factory workers may 'work to rule', babies cry as a way of attracting attention, and so on). Although Giddens rejects the objectivism and determinism of structural linguistics, he explains his use of the term structure by making illustrative reference to Saussure's distinction between wholes (language/or *langue*) and parts (situated speech acts/or *parole*). Structure refers to the 'structural properties' of language (these include the rules of grammar) which have only 'virtual' existence in so far as they have no existence anywhere in time–space; they exist only as 'memory traces', except on those occasions when they are instantiated in speech acts or in written form (Giddens, 1981: 170–1). This illustration serves also to bring out the point that, for Giddens, structure both constrains and enables action: 'every language involves relatively "fixed" categorizations that constrain thought at the same time as they make possible a whole variety of conceptual operations that without language would be impossible' (Giddens, 1981: 171). When these understandings are applied not only to language but to society and social life in general, we are left with a conception of the social in which structure (rules and resources) has no existence in time or space other than when instantiated by people in social settings.[4] Structure is not external to or apart from action: unless structure is instantiated in action, it has no existence other than as memory traces in people's minds (Giddens, 1989: 256). In other words, structures (defined as rules and resources) have no temporality or spatiality. It is often commented that for Giddens it is *systems* as instantiated, reproduced sets of social relations that extend across time and space, and while systems have structural properties, systems, as just noted, are not structures. However, Giddens apparently believes that not only structure but also systems, as he defines them, are 'virtual' until instantiated; although his stance on this matter is somewhat ambiguous, it seems to me that, in effect, Giddens is saying that there is a duality – not a dualism – of action *and* of system (Giddens, 1977: 14, 118; 1981: 172; 1984: 17; see also Archer, 1995: 96; Cohen, 1989: 87–8). Thus while Mouzelis (1995: 118) is correct when he says that for Giddens structure is 'virtual', he is incorrect when he says that Giddens regards systems as actual or 'real' rather than virtual. On this particular issue, my interpretation of Giddens is similar to Archer's (1995: 96; 1996: 690). Therefore I suggest that, like Mouzelis, writers such as Scott (1995: 204) and Hay (2002: 121) err in supposing that, in Giddens's schema, systems have real rather than virtual existence. However, the more general point to be made for the moment is that rather like Berger, Elias, and Foucault (though these theorists, of course, are unidentical in many other respects), Giddens collapses a distinction between agency and structure and he employs a form of theorizing that Archer, who was mentioned earlier, describes as 'central conflation'. Giddens argues for a duality of structure in which agency and structure are viewed as 'two sides of the same coin'. Structure is both the medium and the (largely unintended) outcome of action: instead of regarding action and structure as separable, relatively autonomous elements (a dualism) whose interconnections remain to be empirically discovered in each instance, Giddens dissolves the distinction between these elements. His intention is to avoid giving primacy to either action *or* to structure and this is expressed in his concept 'social practices', a concept which encapsulates Giddens' idea of duality: 'The basic domain of study of the social sciences is neither the experience of the individual actor, nor the existence of any form of social totality, but *social practices* ordered across space and time' (Giddens, 1984: 2, my italics). Social practices are, so to speak, a combination of action and structure: as observed earlier, structure is both the medium and the (largely unintended) outcome of social action/social practices. For reasons that were outlined in the preceding chapter and which will be taken further in the following chapter, there is a good case for suggesting that Giddens's concept of duality should be rejected. In social analysis, agency–structure and micro–macro should be employed as dualisms that refer to distinct, relatively autonomous phenomena. In sum, the major problem with structuration theory is that Giddens collapses, in his terms, structure (rules and resources), systems (reproduced practices across time–space) and agency/social action into an amalgam within which the various elements are fused so tightly together that they cannot be separated. This makes it impossible to investigate these elements separately, to investigate their mutual influences one upon the other over time, or to ascertain the relative impact of each upon any given social situation. Moreover, to attempt to resolve this practical problem of social analysis by means of Giddens's strategy of 'methodological bracketing' merely serves to reintroduce and reinforce the idea of a dualism of structure and action. In other words, dualism is rejected in the ontological phase of Giddens's schema, only to be readmitted in the methodological phase; here, rather than being consistent with each other and regulating each other, ontology and methodology exist in a contradictory relation one to the other.

Codification of some key theoretical concepts and postulates

At this stage of the discussion, it will be helpful if we link together some of the earlier arguments in such a way as to codify a number of interconnected concepts and postulates that form part of the book's overall (meta)theoretical framework. Building upon the arguments developed so far, each of the following will be discussed in turn: (a) the idea of emergence; (b) system and social integration as forms of analysis; (c) the relation of discourses to their social contexts; (d) the concept of structural (or systemic) contradictions; and (e) the notion of recursion ('path dependency').

Emergence

The idea of emergent properties – an idea that is not reificationist so long as we adhere to the definition of actor (or agent) outlined in the Introduction, and which is discussed more fully in Chapter 5 – refers to properties of a social whole (or indeed, of any social phenomena) that are not manifest in any of its constituent parts, properties that arise by virtue of the relation between or interaction among the parts. Emergence can be found at micro-, mezo- and macro-levels of social process. For example, a person has emergent properties – these include human consciousness, a capacity for decision-making, and intentional causal powers – that cannot be found in any of the parts (molecular cells) that constitute the person (Harré, 1981). This rubric ('emergence') also applies to, for instance, committees and organizations: these are entities that can with justification be said to be 'more than' the sum of individual members' personalities, forms of thought, dispositions, intentions, and the like. For example, a formal committee or organization in the public sector is likely to have institutionalized mechanisms of legitimation, resource-attraction and decision-making, and more generally causal powers of a kind that for empirical explanatory purposes cannot be reduced to the level of its individual members (Holzner, 1978; Clegg, 1989: 187–8). Informal groups also have emergent properties in the form of, for example, routinized patterns of interaction, informal systems of rules, and mechanisms of social control that very often emerge simply by virtue of the group's existence. As already noted, emergent properties of social wholes are also to be found at the macro-level of social process. For instance, general cultural values and norms are in varying degrees given expression in everyday practices and routines that for the purposes of social explanation cannot legitimately be reduced to the attributes of individuals; the aggregated outcomes of individual actions are not unimportant, but there are no good reasons for endorsing methodological individualism, which is a reductionist doctrine that attempts to reduce the whole of social explanation to the actions of individuals (Hindess, 1988).

In the Durkheimian tradition, Parsons (1967) insisted that differing types of social phenomena exist at different levels of social reality. For example, he argued that the personality system, the social system, and the cultural system each have distinct properties that are peculiar to the system in question. Hence it is not legitimate to try to explain phenomena which occur at one level of reality (for example, the social) in terms of phenomena that occur at another level (for example, the psychological). The question of emergent properties that relate to a distinction between differing levels of social reality is an aspect of the micro–macro distinction which was discussed in Chapter 2 (also see Chapter 7). Theorists who reject 'micro–macro', such as Law (1994) whose framework blends structuralism with poststructuralism, efface the distinction between micro and macro and thereby obscure the idea that emergent properties may arise at differing levels of social process. It has been argued by classical as well as many modern theorists that such properties require investigation and explanation *at the level of social process at which they occur.* This is exemplified in Durkheim's (1982: 110) methodological prescription which states that we should explain social facts in terms of *other* social facts. The influence of Durkheim is evident in Mouzelis's (1991: 78) insistence that 'macro social facts must primarily be explained by other macro-facts'; here the word 'primarily' serves to temper Mouzelis's injunction, but nevertheless his theoretical position is more Durkheimian than Layder's, whose work is examined in the next chapter. Layder's methodological emphasis (1997: 241–3) is placed precisely on the argument that it is wrong to attempt to explain macro-social phenomena exclusively in terms of other macro-social phenomena, or to attempt to explain micro-happenings exclusively in terms of other micro-happenings. Layder's arguments concerning the existence of a stratified social ontology are based on the idea that social reality is made up of four social 'domains'. These are individual biography/subjectivity; 'situated activity' (face-to-face interaction/intersubjectivity); 'social settings' (the locations in which situated activity occurs); and macro-social phenomena ('contextual resources', in Layder's terminology). Although these are relatively autonomous domains with distinct properties and effects of their own, they interpenetrate and therefore it is necessary to empirically explore links and mutual influences between them (Layder, 1997). The point to be made here is that social enquiry often requires that we work across rather than only within micro-, mezo- and macro-domains of social reality. In other words, recognition of the existence of emergent properties should not prevent us from searching for connections between phenomena (including causal connections) both within and between domains or 'levels' of social reality. It is also worth noting that these theoretical observations can usefully be brought to bear upon the work undertaken by political scientists and policy analysts involved in policy network analysis: as some political scientists recognize, 'policy network' tends to be employed almost exclusively as a mezo-level inter-organizational concept, and there is insufficient work on the exploration of links between this level and the micro- and macro-dimensions of the policy process (Marsh and Smith, 2000). Moreover at a global level, the occurrence of interaction between national government actors and between them and other (for example, subnational and supranational) actors, results in the empirically complex emergent properties that are characteristic of contemporary postnational governance (Sibeon, 2000; Rumford, 2002).

There is another aspect of emergence that calls for comment. This concerns Archer's (1995: 167, 173–4) understanding of emergent properties. Her concepts of 'structural' and 'cultural' emergence (ibid.: 173–9) are in my opinion too restrictive since they refer to 'necessary' relations between two or more phenomena which constitute another, emergent phenomenon. For instance, Archer, like Sayer (1992: 92) observes that the existence of landlords and tenants are 'logically necessary' to the existence of each other and to landlord–tenant relations, and to the existence of rent as an emergent and institutionalized form of economic transaction. Excluded from Archer's definition of structural or cultural emergence, however, are 'new' properties that result from purely contingent interaction among phenomena, as distinct from the special case (that is, phenomena that are 'necessarily' related to each other) which Archer (1995: 173) has in mind. My concept of emergence, which is wider than Archer's and is in some respects similar to Coleman's (1990: 5), makes no assumptions as to whether, say, phenomenon A and phenomenon B are 'necessary' to each other or to the emergence of phenomenon C. If two causally unrelated phenomena (A and B) fortuitously combine and result in a new phenomenon (C) – even though they are not 'necessary' to C, which could have resulted from interaction among elements other than A and B – then, unlike Archer, I regard C as emergent simply by virtue of its being 'more than' the sum of its constituent elements (that is, more than the sum of A and B). This, it should be noted, relates to a more general understanding that social phenomena resulting from diachronic interconnections between agency, structure, and social chance typically exhibit emergent properties; in other words, there is reason to suppose that emergence is ubiquitous.

System integration and social integration

In this section I draw primarily though not exclusively upon Mouzelis's codification and insightful elaboration of Lockwood's (1964) very important distinction between system and social integration. In both theoretical and empirical work it is appropriate to employ a distinction between a *social integration* approach (the study of agency/actors and of social relations – whether co-operative or conflictual – among actors), and a *system integration* approach (which refers to the study of relations between the 'parts' of social systems, including, for example, relations between positions/roles, rules and social institutions). This distinction indicates that society has at least two 'faces' or dimensions. In Mouzelis's (1995: 127) words: 'a social whole can refer both to a system of interrelated actors (to a *figurational* whole) and a system of interrelated rules, roles or social positions (*institutional* whole)'. Put simply, social integration refers to the study of agency and actor–actor relations, system integration to the study of part–part relations. In the social sciences it is necessary to study both dimensions, as well as links between them. If, for instance, we wish to focus attention upon system 'needs' (see the Introduction, note 6) it is important, as Mouzelis (1991; 1995) observes, to draw upon the distinction between social integration (a focus upon agency and figurational wholes/relations among actors) and system integration (analysis of institutional wholes and of relations between institutions or between, say, roles/positions). If the social integration mode of analysis is lost sight of in studies that refer to a social system's conditions-of-existence (system 'needs'), this courts the 'cardinal sins' and results in theoretical and methodological problems, including the problem of reification; in reificationist theories, structural 'parts' (rules, positions/roles, social institutions) are wrongly treated as though they are actors with decision-making powers. In order to avoid teleology (trying to explain, without reference to intentional planning, a cause of something in terms of its effects) and reification (the attribution of agency to entities that are not actors), it is necessary to employ the following principle. When a social system or social network (or any social whole, such as a small group, an organization, a profession, or a society) is inspected in *institutional* terms (a system integration mode of analysis) it is legitimate to enquire into the system's conditions of existence, providing that *figurational* analysis (a social integration approach) is also brought into the picture so as to examine the part played by actors and actor–actor relations in the creation, reproduction or change of the system in question.

A few additional observations are called for. First, the social integration and system integration distinction is not synonymous with the micro–macro distinction. As already noted, system integration and social integration forms of analysis may be undertaken at micro- and macro-levels of social process. Mouzelis (1997) rightly rejects Giddens's (1984: 376, 377) formula whereby social integration refers to situations of co-presence, and system integration to interaction across time–space. However, Mouzelis's particular reason for rejecting Giddens's formulation, is flawed: as argued in Chapter 2, we ought not accept Mouzelis's rather curious and inconsistent claim (1995: 124; 1997) that face-to-face interaction among powerful actors is a macro-phenomenon that should not be regarded as micro-situational interaction. I suggest a more adequate reason for rejecting Giddens's re-working of Lockwood's distinction is that actor–actor relations/ social integration can refer to face-to-face encounters in situations of co-presence; to individual–individual relations across relatively large stretches of space and time; and to inter-organizational relations between social ('organizational') actors (see Chapter 5). Second, I should like to empha-size rather more strongly than Mouzelis that there are 'degrees of system-ness' and that the system integration and social integration distinction is relevant not only in the case of investigation of tightly coupled social systems/social networks, but also situations characterized by relatively inde-terminate or 'loose' configurations of action (see Chapter 6). Third, Mouzelis (1991: 172–93; 1997) is correct to reject Habermas's use of the system integration and social integration distinction. Habermas (1987: 151–2) defines social and system integration in more or less the same terms as those referred to above, but then he proceeds to a dubious theoretical formula which specifies that what he calls the System (polity and economy) should be studied from the standpoint of a system integration approach and that what he terms the Lifeworld (households, relations among kin, friends, neighbours, and so on) should be studied in terms of a social integration approach. For Habermas, the system is steered and co-ordinated in an auto-matic way by the media of power (in the case of the polity) and by money (in the case of the economy); these media do not, so to speak, rely upon agency/actor–actor relations – they are said to work on the basis of systemic mechanisms that express system 'logic' and system functional imperatives ('system needs'). The lifeworld, in contrast, rests on actor–actor relations and should, according to Habermas, be studied exclusively from a social integration vantage point. Habermas's reasoning in connection with this matter, is untenable. Social relations are an important part of political life and of social happenings in public bureaucracies (the 'polity'), and the same is true of private firms and the marketplace (the 'economy'). Conversely, a system integration focus on relations between roles/positions or between roles and social institutions can hardly be excluded from, say, social investigation concerned with households or community life (the lifeworld). Against Habermas, it can be argued that *all* social spheres – including those he labels the System and the Lifeworld – should be investigated from both system and social integration perspectives. These remarks lead to a fourth and more general observation: it should be emphasized, once again, that it is desirable that all instances of concept formation should be based upon critique of the four 'cardinal sins' outlined in the Introduction. Otherwise, potentially useful concepts or conceptual distinctions may be marred or misused by virtue of their being unnecessarily linked to defective forms of theoretical-methodological reasoning. For example, a distinction between system integration and social integration approaches is deployed in Marxism (Mouzelis, 1995: 122) and in, for instance, radical feminism, both of which entail reductionist theorizing. Fifth, it was mentioned earlier that Mouzelis (1995: 80) observes that the question of how figurational and institutional structures (and therefore, social and system integration modes of analysis) are related to each other, is a difficult theoretical problem and that he is unsure as to where its resolution lies. Here Mouzelis is alluding to an aspect of the agency–structure problematic. Part of the solution to the problem to which he refers revolves around theoretical synthesis allied to concept development that builds upon sustained critique of reductionism, essentialism, reification, and functional teleology, and that also explicitly confronts the important question of the relation of discourses to the social contexts in which they are located.

The relation of discourses to their social contexts

With regard to the highly complex matter of the relation of discourses to society or to social contexts, ethnomethodologists along with poststruc-turalists, discourse theorists, and postmodernists believe the former consti-tute the latter, whereas structuralists tend to reverse the direction of determination and to argue that structure determines thought. In regard to this issue, though not necessarily others, my own theoretical position is very roughly similar to that of White (1992: 305) and Law (1986c: 3–4), both of whom regard the relation of discourses to social contexts as a two-way or 'dialectical' process. In Chapter 1 it was argued that the relation of dis-courses (including discursive practices) to social contexts is generally *loosely dialectical* (each to a variable extent influences the other, but without there being any necessary or direct correspondence or 'perfect match' between them; change in the one does not necessarily result in automatic or match-ing change in the other): discourse, using this term broadly to include actors' forms of thought and related practices within any particular field of action, spirals into and out of social contexts in sometimes highly disorderly and unpredictable fashion. That this should be so is not surprising. Discourses are not expressions of some unified social totality; rather, they are quite often mediated in differing ways by a variety of actors, circumstances, and mechanisms that, moreover, may be discontinuous across micro-, mezo- and macro-levels of social process (see Chapter 7). This is not to say there can never be a relatively close correspondence between discourse and context. There may be cases where, for a period of time at least, discourse powerfully shapes context(s), or alternatively, where contextual factors are conducive to the development of, or have a pronounced conditioning effect upon, particular forms of thought: these, however, are contingent occurrences; they are matters for empirical investigation, not for a priori theoretical predetermination of the kind associated with, say, structuralism or poststructuralism/discourse theory or with an exclusive commitment to phenomenology or symbolic interactionism. Recall, too, that from the standpoint of any particular actor or discourse, the social context ('structure') includes *other* actors and other discourses. It is, also, worth observing that Berger and Luckmann's (1971) view of language and society to some extent resembles the conception outlined above, although as we have seen, Berger and Luckmann err in sometimes implying that there is a 'direct link' between discourse(s) and society. With reference to structuration theory and discourse, processes analogous to those discussed here are described by Giddens – in terms of the relation of academic to lay discourses – as 'the double hermeneutic' (1984: xxxv).[5] In regard to postmodernism, it was argued in Chapter 1 that there is a tendency among postmodernists to attempt, contradictorily, to combine two opposed (meta)theoretical claims: on the one hand, it is argued that discourses create or produce social contexts (the postmodern argument here being that there is no pre-discursive, ontologically prior social reality), and, on the other, that discourse is in some sense determined by social context (by, that is, actors' structural location – as 'men', 'white people', or whatever – in the social totality).[6]

In recent years policy analysts have increasingly begun to recognize the significance of language and discourse in the policy process. For example, Thrift (1994: 22–3) in a paper on international monetary systems makes the point that certain forms of thought and practices tend to become institutionalized in policy networks. A similar point is made by Hoppe (1993: 77), and also by Haas (1992: 5) in connection with the relation of the policy process to transnational epistemic communities. An epistemic policy community is a network of socially recognized 'experts' with expertise relevant to a particular policy domain; while members may come from a variety of disciplines or professional backgrounds, they tend to subscribe to a common discourse and to share beliefs about the nature and causes of policy problems, and about possible solutions and desired policy outcomes (Haas, 1992: 3). The issues under discussion here, as shown in these references to policy studies, are not only of interest to theoreticians; they relate closely to the study of empirical processes. It is important to recognize that actors' forms of thought in general, but also systems of thought of the kind that may be found in occupations, professions, and policy communities, are not necessarily internally coherent and highly crystallized. Discourses may to a greater or lesser extent be internally splintered (White, 1992: 305), the extent to which this occurs being an empirical question. For example, the 'same' perspective or ideology may be mediated in different contexts at different levels of crystallization, explicitness, and internal conceptual consistency (Rootes, 1981). Of significance, too, is the point that theories, perspectives, and ideologies have 'publics' (mass media, professional groups, administrators, consumer or client groups, and so on), and ideologies for their survival may, in differing spatio-temporal contexts, have to be flexibly modified in order to meet the demands of different 'publics' (Bouchier, 1977). The part that discourse plays in politics, governance, and the policy process is, then, as indicated in these brief examples, a field of enquiry that is of considerable importance (Sibeon, 1997: 65–8).

It perhaps hardly needs to be said that unresolved conceptual disputes surround the question of the relation of discourses to 'society' or to specific social contexts or situations. These conceptual problems relate to epistemological and ontological issues that were discussed earlier, and in particular, they relate to the question of whether, and if so in what terms, it is legitimate to regard social reality as a product of discourse. Is there an ontologically prior, pre-discursive social reality 'out there'? The argument developed here and in previous chapters rests upon a flexible but realist social ontology, and upon critique of the four 'cardinal sins' in the specific terms that these were defined in the Introduction. My approach to the question of the relation of discourses to their social contexts acknowledges the emergent properties of social systems, of institutions and of other phenomena, and rejects the idea that there is a 'direct link' between subjectivities and the objective dimension of social life, while at the same time recognizing that social reality is in some sense socially constructed: the social fabric consists in part of socially constructed materials that over time have become institutionalized (or 'consigned', in the terminology of actor network theory). An important point that I should like to establish here is that even if we allow that social reality is, as poststructuralists and postmodernists claim, discursively constituted, there nevertheless is a (socially constructed) reality 'out there'. As Mouzelis (1995: 61) observes, discursively constituted arrangements (for example, the notion that formal paper qualifications are necessary for entering the teaching profession or for practising as a surgeon) may over the course of time become firmly established social patterns that to all intents and purposes are irreversible: '"discursivity" by no means always entails fragility or malleability; it is compatible with institutionalized arrangements with high degrees of immutability'. Once socially constructed – and I have already clarified that, like Layder (1997), I am not suggesting there is a direct link between subjectivities/action and institutional social orders – the social world may over time acquire an objective facticity in the form of, in particular, social institutions, rules, roles/positions, and resource and power distributions. In regard to these ontological issues, my own theoretical position, as indicated earlier and also in the later chapters, endorses Mouzelis's insistence upon recognition of the significance of systemic phenomena, while also acknowledging, in rather less systemic vein, what Stones (1996: 232) calls 'sophisticated realism': that is to say, the social world is 'real', but at the same time it is often highly variable, and empirically 'messy'. The central point for emphasis here, however, is that elements of a discursively constituted social world, if and when they are stablized ('institutionalized') across time and space, can legitimately be said to be real and to be objective elements of social structure: such elements are ontologically prior to, though in principle they may be open to modification or transformation by, the discursive, interpretative, and practical activities of any particular actors who encounter them.

Structural contradictions

Marxist theorists, including structuralist Marxists such as Poulantzas (1973) and Althusser (1965; 1971) argue that we should be aware of the existence of socially and politically important phenomena known as 'structural contradictions', and that these are inherent features of capitalist society. It is argued, in objectivist terms, that there are incompatibilities or contradictions between the various elements or 'parts' of the (capitalist) social system, as distinct from contradictions that are perceived and experienced by actors; in terms of this objectivist notion of structural contradictions as phenomena that exist among and within the parts of social systems (parts such as economy, polity, and culture), it is structures *themselves*, not actors' experiences, perceptions, intentions, and activities, that are said to be in tension. An opposing, subjectivist conception is developed by Berger and Luckmann (1971: 80–2, 224) who, in rejecting notions of institutional, systemic or functional 'logic', deny that an external observer can determine the degree of integration (or malintegration) of a social system. In Marxist objectivist theories it is, as just noted, the structures themselves that are said to be in tension. Phenomenologically oriented theorists such as Berger and Luckmann (1971: 224) reject both Marxist and structural-functional concepts of contradiction, malintegration or integration: '"functional integration", if one wants to use this term at all, means the integration of the institutional order by way of various *legitimating processes*. In other words, *the integration lies not in the institutions but in their legitimation.*' On this view, neither structural contradictions or, conversely, structural compatibilites can have an independent existence of their own within or among structures. In opposition to Marx and Parsons, Bergerian sociology supposes that 'contradictions', or alternatively 'compatibilities' among the elements of social systems, lie in the eyes of actors who perceive and experience them, and *not* in the structural elements themselves. For Berger and Luckmann the converse of 'legitimation' in the sense just referred to is that any 'crisis' of structural arrangements – as in, for example, the proposition, which gained currency in the 1980s, that there is a 'legitimation crisis of the welfare state' – is not a matter of 'contradiction' among or within the structures themselves, *but a crisis of legitimation of those structures by actors*. The problem here, however, is that in rejecting objectivist theorizing, Berger and Luckmann (1971: 82) go to the other extreme and endorse subjectivism; it is argued that the integration or malintegration of an institutional order 'can be understood *only* in terms of the "knowledge" that its members have of it' (my italics). This statement encapsulates the subjectivism associated with Bergerian sociology and with phenomenological sociology in general.

Giddens employs a concept of structural contradictions; his concept, however, is somewhat ambiguous. In some of his writings he gives the impression that he rejects objectivist theories of contradictions in favour of a subjective, actor-oriented definition (1976: 127–8; 1993: 134). However in *The Constitution of Society*, where he refers to objective and subjective elements, he develops a concept of structural contradictions that inclines to the former (1984: 198–9). He makes a distinction between *structural contradiction* ('disjunction of structural principles of system organization') and *conflict* ('actual struggle between actors or groups'). Here Giddens, in contrast to Berger, appears to be suggesting – in terms that sit uneasily alongside his commitment to a *duality* of action and structure – that structural contradictions can exist objectively (1984: 315) even where they are not perceived, experienced or acted upon by actors who, for whatever reason, remain unaware of their 'interests' (ibid.: 199, 318). Implicit in these references to Giddens's theory of 'structural contradictions' are unresolved problems surrounding not only his conception of a duality of action-and-structure and of action-and-system as he defines these terms, but also a lack of clarity concerning his commitment to the idea of 'unacknowledged interests' (ibid.: 198-9, 318) (see the discussion of power and interests in Chapter 5). Another major contemporary sociological theorist referred to earlier, Mouzelis, attempts to balance objectivist and subjectivist notions of systemic contradictions. However despite his frequent critical references to the 'denial' of agency by poststructuralists, structuralist Marxists and structural-functionalists, when it comes to the topic of 'structural contradictions' he argues, in effect, that structural or systemic incompatibilities/contradictions are 'objective' (1995: 77–8) and can be said to exist even where actors are subjectively unaware of their existence (ibid.: 122); it is true that Mouzelis does insist that, in accordance with his use of the system integration and social integration distinction, it is necessary to also take account of actors' perceptions of or responses to systemic or structural contradictions, but for him a (systemic) contradiction is ontologically prior to actors' experience of and responses to it. Although Mouzelis's position is nuanced in the terms just described, he tends to incline towards the objectivist position. Also of interest is Archer's analysis. With reference to the work of Weber, Lockwood and others, she discusses (1995: 219–21) 'necessary compatibilities' between the components of social systems (such as, in Ancient India, compatibilities between caste, religion, polity, and law) and 'necessary incompatibilities' between system parts, as in the case of societies based on patrimonial bureaucracy with an in-built contradiction between bureaucratic centralization, and economic and societal pressures for decentralization. Archer's and others' notions of 'necessary' and 'objective' compatibilities/incompatibilities between the parts of social systems should be viewed extremely cautiously (it can be argued that there *is* an objective element in social life, but this is interwoven with subjectivity; see later); nevertheless Archer (ibid.: 214–15) is aware of at least some of the subtleties of the dialectics of agency and structure in so far as she recognizes that to some extent systemic compatibilities and incompatibilities are the partly intended, partly unintended outcomes of actions.

We cannot duck the issues that are under discussion here. Structural or systemic tensions of various kinds are recurrent features of social life. Some of these occur at the macro-level of social process. For example, it is perfectly clear that in India there has been a certain amount of contradiction or incompatibility between the traditional caste system and aspects of the industrialization process (Gould, 1987). System incompatibilities of this kind (like social structure in general) are not reducible to agency, that is, they are not reducible to the intentions and activities of any particular actors. Macro-structure in general (including structural compatibilities/incompatibilities) stretches in time and space away from any particular actors or any particular encounters or activities. An example at the mezo-level of social process concerns policy sectors where there may arise structural incompatibilities that are akin to tension within what Merton (1968) has described as role sets: it is legitimate to speak of certain positions/roles (those of, for instance, hospital administrators, on the one hand, and physicians, on the other) as existing in a state of tension with each other, tensions which outlive the individuals who happen to occupy the roles at any particular point in time. And yet behaviour is not wholly role-determined; to some extent, it is role-determining. Therefore it is appropriate, I suggest, to regard system incompatibilities/tensions such as inter-role tension (or 'contradiction') as part of the dialectics of agency and structure whereby action and structure influence each other, this being a dialectic which departs from Bergerian sociology in so far as it is not claimed that there is an invariant or 'direct' link between action and structure, but that there is a more or less loose interweaving and interpenetration of these elements. Importantly, the interweaving of structure and activities – and this would apply irrespective of whether the focus of analysis happens to be system compatibilities or incompatibilities – should be investigated in an ontologically flexible fashion without recourse to theories which entail reductionism, essentialism, reification or functional teleology. This means that, for example, theories predicated on methodological individualism or methodological collectivism should be avoided; and I have already argued the case for structure-action dualism, not duality. Though not identical to Layder's (1997) theory of social domains (this is discussed in the next chapter), my approach to structural or system contradictions is in some respects compatible with Layder's. What I am proposing here is a conception of structural contradictions (or conversely, compatibilities) that is neither objectivist nor subjectivist. Structure, including incompatibilities/contradictions among structural elements such as roles, predisposes or conditions certain kinds of action and the latter intentionally and/or unintentionally reproduces or elaborates structure, including any incompatible elements of structure such as recurrent role–role tensions or incompatibilities. In any given field of action, structure/social context partly shapes and is partly shaped by activities, as part of an ongoing diachronic interplay between structure and agency/action. It is not difficult to conceive of situations, as in Merton's (1968) classic example of role set conflict, where current actors are confronted by institutionalized role conflicts and contradictory expectations; patterned, ongoing conflicts and contradictions inherited from the past are elements of structure (relatively enduring conditions-of-action) that confront current actors. Also, where patterned, reproduced incompatibilities ('contradictions') between roles, rules or between social institutions have a long history, it is likely that at various times in the past certain compromises will have been struck by contending parties who are involved in the contradiction(s) (which is to say that agency has a part to play in the history of structural contradictions). Some of these compromises, though in principle open – to a greater or lesser extent – to re-inspection and re-negotiation, may have become institutionalized and therefore these too become an established part of the structure or social context that confronts present-day actors. I am suggesting, in other words, that patterned compatibilities and incompatibilities (of values, of roles, of perspectives, social practices, and so on) are part of an action–structure dialectic: actors' forms of thought, preferences and actions spiral into and out of contexts, and we have seen that a social context may exhibit significant recurrent compatibilities or incompatibilities among its constitutive elements and that these are objective elements of the social that are not reducible to the actions of any particular individuals. Present-day structure, as noted above, may also include institutionalized mechanisms that in the past were designed to attempt to contain or deal with experienced structural contradictions. The more general point to be made here is that the idea of structural (or system) contradiction cannot legitimately be ignored or side-stepped by social investigators: the term – along with the opposite notion of structural compatibilities – refers to important kinds of phenomena that arise from the interplay of activities and structures over time and which are neither wholly objective nor wholly subjective components of social reality.

Recursion and path dependency

The concept 'recursion' (sometimes known as path dependency) refers to self-reproducing or self-generating tendencies (Law, 1994: 14–16) that occur at the micro-, mezo- and macro-levels of social process and which are associated with, in particular, social systems or social networks (see Chapter 6). The theoretical and methodological principle that is involved here, a principle implicit in much of the earlier discussion, is that the existence of temporal or spatial continuities cannot be presumed in advance of empirical enquiry. Should any particular set of social conditions be reproduced across time and space, this is a relatively fortuitous and unpredictable outcome arising from conjunctions of agency, structure, and social chance (the latter is discussed in Chapter 5), rather than the automatic unfolding of some putative structural exigency; nevertheless, in certain circumstances – including those where recursive tendencies exist – some outcomes are more likely than others.

Where social stability is a feature of any particular context of action, it is probable that one of the factors involved in the process of social reproduction is recursion. Some versions of this concept, it can be argued, should be rejected for the reason that they are a form of reification, as in Luhmann's (1982; 1989) claim that tightly coupled social systems are 'autopoietic' or self-sustaining in a sense that implies systems exhibit agency (in effect, Luhmann proposes that systems are actors in the terms that actor was provisionally defined in the Introduction, where it was argued than an actor or agent is an entity that in principle is able to formulate, take, and act upon decisions). Similarly, in discussing governance, public policy, and recursion, Mayntz does not examine the concept *agency* and she exposes herself to the charge that, like Habermas, she employs a reified conception of social systems. She claims that social systems and social networks 'under certain conditions are able to define their own boundaries, and to actively protect themselves from external intervention' (1993: 17), and that systems have an 'ability to organise ... capacity to act' (ibid.: 18). Mayntz's claims are open to challenge: to say that an entity – such as a social system – may have recursive tendencies is not to say that the entity in question is thereby an actor or agent. When compared with Luhmann and Mayntz, my use of the concept ('recursion') is somewhat closer to – though far from identical with – its applications in symbolic interactionism, in Elias's process sociology, and in Giddens's structuration theory (see Law, 1994: 97, 112).

Some of the better accounts of recursion are to be found in the disciplines of political science and public policy. An example is Wilsford's (1994: 269) path dependency model of recursion: 'In a path-dependency model, existing policy (that is, the institutions and the rules of the game in place in a particular policy domain at a particular moment) acts as a focusing device for policy ... to channel future policy movement along a certain path.' Wilsford (ibid.: 253) also brings out the point that a path dependency model (the idea that events, circumstances, and decisions predispose future events) is not the same thing as historical determinism. Though he rightly rejects the idea of historical and structural predetermination, he provides little conceptual underpinning for this rejection. However, what seems clear from his paper is that he is critical of theories of structural predetermination without wanting to replace such theories with the equally problematical assumption that the social world is entirely 'chaotic'; instead, though he does not state the matter in quite these terms, he recognizes that time–space stability and policy continuities occur, but that these are contingently reproduced continuities and not (despite claims to the contrary in various reductionist and functional teleological theories) necessary effects of the social totality. Policy network theorists and researchers have emphasized that some policy networks (see Chapter 6) are conducive to the development of recursive patterns of public policy and practice. M.J. Smith (1993: 72) observes that once in existence, systemic patterns in policy communities tend to be reproduced via institutionalized rules, regularized inter-organizational interaction among a small cohort of state and non-state actors, and 'standard operating procedures'; in these ways policy networks enstructure certain perspectives, objectives, and interests within the policy process (1993: 234). Recursion and path dependency is also relevant to an understanding of political and policy processes associated with postnational governance (Sibeon, 1997; 2000). In the European Union (EU), for example, when subnational actors (such as local authorities or regional bodies within member states) and national actors (such as national governments or actors who are a part of national government) commit themselves to programme or policy agreements with actors from other member states or perhaps with the EU itself, it sometimes happens that massive 'sunk costs' make policy reversal or withdrawal unattractive, even in circumstances where – had such costs not existed – the actors would have preferred (because of a change in preferences or perhaps, for example, because of a new awareness of unanticipated consequences arising from earlier policy decisions) to reverse policy or even withdraw from the policy programme (Pierson, 1998: 316). Political and policy actors, that is to say, sometimes become 'locked into' a particular set of political, planning or resource arrangements or frameworks.

> Recent work on path dependence has emphasized the ways in which initial institutional or policy decisions – even suboptimal ones – can become self-reinforcing over time. These initial choices encourage the emergence of elaborate social and economic networks, greatly increasing the cost of adopting once-possible alternatives and therefore inhibiting exit from a current policy path. (ibid.)

One aspect of recursion in the EU policy process is to do with what political scientists and policy analysts call 'the spillover effect'. Schmidt (1996: 234, 236) is one among many observers who have pointed out that a supranational approach (that is, an approach to governance and policy that is shaped more by the EU as a supranational body than by inter-governmental negotiation among member states) in one policy sector – such as agriculture or competition policy – may 'spill over' and engender a supranational orientation in other policy sectors; once a supranational organization such as the European Union is created, it tends through various recursive processes to expand its influence to a range of policy sectors.

Recursion, defined as self-reproducing or path-setting tendencies within any particular field of action, is in some sense an outcome of interaction between agency, structure, and social chance (the idea of interaction between these elements is developed in some detail in Chapter 5). As we saw in the examples drawn from politics, governance, and the policy process, recursive tendencies among social phenomena are not outcomes that are structurally or historically predetermined and nor are they simply a product of agency. There are, then, grounds for suggesting that the concept *recursion*, if appropriately employed, is capable of contributing to the construction of well-founded empirical accounts of social stability within any given field of action.

Summary

The first part of this chapter, bearing in mind problems and themes identified in the preceding chapter, examined four major theorists' efforts to address agency–structure and micro–macro.

●

The dialectical approach of Peter Berger is an imaginative attempt to theoretically and methodologically integrate the investigation of micro- and macro-realms of society. In Bergerian sociology, actors' meanings are objectivated (institutionalized) and 'become' a macro-social order which is then absorbed or re-appropriated by individuals; people are both creators and products of society. Though a thought-provoking effort to 'integrate' micro and macro, Berger's synthetic framework is in some respects contradictory and fails to avoid pitfalls associated with upwards and downwards conflation.

●

Norbert Elias's figurational (or 'process') sociology, like Berger's work, is insightful and directs our attention to important dimensions of the social. Elias's processual conception of social life, his thesis on the unintended nature of society, and his ideas on power, are of considerable importance; but Elias wrongly implies there is a 'direct link' between activities and social structure, and tends to neglect the significance of the institutional dimension of society and its relation to the figurational.

●

Michel Foucault, along with each of the writers whose work is discussed in this chapter, has provided an original and significant contribution to our understanding of agency–structure and micro–macro. His wide-ranging writings on discourses, power, and the self illuminate certain aspects of social life. There are, however, unresolved problems in Foucault's approach. His method of analysis tends towards essentialism and the 'grand theory' style that he says he wishes to avoid; he collapses distinctions between agency and structure, and micro and macro; and some of his theorizing inclines towards reification and social determinism.

●

Anthony Giddens's concept of a duality of action and structure is part of his general (meta)theory of structuration. Examination of the conceptual components of structuration theory is instructive and there is considerable merit in Giddens's extensive critique of theories of agency–structure and of micro–macro. However, an argument set out in this and later chapters is that the relation of structure to action is a dualism, not a duality, and that Giddens's duality schema extends not only to his concept of structure but also to his concept of system(s).

•

The second part of the chapter expanded upon certain themes referred to earlier, and directed attention to (meta)theoretical concepts and postulates that, it was argued, are of major importance to the future development of metatheory and substantive theory, and to the conduct of empirical studies.

•

Emergence refers to those properties of social phenomena that are not manifest in constituent parts of the phenomena in question, properties that arise by virtue of the relation between or interaction among the parts. The existence of emergent properties at the micro-, mezo- or macro-levels does not prevent us searching for causal or other connections among phenomena within but also across levels of social process.

•

The *social integration/system integration* distinction is an indispensable analytical tool, though it has been misapplied by, for example, Giddens and Habermas. A social integration approach concentrates on the study of agency and actor–actor relations (whether co-operative or conflictual), a system integration mode of analysis being concerned with the study of part–part relations (that is, relations between the parts of social systems and structures, such as relations between positions/roles, rules, and social institutions). How figurational and institutional structures and social and system integration forms of analysis are related to each other, are important questions.

•

The *relation of discourses to social contexts* is another unavoidable metatheoretical issue that social theorists and empirical investigators must necessarily address – either implicitly, or preferably, explicitly and reflectively – during the course of their work. It was argued, further to the discussion of this point in Chapter 1, that there are no invariant or 'direct' links between discourses (whether academic, political, professional, cultural, or other discourses) and social contexts, though empirically contingent and more or less loosely dialectical links may develop between discourse and context; that the social fabric is 'real' albeit in some sense socially constructed; and that society – even though it is partly discursively constituted – has emergent and unintended properties that are not reducible to any particular discourses.

●

The concept *structural contradictions,* which is another concept that cannot legitimately be side-stepped by social investigators, refers to 'objective' tensions between the parts of social systems or structures. It is argued that objectivist and subjectivist notions of structural contradictions should be replaced by a conception of structural compatibilities/incompatibilities that entails an ontologically flexible and loosely dialectical postulate of agency–structure and of links between social integration/figurational and system integration/institutional dynamics.

●

The concept *recursion* (or 'path dependency') is important in so far as it refers to self-reproducing or self-generating tendencies at the micro-, mezo- and macro-levels of social process; it is argued that recursion, like social structure in general, should be regarded as an outcome of interaction between agency, social structure, and social chance.

Notes

1 The emphasis in Bergerian sociology on the subjective element of a person–society dialectic can be illustrated with reference to the concept 'structural contradictions', which is discussed later in the chapter. Berger is opposed to Marxist or functionalist notions of 'objective' or 'structural' contradictions/incompatibilities or tensions within or between the elements or 'parts' (institutions, systems of rules, roles, and so on) of social systems, and where the parts and the systems are seen as having a separate ontological existence from individuals. Berger and Luckmann (1971: 82) reject any such ontological separation: they argue that the question of whether institutions are integrated (or 'hang together' as they put it) or else are 'malfunctioning' (as in situations of 'legitimation crisis') is not a matter of institutional or functionalist 'logic' but a question of how the institutions are *perceived* by individuals.

For reasons implicit in the earlier chapters, there are grounds for taking the view that Berger and Luckmann are indeed correct to acknowledge the subjective dimension of what are often called 'structural' (or 'systemic') 'contradictions'. However, for the social analyst it also becomes necessary – when systems are regarded as having an emergent and relatively autonomous existence that is at least partly independent of individual subjectivities – to find an adequate way of accounting for the *objective* dimensions of 'contradictions'; this Berger and Luckmann fail to do. Later in the chapter with reference to structural contradictions and the system/social integration distinction, it is argued that subjective and objective dimensions can be suitably incorporated into social analysis without recourse to reductionist and reified notions (as in Marxism and teleological functionalism) of 'objective' structural or systemic contradictions.

2 This ambiguity in Berger's theoretical position, an ambiguity which seems to stem from theoretical contradiction, is reflected in the existence of three conflicting interpretations concerning the question of whether Berger employs a Durkheimian, materialist, and social determinist framework (an interpretation of Berger that is voiced by Hamilton, 1974: 139), or conversely an idealist mode of analysis (Wuthnow et.al. 1984: 28–9); or whether he steers a middle course that 'avoids the distortions of one-sidedly "idealist" or "materialist" interpretations' (Hunter and Ainlay, 1986: 40).

The above connects to the 'duality versus dualism' debate. In the case of language, Berger and Luckmann (1971: 53) subscribe to a dualism of agency and structure that is positively Durkheimian: 'language has the quality of objectivity. I encounter language as a facticity external to myself and it is coercive on me. Language forces me into its patterns.' And yet, throughout *The Social Construction of Reality* the predominant emphasis is on subjectivity and the ways in which the objectified social world is not 'objective' *per se*, but rather, 'appears' to be objective to individuals who have mistakenly 'reified' the social (Berger and Luckmann, 1971: 106). It is, then, perhaps not surprising that there are conflicting interpretations of the matters under discussion here. As already noted, Archer (1995: 13, 63), who is critical of Berger and Luckmann, regards their work as an idealist 'central' 'conflation' of agency and structure (that is, a duality), whereas Mouzelis (1991: 78), who is mindful of Berger and Luckmann's concepts of 'externalization' and 'objectivation', sees in their work a paradigmatic dualism in which there is a dialectical relation between subjectivity and social institutions: alternatively, Bhaskar (1979) believes that in trying to avoid what Archer terms 'upwards' and 'downwards' conflation, Berger and Luckmann end up by contradictorily incorporating *both* conflations into their framework.

3 See the Introduction, note 6.

4 In the case of resources such as land it is difficult – in terms of Giddens's concept of structure as 'rules and resources' – to apply Giddens's rubric that resources have only a 'virtual' existence. In fact, many if not most discussions of Giddens tend to refer to structure as rules, rather than rules and resources. This is consistent with Giddens's idea that rules often entail the mobilization of resources and with his insistence (1984: 18) that 'rules cannot be conceptualized apart from resources'. Moreover, Giddens (ibid.: 33) himself makes the point that allocative resources such as land, though they might seem to have 'real' existence in a way that he denies to structure, are only resources when linked to and defined by rules. The net effect, according to, for example, Mouzelis (1995: 195) is that resources are certain kinds of rules and we may assume that structure, for Giddens, amounts to a set of rules.

5 I am inclined to agree with Layder's (1998a: 96) observation that 'the double hermeneutic' exaggerates the degree to which social scientific discourse enters into the everyday world. That said, research concerned with the study of the relation of academic knowledge to the formulation and implementation of public policies indicates that some conceptual schemas 'travel' from academia into policy communities (Weiss, 1986; Stenson, 1993: 49). And in regard to popular culture, while it may be

true that Giddens has a tendency to over-estimate the extent to which social science concepts are incorporated into 'lay' discourses, it should not be overlooked that there are a variety of routes – for example, professional training, the work of writers engaged in the popularization of academic ideas, media accounts of research findings or of newsworthy conference reports, and so on – by which at least some concepts developed in such disciplines as psychology, sociology, and economics filter into everyday language.

6 The 'society shapes discourse' variant of postmodern theory, which often is concerned with radical cultural politics, tends to borrow from rather crude 'modern' theories of social inequality, and at times comes close to replication of archetypal modernist and reductionist versions of the oversimple and determinist notion that actors' forms of thought and interests are determined by what is taken to be their structural location (as 'middle-class people', 'heterosexuals', 'white people', 'men' 'colonialists', or whatever) within the social totality. Here, Hindess's excellent critique (for example, 1987a; 1987b; 1988; 1989) remains relevant. Some of the ambiguities and theoretical contradictions that arise from an unfortunate theoretical fusion of 'emancipatory' postmodern cultural politics with crude versions of modernist theorizing, are set out in Antonio (1998) and in the trenchant critique by Rojek and Turner (2000). A generally thoughtful and useful introduction to some of the issues touched upon here is provided by Nash (2000) in her text on political sociology.

4

Three Major Contributors to Contemporary Sociological Theory: Archer, Mouzelis and Layder

Most of the themes featured in the previous chapters are taken up in the work of three writers who – though they have not, as yet, attracted the amount of attention that their work merits – are significant figures in the recent movement towards a renewal of sociological theory; the authors whose work will be considered here (Margaret Archer, Nicos Mouzelis, and Derek Layder) have made incisive inroads into still unresolved problems that require attention if sociology – which, as observed in Chapter 1, was much criticized during 'the cultural turn' – is to continue to convincingly demonstrate its theoretical and empirical explanatory potential in the period 'after postmodernism'. Although the recent work of these writers is, in my view, of considerable importance to the future theoretical and methodological development of the discipline, their contributions are, as we shall see, by no means satisfactory in all respects. Throughout the book numerous references are made, often in approving fashion, to various aspects of the work of these writers, therefore, here I shall give rather more attention to critique than to exposition; it is hoped this does not convey an impression of their work that seems more critical than I intend.

Comparative (meta)theoretical analysis of the writings of Giddens, Archer, Mouzelis, and Layder – at the present time, remarkably little comparative analysis of their work exists – reveals a number of rather intricate threads of similarity and difference in their approaches, and it is important that these should be unravelled; therefore as well as an element of relatively straightforward description and also critique of theoretical positions, in what follows it will in places be necessary to attempt to unpack some quite complicated conceptual variations and nuances of theoretical meaning in the writings of these major contemporary sociological theorists.

Margaret Archer: morphogenetic social theory

Archer's main contributions to theoretical sociology (1982; 1988; 1995; 1996) centre on her morphogenetic social theory: 'The "morpho" element is an acknowledgement that society has no pre-set form or preferred state: the "genetic" part is a recognition that it takes its shape from, and is formed by, agents, originating from the intended and unintended consequences of their activities' (Archer, 1995: 5).[1] *Morphogenesis* refers to the elaboration of structural forms, and *morphostasis* to their maintenance (Archer, 1982). I have reservations about certain features of Archer's framework. For example, in Chapter 2 I criticized her unusual notion of micro–macro, and in Chapter 3 it was suggested her conception of structural and cultural emergence is too restrictive by virtue of focusing only upon 'necessary relations' among phenomena. And later, I shall express some reservations about her use of the notion of activity dependence. In general, however, her approach – which builds upon her anti-conflationist formulations – has much to offer the future development of sociological theory and method.

Archer (1995: 46–57) rejects what she describes as 'downward conflation', a mode of analysis which is associated with methodological collectivism. In downward conflationist theorizing, agency is explained *in terms of* structure: for example, in Parsons's later work the central value system is said (with reference to structure and social system) to induce compatibility among institutions and (in terms of agency) to socialize agents so that they energize the social system. Downward conflation rests upon a notion of structural determinism, as distinct from a less strong 'structural conditioning' (ibid.: 216): in downward conflationist paradigms actors are portrayed as unreflective, socialized beings who lack creative or innovative capacities of the kind that may shape structure. In such theories, as Archer critically observes (1998: 83), there is little or no sense of society as something which in its existing form may be desired by no one; society, Archer argues, is an unplanned outcome of inter-group conflict, negotiation, and compromise. Rather than allow that interaction can have intended and unintended consequences that lead to emergent structural properties, some of which may be large-scale, it is argued by some Marxists, structuralists, structural-functionalists, and other downward conflation theorists that society is the effect of in-built systemic forces or tendencies. In contrast, in 'upward conflation', to the extent that Archer associates this with interpretative sociology, the larger social system ('society') is portrayed as an aggregation of micro (face-to-face) interactions.[2] Archer associates upwards conflation with interactionist sociology (Archer, 1995: 60), with 'the neo-phenomenological school' (ibid.: 84), and with methodological individualism (ibid.: 34–46). She argues that upward conflationist ontology wrongly treats structure as the product of agency exercised by current as distinct from previous actors, and wrongly assumes that structure is no more than 'other actors' and their activities. She observes that these postulates erroneously disallow the proposition that structures have aggregative and emergent properties that are 'more than' the sum of the interacting individuals and their decisions and actions, such properties having a shaping or 'conditioning'[3] influence upon actors' forms of thought and activities (and very often, structure operates as a major constraint upon certain types of action); relatedly, upward conflation theorists tend to see structure as readily alterable by actors, providing they have the necessary motivation and information to promote social change. In both upward and downward forms of conflation, relative autonomy is withheld from agency and from structure: primacy is erroneously given to agency *or* to structure as the ultimate constituent of society, rather than investigating 'the two-way interplay between them' (Archer, 1998: 74). A third mode of reasoning rejected by Archer (1995: 167–8) is what she terms 'central conflation' (ibid.: 61), which she associates, in particular, with Giddens. In rejecting duality theorizing of the kind found in structuration theory, Archer, drawing on Bhaskar's (1989a; 1989b) critical realism, insists that individuals and society, far from being 'two sides of the same coin', are different kinds of phenomena: '[Individuals and society] do not constitute two moments of the same process. Rather, they refer to radically different things' (Bhaskar, 1989a: 33). Archer (1995: 101) is of the view that Giddens's concept of 'social practices' does not do justice to either action or structure; the concept decentres agency in favour of practices, and also downplays structure which is seen as not real but only 'virtual' until instantiated by agency. In structuration theory, relative autonomy is granted to neither agency or structure and both are seen as inextricably bonded together; therefore there is no possibility of investigating their interplay, or of ascertaining the relative importance of each in any particular situation (Archer, 1998: 75, 81). In Archer's analytical dualism, in which agency and structure are distinct, separable phenomena, *temporality* is seen as a central aspect (1995: 92) of the mutually shaping relation between agency and structure; structure precedes action which in turn leads to structural reproduction or elaboration, and the cycle is then repeated (ibid.: 157–8, 192–4). Archer's argument is that structuration theory is flawed by the failure to acknowledge temporality in the sense to which I have just referred, resulting in an inability to conceptually separate agency and social structure in a way that might allow us to study links between the two and allow us to assess the relative influence of each in any given social context. For Archer, then, Giddens is an 'elisionist' (ibid.: 93) who collapses agency and structure together – structure has no existence outside of its instantiation by agency – and who denies that structure has emergent or autonomous properties, and that structure precedes action (ibid.: 93–101).

Arising from Archer's involvement in the 'duality versus dualism' debate it should, to take up a point made in the previous chapter, be observed that miscommunication and misunderstanding among contemporary theorists is undoubtedly related, at least in part, to the fact that certain terms which are central to the debate are sometimes defined and handled in quite different ways. For example, Archer rejects Giddens's duality concept and argues that social science should be predicated wholly upon dualism. However, Mouzelis, whose work is discussed later, does not reject so much as reconstruct and extend structuration theory: employing the term duality to refer to unreflective orientations of actors to structure, and dualism as a term for describing actors' reflexive orientation to structure, Mouzelis, *contra* Archer, claims structuration theory is not wrong but *incomplete* and that what sociological theory and method require is both duality *and* dualism (in, that is, the particular terms that these are defined by Mouzelis). Thus, for Archer, whose position entails outright rejection of Giddens's concept of duality, dualism refers to a temporal separation between action and an ontologically prior structure which is subsequently reproduced or elaborated by action; whereas for Mouzelis, who attempts to *reconstruct* structuration theory, duality and dualism refer to differences in actors' mental orientations – reflexive or otherwise – to social structure. There are here fundamentally different uses of the terms duality and dualism, and it is important that these differences should be made explicit; this is something to which I shall return shortly, with reference to Mouzelis's theorizing.

I suggested earlier that Archer's extensive conceptual framework – which I cannot do full justice to within the confines of this chapter – is capable of contributing significantly to the development of sociological theory and methodology. In particular, her clarification of the grounds for rejecting upwards, downwards, and central conflation, is invaluable, as also, for example, is her concept (discussed in Chapter 1) of a flexible but realist social ontology allied to her epistemological and methodological arguments; her work on a stratified conception of the actor; and her work on 'positional interests' (see Chapter 5) and on the dialectics of agency and structure. However, there is one aspect of her framework that, in addition to those mentioned earlier, is open to criticism. Archer's view of the 'activity dependence' of social structure rests on an argument that current structures are the effects of actions taken by people who, as she puts it, are 'long dead' and there is, therefore, a 'temporal escape' of structures from past actions (Archer, 1995: 147, 148, 253). She argues that the activity dependence of, for example, demographic structure is 'past tense': in her words, 'Here the activity dependence of such structures can be affirmed in only one accept- able way: by reference to the activities of the long dead' (ibid.: 143). And in more general terms it is claimed that: 'we are all born into a structural and cultural context which, far from being of our making, is the unintended resultant of past interaction among the long dead' (ibid.: 253). Archer's insistence that present structures are effects of *past* actions is linked to a confusing conflation of, first, the relation of present-day actors to current structures, and, second, the relation of present-day actors and structures to previous actors and previous structures. Both of these dimensions – which refer to synchronic and diachronic dialectics of action and structure (for a convenient sketch, see Ritzer, 2000: 48) – are undoubtedly important, but Archer tries to run them together in a way that wrongly downplays the extent to which present-day social contexts may be dependent upon the activities of current actors. Archer recognizes that current activities in aggregate have the effect of unintentionally reproducing or modifying society (for example, ibid.: 72): and yet in her discussion of the activity dependence of society she seems to paint current actors out of the picture. Archer is right to refute methodological individualism as a form of upward conflation (1995: 77; 1998: 76–8), but this should not be allowed to obscure the extent to which the activity dependence of current contexts or structures may relate to current activities. She says that the activity depen- dence of social structures may be 'present tense *or* past tense' (1995: 145), this being an empirical question. Thus there are, according to Archer (ibid.: 145), some present-day social structures that are 'ontologically *independent* from the activities of those people here present' (my italics). This is taking things too far. As I have already suggested, it is legitimate to refute method- ological individualism, to argue that structures have emergent properties, and to observe that the activity dependence of present structures relates to past actions; but these statements should not be taken as far as Archer's extreme claim that some current structures may be *entirely independent* of current actors. It seems that here, in a way that sits uneasily alongside some of the implications that may be thought to arise from what Archer (ibid.: 141) elsewhere calls the 'no people; no society' truism, she wants to iden- tify situations where, in her view, there is a total separation of current struc- ture from current action (in contradistinction to Giddens's opposing schema where structure/system and action are mutually constitutive to such an extent that it is impossible to separate them). When compared with Archer's formulation of the activity dependence of society, an in some ways more satisfactory stratified social ontology is provided by Derek

Layder; selected aspects of his theoretical framework will be outlined in the final section of the chapter.

Nicos Mouzelis: 'back to sociological theory'

The frequency of my earlier brief references to Mouzelis – one or two of which, however, departed from certain aspects of his conceptual framework – reflects his position as one of the leading figures in the contemporary movement towards a reconstruction of sociological theory (for example, Mouzelis, 1989; 1991; 1993a; 1993b; 1994; 1995; 1997; 2000). Mouzelis's *Back to Sociological Theory* (1991) is a landmark in the movement to reject postmodern theory while at the same time re-appraising traditional sociological concerns in the light of recent theoretical developments. Within the space available for this chapter, what follows is an abridged review of but two strands of his extensive theoretical work. The first refers to Mouzelis's useful codification of three significant dimensions of social action; the second is in the nature of a critique of his handling of the 'duality versus dualism' debate.

Three dimensions of social action: positional, dispositional, and situational

Highly significant aspects of agency–structure and micro–macro are to be found in Mouzelis's (1991: 196–200; 1995: 136–7) typology which distinguishes between role/positional, dispositional, and situational-interactional dimensions of social action. He emphasizes that in social analysis it is necessary to focus on each of these. Analysis which gives emphasis to the *role/positional* dimension is, following the Durkheimian/Parsonian tradition, a form of analysis that is mainly concerned with investigation of the ways in which social positions and more or less predefined role scripts which are part of a macro-institutional order, are significant factors that shape local interaction. Mouzelis (1991: 106) illustrates his typology with reference to the role-scripts of teacher and pupil, and shows that at least some aspects of what goes on in the classroom are shaped by the roles/positions of the participants. The *dispositional* dimension of social life, the second dimension in Mouzelis's typology, borrows from Bourdieu's (1977, 1990) concept of 'habitus'. This refers to actors' general 'dispositions' (attitudes, skills, norms, and so on) that do not derive from specific roles – the roles of teacher and student in Mouzelis's example – but rather, from the actor's wider experiences of life in regard to social class, ethnicity, religion, gender, attendance at specific educational establishments, and so on. The actor brings to any specific encounter (for example, teacher–student) those acquired generalized aspects of self which, though not derived from the specific roles involved in the encounter, nevertheless partly shape the pattern of interaction that develops among the participants. The point here is that *general* life experiences affect how we act in any *particular* situation and the dispositional dimension helps us understand, for example, why it is that, though there may be many similarities in their role performances, no two teachers ever perform the role of teacher in *exactly* the same way. The third dimension of interaction, the *situational-interactional* dimension which is described in the work of Mead (1967) and other symbolic interactionists, refers to emergent and contingent features of the interactional situation itself, and in particular to situated meanings that come into existence *during*, and as an outcome of, the process of interaction within a micro-setting such as a classroom; these are emergent features of social action and interaction that derive neither from positions/roles nor dispositions.

Assessed in terms of its usefulness as an analytical tool, Mouzelis's typology of social action is in my view heuristically important to the development of substantive theories and to the design of empirical studies, particularly if it is broadened to include social ('organizational') actors and inter-organizational relations (Sibeon, 1997: 77–80) (see Chapter 5), and if extended to include a more explicit focus on time–space and material diffusion processes (this is discussed in Chapter 6).

Duality plus dualism?

A remarkable, and relatively unexamined degree of complexity and variation surrounds the ways in which the 'duality versus dualism' debate has been handled by contemporary sociological theorists. It was observed earlier that Archer (1995; 1998) rejects Giddens's concept of a duality of structure, and argues instead for a dualism of structure and action. By dualism, Archer means that there is a temporal separation between structure and action: structure precedes the action which reproduces or elaborates it. For her, theorizing should always (1995: 101) be premised on dualism; in her view, duality is a form of central conflation that should be entirely excluded from social analysis. In contrast, Mouzelis, employing the terms duality and dualism differently from Archer, argues that there *is* a place for duality in social analysis, but that dualism is also necessary: that is to say, Mouzelis does not reject Giddens's structuration theory (where structure is 'rules and resources'), instead he reconstructs it so as to embrace both duality and dualism. In doing so, Mouzelis retains Giddens's definition of structure: he states, 'I shall continue to use the term "structure" in the way Giddens has defined it' (1995: 196). However, Mouzelis defines duality as a concept that, paradigmatically speaking (see later), refers to situations where actors have no cognitive distance from 'rules' (he has in mind situations where there is an unreflective, routine drawing upon rules); and dualism for Mouzelis is a term that indicates, again in a paradigmatic sense, scenarios where actors draw reflexively upon rules for theoretical-analytical, strategic or monitoring purposes. There are here some (meta)theoretical disjunctions that have received little attention in the literature. Giddens (1993: 3, 6), it should be noticed, acknowledges Mouzelis's observation that reflexivity ('distance from rules') is significant, but says Mouzelis has misunderstood structuration theory's concept of the duality of structure and that reflexivity should not be equated with dualism. For Archer, dualism refers to a temporal separation of structure and agency, and duality to a collapsing of this separation; for Mouzelis (and for Giddens, claims Mouzelis) the duality–dualism distinction refers to differences in actors' orientations – reflexive or otherwise – to structure. In regard to this matter, I am closer to Archer than to either Giddens or Mouzelis. That said, Mouzelis's quite complex theoretical formulation of duality–dualism does raise, as indicated below, a number of interesting and important questions.

Mouzelis (1995: 120) evidently considers that he remains fairly close to structuration theory, in so far as he refers to a distinction between structure as '*virtual* rules' (my italics) and system as '*actual* social games or systems' (my italics). Many commentators appear to share this understanding of Giddens's theory of structuration. (Whereas, as noted in Chapter 3, my dissenting interpretation – like Archer's (1995: 96; 1996: 690), although she does not amplify the point – is that Giddens's notion of duality applies both to his concept of structure *and* to his concept of system: were this not so, probably much of the controversy surrounding structuration theory would not have arisen, since it is commonplace in social science to assert both that actors employ forms of thought that are carried in the head (the 'virtual' element) *and* that there exist real ('actual') material things such as social systems or networks that, though ultimately dependent upon activities, are relatively autonomous and external to individuals and to any particular activities.) The virtual/actual distinction refers to paradigm and syntagm (paradigmatic and syntagmatic being terms drawn from structural linguistics). That is, Mouzelis (1995: 118) says Giddens's 'structure' refers to a virtual set of rules that, like Saussure's *langue*, exist outside time and space (as memory traces in actors' minds), and that this notion of structure refers to the paradigmatic dimension of social life; on the other hand, says Mouzelis, Giddens's concept of system refers to syntagmatic, 'actual' patterned relations in time–space. It is via the processes of structuration that the paradigmatic becomes syntagmatic: 'the term structuration ... signifies the process by which structures lead to the constitution of social systems' (Mouzelis, 1995: 118). Mouzelis (ibid.: 120) states that actors can relate to the former (structure as 'virtual rules') in terms of duality (a view that Mouzelis ascribes to Giddens), and in terms of dualism (which, Mouzelis says, is denied by Giddens); also, actors may relate to the latter ('actual' social systems or social games) in terms of duality and dualism – therefore these two concepts, duality and dualism, are 'both equally indispensable' (ibid.). In effect, Mouzelis extends and reconstructs – but does not reject – Giddens's duality of structure. He does this by arguing that actors' relation to structure (defined, after Giddens, as 'rules') and to social objects in general, is more varied than is implied in structuration theory (Mouzelis, 1995: 119). Mouzelis, then, distinguishes between paradigm (general rules that are 'virtual') and syntagm ('actual' and observable instances or applications of rules) and he argues that in both cases – the paradigmatic and the syntagmatic – actors may, depending on the circumstances, relate to social objects in terms of a subject–object duality or in terms of a subject–object dualism. Here, as I have already pointed out, Mouzelis is not rejecting Giddens's concept of a duality of action and structure, since he believes Giddens's concept is entirely legitimate; rather, and the point bears repeating, Mouzelis is arguing that structuration theory, in so far as it employs the idea of duality to the exclusion of dualism, is incomplete: for Mouzelis, the paradigmatic and syntagmatic dimensions of the relation of actors to social structures and to social objects involve both duality and dualism. This leads Mouzelis to a fourfold classification – with the elements regarded as continua rather than either-or states of affairs (1991: 100) – which refers to variation in the relation of actors to 'virtual' structures (as 'rules') (the paradigmatic aspect) and, syntagmatically, to 'actual' social objects or systems (1991: 99–100; 1995: 119–21). *Paradigmatic duality*, Mouzelis suggests, is associated with Giddens's duality of structure, whereby actors unreflexively enact ('instantiate') rules, and where rules are both the medium and outcome of social action; there is, so to speak, a 'lack of distance' between subject and object (Mouzelis, 1991: 99). Mouzelis says this is akin to structuralism, where actors are seen as 'drawing on more or less "hidden" rules in a natural-performative manner' (1995: 121); and 'it is on this partial case [that is, paradigmatic duality] that Giddens bases his duality-of-structure notion' (ibid.: 121). *Paradigmatic dualism* is where actors, for theoretical-analytical, strategic, or monitoring purposes distance themselves ('stand back') reflectively from a 'virtual' body of rules (that is, in Giddens's and Mouzelis's terms, from structure). For Mouzelis the essence of paradigmatic dualism is distance between actors and rules, and 'This distance can be *vis-à-vis* rules known and followed by the subject, in which case the actor's reflexivity is enhanced; or the distance may be *vis-à-vis* rules that other agents adopt and follow and which the actor wants to explore and/or change' (1991: 99). *Syntagmatic duality* is where the actor is vital to the existence of a social context (that is, to the existence of an 'actual' – not virtual – social system, social context or social game(s)). Where there is syntagmatic duality, the actor contributes very significantly to the construction and reproduction of interaction in a social system (Mouzelis, 1991: 100). Here the context is not 'external' to the actor, an example being a factory worker's relation to a small shopfloor work group of which he is a member (1995: 120). Syntagmatic duality is associated by Mouzelis with the writings of Mead and Schutz, where systems and actors' activities are seen as inseparable (ibid.: 121). *Syntagmatic dualism* refers to states of affairs where the actor is not vital to, or has little effect upon the social context (for example, an office cleaner or junior clerk in a multinational corporation), and therefore, says Mouzelis, the context is 'external' to the actor in the sense implied by Durkheimian sociology where society is regarded as external to individuals (ibid.: 121). As Mouzelis puts it, syntagmatic dualism applies where 'actors' orientations focus on interactions or social systems to the production or reproduction of which they contribute but slightly' (Mouzelis, 1991: 100).

It is important not to lightly dismiss Mouzelis's distinction between paradigmatic duality, paradigmatic dualism, syntagmatic duality, and syntagmatic dualism: these analytical categories draw our attention to important dimensions of the social, and more narrowly, they open up some interesting questions about structuration theory and its critics. However, it is difficult to avoid the conclusion that Mouzelis's typology, for all its apparent conceptual sophistication, is ultimately unsuccessful. The notion of duality as understood by most commentators (myself included) and as advocated by Giddens is, I argued earlier, seriously flawed, and here I would wish to endorse Archer's critique of central conflation, but equally, Mouzelis's notion of duality–dualism as a way of describing the extent to which actors are essential to a (syntagmatic) social context and of describing the degree to which actors' orientations to (paradigmatic) rules or discourses are reflexive, rests upon a confusing and unnecessary re-definition of the terms 'duality' and 'dualism'. There is, I suggest, a temporal separation (a dualism) between pre-existing structure (the 'conditions-of-action') and the action which reproduces or elaborates structure, *irrespective* of whether, in regard to the paradigmatic dimension, the action is reflexive (where actors draw upon rules or discourses in a reflective way) or unreflexive (where discourses or other elements of the conditions of action/social context are drawn upon unreflectively, or in a habitual kind of way). Nor is any useful analytical purpose served by Mouzelis's notion of syntagmatic duality and dualism, where the duality–dualism distinction becomes a way of denoting whether or not some particular actors are 'essential' to the reproduction of a social context. It also seems clear that Mouzelis is wrong to infer that

Giddens regards structure ('rules') as virtual/paradigmatic, and systems (for Giddens these are reproduced social relations) as 'real' or 'actual' (syntagmatic):[4] as argued earlier, there are passages in Giddens's writings which suggest, despite some ambiguity in his formulation of duality, that he sees both structure *and* systems, as he defines these, in virtual/duality terms. Mouzelis (1995: 197), in suggesting structuration theory's duality is not wrong but incomplete and should be complemented by dualism, states that he agrees with Archer's and Layder's criticism that Giddens's rejection of the agency–structure distinction means Giddens cannot examine how far, in concrete situations, actors are influenced or constrained by social contexts. Here we witness, in the terms outlined above, a degree of potential conceptual confusion arising in part from theoretical dialogue involving concepts that are defined and used in different ways by the parties involved: as we have seen, Archer (1995: 96) is of the view that Giddens sees systems (rather than only structure) in duality/virtual terms, and she also argues that duality should be completely abandoned rather than, as in Mouzelis's approach, retained but complemented by a focus on dualism; and Giddens, as noted earlier, refutes Mouzelis's ascription of reflexivity to action–structure dualism and hence refutes Mouzelis's ascription of a lack of reflexivity to Giddens's concept of duality of structure. It seems appropriate that future work should address more closely the (meta)theoretical discontinuities highlighted above. For the present, however, it should be noted that Layder, as I shall show in the next section, in some respects departs from the theoretical positions of both Giddens and Mouzelis, while endorsing certain aspects of Archer's framework.

Derek Layder: the theory of social domains

Layder's writings often give special emphasis to the relation of theory and social ontology to sociological methodology (for example, 1993; 1998a), and even where his primary concern is theory and metatheory (for example, 1994; 1997; 1998b) the question of how theory and method relate to each other is never entirely absent from his work. A focus on connections between metatheory and methodology is certainly not unimportant (see Chapter 7). However, in what follows, given the concerns of the present chapter, it is Layder's metatheorizing, particularly his (meta)theory of social domains, that is the main focus of attention. Like Mouzelis and Archer, Layder is an enthusiastic advocate of sociological renewal in terms that are critical of poststructuralist and postmodern relativism while at the same time attempting to steer clear of modernist 'grand theory' paradigms. He favours a 'modest', circumscribed approach to social explanation, an approach which – though retaining an epistemological commitment to realism – recognizes that social reality is multiform, relatively indeterminate and unpredictable, and that, therefore, reductionist single-order theories and notions of original or prime causes are unlikely to achieve explanatory success. Layder, though he draws elements of contrasting paradigms and perspectives into his synthetic metatheoretical schema, is critical of certain aspects of the approaches that he borrows from. This relates in part to his criticism of the three forms of conflation – downwards, upwards, and 'central' – that Archer also strongly opposes. Layder is, for example, opposed to the notion of duality and to any approach which collapses distinctions between agency and structure and between micro and macro. Symbolic interactionism, structuration theory, and Foucauldian theorizing are criticized for having a flattened ontology that ignores 'vertical' differentiation of the various spheres (or 'domains') of social reality. For Layder, the social world is made up of differing *kinds* of phenomena – including those that are subjective or objective, and micro or macro – and it is this ontological multidimensionality which dictates that social reality cannot adequately be accounted for in terms of any single, unidimensional principle of explanation such as 'intersubjectivity', 'habitus', 'figurations', or 'social systems' (Layder, 1998b: 86–7).

Layder's theory of social domains is an attempt – a largely successful one, in my opinion – to develop a flexible, non-reductionist social ontology as a means of addressing agency–structure and micro–macro. Terms that Layder uses interchangeably with 'domains' or 'social domains' include 'dimensions' or 'orders', or sometimes 'layerings' so as to emphasize the stratified nature of his social ontology. Implicit in my earlier remarks is Layder's contention that no domain has analytical primacy. Another feature of his framework is that the domains are interwoven and interdependent, but at the same time each has relative autonomy (that is, each has distinct properties and effects of its own). Layder argues that social reality is made up of four social domains, which relate to the subjective and objective realms of the social. The subjective dimension of social life consists of two domains, the individual–subjective which Layder refers to as 'psychobiography', and the intersubjective which he terms 'situated activity': the objective or systemic dimension consists of 'social settings' (these are the social contexts or locations in which situated activity occurs) and 'contextual resources' (a term which Layder uses to refer to widespread cultural phenomena, and to the distribution of resources relating to, for example, social class, gender, ethnicity, and other sources of inequalities and power differences). Central to Layder's conception of society is his understanding, which is described below, that 'objective' systemic factors influence though do not determine the subjective dimension (the domains of psychobiography and situated activity); conversely, psychobiography and situated activity partly shape but do not determine social settings and contextual resources (as just noted, these in Layder's scheme constitute the objective dimension of the social).

Psychobiography is the term that Layder uses to refer to largely unique, asocial components of an individual's dispositions, behaviour, and self-identity, these being aspects of the individual that are relatively independent of face-to-face interaction and of the macro-social sphere. It is worth noting that his concept of psychobiography (Layder, 1997) in some respects is a forerunner of the recent renewal of sociological interest in agency and the self; this interest is reflected in, for example, McNay's (2000) work on gender and agency, Turner and Rojek's (2001) conception of society and culture, and Archer's (2000) text which builds on her 'morphogenetic' theoretical foundations as described earlier and which gives special attention to agency. When Layder (1997: 26) refers to 'the dialectic of separateness and relatedness', he means that individuals are made up of unique elements of cognition, emotion, and behaviour that are in some sense separate from the social world, yet at the same time those elements of self are related in various ways to social conditions and social experiences. Layder's insistence upon the relative autonomy of psychobiography causes him to strenuously resist poststructuralist and postmodern attempts to 'decentre the subject' and to portray people as effects of discourses (here Layder's argument is that psychobiography is a highly significant mediating factor that influences the manner in which discourses are handled by individuals). And while he is generally sympathetic towards symbolic interactionism, he criticizes interactionists' failure to recognize the significance of psychobiography/subjectivity, which is not reducible to interaction/intersubjectivity. He is critical, too, of Elias for over-reaction against individualist conceptions and thus for failure to acknowledge the unique aspects of individuals. Similarly, while Bourdieu's concept of 'habitus' is not rejected by Layder, its emphasis upon the type of dispositions ('social' dispositions) that are acquired through group memberships and social experiences is, for Layder, incomplete in so far as no attention is given to individual psychological dispositions that are more to do with individual psychobiography than with social experiences.

The second domain that forms part of the subjective realm of society is *situated activity*, which refers to face-to-face interaction/intersubjectivity. This is the domain that figures in the symbolic interactionist literature (Joas, 1988). Following Goffman (1983: 4), Layder (1997: 88, 93) sees situated activity in terms of situations of co-presence where two or more individuals are able to monitor and reflectively respond to unfolding action; this excludes larger gatherings such as crowds, audiences or, say, mass political demonstrations of the kind, for example, that contributed to the overthrow of Communist governments in Eastern Europe in 1989/90 (though this, of course, is not to deny that instances of situated activity may occur within the context of larger gatherings). Situated activity subsumes three types of encounters (Layder, 1997: 133): transient, intermittent, and regularized. Transient, one-off encounters (ibid.: 94–5) include encounters between strangers in public places (on the street, on trains or buses, in queues, and so on); the expression 'intermittent encounters' (ibid.: 96–7) describes, for example, meetings between spatially dispersed acquaintances, friends, or family members who periodically make contact with each other; 'regularized' encounters (ibid.: 97–9) are ongoing interactions among, say, family members or work colleagues. The domain of situated activity, which forms part of what Goffman calls 'the interaction order', is described by Layder (ibid.: 245) as a volatile 'hotbed of creativity'; here Layder makes the point, however, that the innovative, creative new meanings that frequently emerge in situations of co-presence very often remain within the location in which they arise (in non-routine situations new, emergent meanings may 'travel' across time–space and have implications for the macro-social order, but in routine situations, argues Layder, the new meanings that emerge in locales generally have no implications for other locales or for the macro-social order).

In Layder's terminology, *social settings*, which together with contextual resources (see below) form part of the objective realm of society, is a term that refers to the locations – the home, the street, schools, restaurants and shops, workplaces, theatres and sporting stadia, and so on – within which situated activity occurs. Although situated activity intertwines with settings, the latter are relatively autonomous (Layder, 1998a: 158). Settings vary in terms of the extent to which they are formally organized: some settings (for example, a court of law) exhibit highly formalized rules, practices, and authority relations, whereas others (for example, family settings) are less formalized, although *all* social settings, Layder notes (1997: 3), are underpinned by 'an elaborate social fabric of rules, understandings, obligations and expectations'. He emphasizes the importance of differentiating situated activity from social settings, the latter, as just noted, being *locales* of activity (1998a: 157). Settings, to repeat, are locations of activity that are relatively independent of face-to-face activities, and of the macro-social order. In other words, within settings we encounter conditions of action – discourses, resource patterns, social positions/roles, and more or less institutionalized practices – that are inherited from the past and which, though domains interpenetrate and influence each other, are not reducible to any of the other domains.

The domain that Layder calls *contextual resources* is comprised of two elements. First, 'society-wide' (1997: 4) distributions and ownership of resources – money, homes, material possessions, health care, and the like – associated with, for example, divisions of social class, gender, and race; and, second, widespread cultural understandings, discourses (including legitimatory discourses), and social practices. In other words, 'contextual resources' is a macro-domain that, for Layder, is to do with large-scale patterns of power, domination, and material inequality, as well as widely dispersed and patterned cultural phenomena (discourses, cultural values and beliefs, and so on).

In light of the issues that have been raised for discussion in this and previous chapters, Layder's theory of social domains prompts the following observations. First, the point has already been made that while each domain is relatively independent of the others, the domains interpenetrate and overlap. There is no simple correspondence or causal connection between domains (for example, interaction in local settings may, depending on the circumstances, tend to subvert or support the macro-social order): in other words, social investigators should be alert to the development of contingent – as opposed to structurally predetermined – links between domains. Second, and closely related to the point just made, none of the domains has analytical primacy; Layder's approach is ontologically flexible and empirically 'open'. Third, Layder's (meta)theory has the advantage that it incorporates subjective and objective dimensions of the social. This is important, since any social ontology that neglects one or other of these dimensions will, at best, be lopsided and incomplete. Fourth, Layder has a well-developed conception of certain aspects of time–space. For example, he notes (1997: 77) that it is not possible to adequately represent his theory in diagrammatic form. We can think of social processes over time as existing in a 'horizontal' plane, but this obscures the 'vertical' layering of the four domains, and even more complexly, such layering is itself dynamic and always in 'process' (1997: 24). Also, there exist differing time frames. Interconnections of objective and subjective aspects of social reality, and of agency–structure, are complex conjunctures of time–space where the relatively short time-frames of face-to-face interaction (situated activity) meet the extended time-frames of long-standing institutional conditions that extend from the past into the present (1998b: 88). Fifth, in the preceding chapter it was briefly noted that Mouzelis is close to Durkheim when he asserts that 'macro social facts must primarily be explained in terms of *other* macro-facts' (Mouzelis, 1991: 78) whereas Layder's stratified social ontology and his conception of relatively autonomous but interpenetrating domains that influence each other, cause him to stress (Layder, 1997: 241–3) that it is an error to try to explain macro-social phenomena exclusively in terms of other macro-social phenomena; we have here a difference of emphasis, with Layder giving more weight than

Mouzelis to the notion of a stratified social ontology in which social phenomena may legitimately be partly explained in terms of other phenomena that exist at differing levels of reality. Of the two, Layder's rather than Mouzelis's is, in my view, the more correct emphasis (and this is a question of emphasis, not an either/or choice: moreover, the precise extent to which social explanation should be concerned with causal connections or influences within *or* across levels of social reality is something that may vary from case to case). Sixth, Layder argues – in terms with which I have much sympathy, although my approach (for example, Sibeon, 1999a) differs from his in certain respects – that while society is, as Archer (1995: 72) observes, activity-dependent, there is no *direct link* between action and structure. This relates, of course, to the debate of duality versus dualism. Layder observes that there is a 'loose coupling' between the relatively independent domains described above. He argues (1997: 99, 236) that failure to adequately take into account the relative autonomy of the interaction order is a factor in the misplaced tendency of some theorists – including Giddens, Bourdieu, Habermas, Berger and Luckmann, and Elias – to suppose that there is a direct link between action and structure (or system). Layder acknowledges that system reproduction is dependent upon routine, reproductive activities in situations of co-presence; however, the extent to which system reproduction is dependent upon any particular situated activities is an empirical variable, not a constant factor. In regard to the aspects of agency–structure under discussion here, I am, in general terms, at one with Archer and Layder. It surely is the case that 'no people: no society' and that society is in some sense utterly dependent upon activities but, and this is the reason why it is necessary to acknowledge subjective and objective dimensions of society and to incorporate these into social explanation, *relatively enduring social conditions ('structure') stretch in time and space away from any particular activities or specific encounters*, and have *emergent* properties that are not reducible either to activities/interactions in general nor to any particular individuals or particular interactions; and in turn, emergent structures have a conditioning influence upon (though do not determine) social activities.

Summary

The theorists discussed in this chapter are major figures whose contributions to sociological theory are, it was argued, centrally relevant to the future development of social theory and social science.

Margaret Archer: morphogenetic social theory

There is considerable merit in Archer's conceptual framework, which in large part is built upon critique of three forms of conflation: downward conflation (which is associated with methodological collectivism) mistakenly attempts to explain agency in terms of structure; upward conflation, which Archer identifies with methodological individualism, interactionism, and phenomenology, is a defective form of reasoning that treats current structures as products of present as distinct from past activities, and assumes structure is no more than 'other actors' and their activities; central conflation, which Archer associates with, in particular, Giddens's theory of structuration, is rejected by Archer for its commitment to a duality of structure and action rather than a dualism in which there is a temporal separation between structure and the action that reproduces or elaborates it. Other important aspects of Archer's work include her flexible but realist social ontology and her work on 'positional interests' (see Chapter 5). However, her conception of the activity dependence of social structure pushes her rejection of upward conflation 'too far', to the point of claiming that some current structures may be entirely independent of current activities.

Nicos Mouzelis: 'Back to Sociological Theory'

A highly significant contribution to our understanding of agency–structure and micro–macro is Mouzelis's codification of a typology that – drawing respectively on Durkheim, Parsons, Bourdieu, and Mead – identifies three types or dimensions of social action: these are positional/role, dispositional, and situational-interactional. This schema – like Mouzelis's insightful elaboration of the system and social integration distinction discussed in the previous chapter – is developed by Mouzelis into an invaluable analytical tool. Also, its usefulness is capable of being enhanced by the inclusion of social ('organizational') actors in addition to individual human actors (see Chapter 5), and by including an explicit focus on time–space and material diffusion processes as discussed in Chapter 6.

•

However, Mouzelis's contribution to the 'duality versus dualism' debate is a mix of, on the one hand, thought-provoking and potentially illuminating insights, and on the other, flawed (meta)theoretical interpretations; the latter are such that, in the final analysis, his handling of duality/dualism has to be adjudged unsatisfactory. Mouzelis retains Giddens's concept of structure, but instead of regarding dualism as a temporal separation between structure and action and duality as a collapsing of this separation, Mouzelis defines duality as an unreflexive actor orientation to structure and dualism as reflective actor orientation to structure (here Mouzelis, as Giddens observes, has misunderstood Giddens's concept of duality). Unlike Archer and Layder, Mouzelis's thesis is that duality and dualism (as defined by him) both have a part to play in social analysis: this postulate is combined with a virtual/actual distinction that refers to paradigm and syntagm, to produce a fourfold typology that encompasses analytical categories that Mouzelis identifies as paradigmatic duality, paradigmatic dualism, syntagmatic duality, and syntagmatic dualism. These formulations by Mouzelis, though they point to interesting questions, are ultimately unsuccessful — as they stand, they serve no useful (meta)theoretical or methodological purpose.

Derek Layder: the theory of social domains

Like Archer, Layder's conceptual framework entails a form of (meta) theorizing that is critical of upwards, downwards, and central conflation. In regard to the latter, Layder's commitment to dualism relates to his contention that social reality is best described in terms of a stratified or 'depth' social ontology that involves rejection of any attempts to collapse distinctions between micro and macro (or between agency and structure). By way of an extension and reformulation of the idea of micro-, mezo-, and macro-levels of social process, Layder's ontology refers to four 'layers' or 'domains', none of which has analytical primacy and each of which has relative autonomy (in Layder's terms, each has distinct properties and effects of its own), although the domains interpenetrate and overlap.

●

Two of the domains ('psychobiography' and 'situated activity') constitute the subjective dimension of the social, and two ('social settings' and 'contextual resources') refer to the objective or systemic dimension. Psychobiography is to do with the individual-subjective realm that is comprised of largely unique, asocial components of self; situated activity is to do with intersubjectivity and interaction; social settings are the locales within which situated activity occurs; and the expression 'contextual resources' describes macro-distributions and ownership of resources, together with widespread discourses and practices.

●

Layder argues there is no simple correspondence or causal connection between domains — any links between them are likely to be in the form of 'loose couplings' that are relatively contingent and not structurally predetermined: put another way, there are no 'direct links' between domains – this being a point that Layder emphasizes as part of his criticism of aspects of the writings of Giddens, Bourdieu, Berger and Luckmann, Elias, Habermas, and Foucault.

•

The four domains have 'vertical' and 'lateral' dimensions and the domains are, argues Layder, complex conjunctions of time–space. Of particular significance is Layder's handling of the ontological premise that society has emergent properties – large-scale structures, though ultimately activity-dependent, stretch temporally and spatially away from any particular individuals, activities or encounters.

Notes

1 Structural reproduction and elaboration for Archer are largely unintended outcomes of action. This is reminiscent of Elias's conception of the social fabric (though Archer does not endorse Elias's 'compression' of individual and society). Any alteration of structural properties is likely to be a largely unplanned outcome of struggle, adjustment, and compromise among various groups and actors; the elaboration of structure within any particular field of action, or within society more generally, is likely to have been planned and intended by no-one and perhaps wanted by no-one, this being, as Archer observes, an outcome that continuously motivates actors to *continue to struggle* in an effort to secure outcomes that accord more closely with their interests (Archer, 1998: 83).

2 A rejection of Margaret Archer's morphogenetic social theory, and a defence of what she critically dismisses as 'upwards conflation', are provided by King (1999). His critique is of interest, since it relates to some of the central themes of this chapter. King is a supporter of Randall Collins's (1981; 1983; 1988) methodological situationalism, which is based on a micro-reduction of 'macro' phenomena. King's largely one-sided commitment to the interpretative tradition and the subjective element of the social causes him to reject Archer's conception of an objective social structure that, though it originates from the intended and unintended consequences of people's activities (Archer, 1995: 5), is emergent, ontologically prior to current actors, and relatively independent of past and present activities. In a nutshell, King's argument is that structure/social contexts are indeed relatively independent of *any one individual*, but not of *all* (past and present) individuals and their interaction. Against Archer, then, King defines social structure as 'other people' and their activities and interactions in the past and the present.

King, in my view, makes some worthwhile points. He rightly argues that sometimes Archer erroneously blurs the distinction between methodological individualism and symbolic interactionism/phenomenology (in one or two parts of his paper, however, King himself veers towards such blurring); and that Archer in her major work on morphogenetic theory (1995) engages in hardly any discussion of the conceptual details and empirical work of interpretivists (she alludes critically to interpretivism in a highly generalized sort of way that does not get to grips with interactionist and phenomenological concepts). He is, in my opinion, also correct in his assertion (1999: 205) that Archer has a tendency to overlook that the interpretivist tradition, despite her implied claim to the contrary, is *not* oblivious to the constraints of the past – such as pre-existing typifications and social routines – and their impact upon present actors. (What King, though, does not go on to properly acknowledge is, first, that the 'constraints from the past' that he is talking about are not the same as Archer's and, second, that micro-social perspectives are a necessary but not a 'sufficient' *modus operandum* for social science; see Chapter 7).

In the end, King's critique of Archer is impaired by its adherence to what Archer terms 'upward conflation'. It is, of course, the case that, as Archer (1995: 141) crisply put it, 'no people: no society': but as she says, this is a truism that – for the purposes of social enquiry – has limited *explanatory* value; this is discussed in the present chapter. While society cannot exist without people and social activities, there is no '*direct link*' between individuals and their activities, and society (Layder, 1997); on this, see the critique of Berger and Luckmann in Chapter 3. Emergence, and the relative autonomy of and temporal separation between structure and action, mean that the social is not reducible to the activities of previous and current actors. Against King, there are good reasons for holding to a conception of the social in which there *are* ontologically prior social structures (the 'conditions of action') that temporally precede the actors who engage with them, and which are 'more than' 'other people' and their co-present interactions. Indeed, at the end of his paper, King somewhat ambiguously concedes the ontological dualism which his paper strives to avoid: he suggests (1999: 223) that, despite his earlier arguments, a 'heuristic' notion of social structure, a notion *not* associated with micro-reduction, may after all be necessary for the purposes of practical social analysis. The contradiction here is evident: in King's approach, micro-reduction of the social is advocated at the level of metatheory/social ontology, only to be rejected at the level of methodology. This relates to my argument in Chapter 1, where it was suggested metatheory/social ontology, substantive theory, methodology, and data interpretations should (a) be *consistent* with each other and (b) should regulate each other.

3 In Archer's theoretical scheme there is no structural determination of agency, but rather, there is 'structural *conditioning*' (1995: 216). Structure provides 'strategic guidance' for actors (ibid.: 215–16). This relates to actors' *interests*: 'situational logics … predispose agents towards specific courses of action for the promotion of their interests' (ibid.: 216). For example, capitalists have a vested interest in the maximization of profits (ibid.: 204). Structural conditioning of agency and interaction occurs in the sense that structure shapes the situations and positions/roles in which actors are involved, and attaches particular interests – to do with, for example, occupation or social class – to particular positions, thus predisposing (but not 'compelling') actors to adopt one course of action rather than another (ibid.: 203–3, 254; 1998: 82). Archer's idea of 'vested' (or 'positional') interests is, potentially at least, analytically fruitful; however, it will be necessary to assess how far her concept 'vested interests' represents a shift away from the largely discredited notion of 'real' ('objective') interests (see Chapter 5, particularly the section on power and interests).

4 In a later paper Mouzelis (2000: 760) again notes that critics have accused Giddens of engaging in 'central conflation' (to use Archer's apt expression); he once

again suggests the critics are wrong and he repeats his assertion that Giddens applies 'duality' to structure (as rules/the paradigmatic dimension) but not to systems/the syntagmatic dimension, and that, therefore, argues Mouzelis, Giddens does not conflate or 'merge' the situated actor and the environment of action. As I have observed in this chapter, Mouzelis's criticism of Giddens is that Giddens's approach should be broadened so as to include the idea that in the paradigmatic and syntagmatic dimensions actors may relate to objects in terms of both subject–object duality and dualism. Mouzelis's schema here is in some respects sophisticated and he raises very interesting theoretical questions: in the end, however, for the reasons I have given, his approach to these theoretical matters is unconvincing.

5

Social Action, Power and Interests

The previous chapters gave expression to the premise that social theorists, in seeking to reflect systematically upon the nature of the social, invariably find it necessary to in one way or another confront the metatheoretical themes that were identified in the first chapter. In relation to those themes the discussion thus far has tended to concentrate on concepts and theoretical issues to do with agency–structure, and to a lesser extent micro–macro; in the present chapter, while continuing to recognize agency/action and social structure as major dimensions of social reality, it is proposed to broaden the scope of the earlier analysis by addressing the idea of *social chance*, and also by examining conceptions of *power* and *interests*. As in all the chapters, the postulates and concepts developed in the following pages subsume critique of the four illicit forms of theoretical and methodological reasoning – reductionism, essentialism, reification, and functional teleology – that were defined in the Introduction (other, less appropriate definitional terms are sometimes applied to these forms of reasoning): as demonstrated earlier, versions of these problematical modes of theorizing continue to exert a damaging influence upon social theory and social science.

The chapter opens with some preliminary remarks on agency and social action, the intention being to ground the later discussion in a restatement and extension of a number of earlier observations concerning agency and the important concept *actor* (or agent).

Agency and social action

In their account of the nature of sociology as an academic discipline, Turner and Rojek (2001: 144) rightly observe that 'the tension between determinism and voluntarism is integral to sociological analysis'. Central to this tension, of course, is the debate of agency and structure. I suggested earlier that the notion of *actor* – and therefore, agency – has tended (despite countless references to the term in social science literature) to become something of a received notion in social theory and in the social sciences.[1] To insist upon an explicit, non-reified concept of actor, and on a concept of agency as a conditioned though not structurally determined capacity to formulate and carry out intentional acts, is not to engage in a sterile form of metatheorizing; rather, it is to insist, at the metatheoretical level, on conceptual clarity of a kind that helps us avoid reification when we engage in practical social analysis. It is, for example, worth reiterating that certain aspects of the concept actor – such as the notion of responsibility for actions or for outcomes – are highly significant in political analysis and in studies of public policy and the policy process. For instance, in confronting problems surrounding the theme 'democracy and governance', a number of political scientists have recently been concerned to address issues relating to the development of a conception of agency and of causal responsibility for political and policy outcomes (Hay, 1995; 2002; Rhodes, 1996; 1997). The ostensibly simple but in fact highly complex idea that agency is associated with causal responsibility for public policies is implicit in Richardson and Lindley's reference to 'possibly the *ultimate question* for all of us concerned with public policy, *i.e. who is accountable and responsible for public policy*' (1994: 3, my italics). Classical 'top-down' models of state steering of society ('government') do not capture the empirical reality of 'governance' (Pierre and Peters, 2000; Richards and Smith, 2002; Kooiman, 2003). Under the complex, multi-level conditions of contemporary European governance there are empirical difficulties in determining which individual and social ('organizational') actors did influence, or in principle were able to influence which political decisions and policy outcomes (Sibeon, 1999b), a situation which raises questions about the nature of democracy and political accountability. Nowadays policy tends to be constructed in sectoral policy networks (agriculture, education, health, environmental policy, foreign policy, and so on) in which a variety of state and unelected non-state actors (and sometimes, supranational actors such as the European Union) jointly formulate and implement policy through a process of 'governance' that entails interaction, negotiation, and compromise, and it is therefore sometimes extremely difficult to ascertain who was responsible for which decisions or outcomes (Rhodes, 1996). The purpose of these policy-related and political illustrations is to bring out the point that running alongside the existence of empirically complex investigative tasks focused on agency (and its interplay with structure), there is a need for conceptual clarity at the metatheoretical level in regard to the concept 'actor'; it is no use asking which actors were responsible for what, or which actors, in principle, might reasonably be held responsible and accountable for particular outcomes if, at the outset, we are not clear what an actor *is*. Here I am not, incidentally, suggesting all outcomes are intended effects of particular agencies; on the one hand it is true that many social scenarios – including 'society' – cannot legitimately be regarded as intentionally produced by any particular actors (Elias, 1978; Archer, 1995; 2000). But on the other, it is also the case that there are periods when some actors have greater influence in particular social spheres than other actors, and the question of causal responsibility for outcomes – which in turn raises the question of what sorts of entities can properly be said to be actors/agents – is therefore significant both analytically and politically.[2]

Many of the earlier arguments are relevant to the present discussion and it will, I think, be helpful at this stage to recall the main elements of the conception of actor and agency set out in the Introduction. I employ an equivalent of what Brubaker (1984: 92) and others call a philosophical anthropology, by which is meant a conception of the essence of what it means to be a human being or individual actor (as distinct from, say, social structures, machines[3] or nature), although my theoretical scheme refers both to individual human actors and social ('organizational') actors.[4] Hindess's (1986a: 115) definition of actor, which informs my conception of agency, is worth repeating: an actor is 'a locus of decision and action where the action is in some sense a consequence of the actor's decisions'. An actor is something that has a capacity to formulate and take decisions and to act on some of them, the question of which decisions are acted upon, or can be acted upon, being an empirical matter. Like Hindess, I argue that there are two main types of actors: individual human actors and social actors (Hindess, 1986a: 115) or supra-individuals (Harré, 1981: 150–2) such as committees, families, small groups, and crucially, organizations in the state, private, or voluntary sectors, including interest groups, political parties, universities, trade unions, professional associations, private firms, central government departments, local authorities, and so on. Most theorists and researchers, when they refer to agency, and when they do not engage in reification, suppose that only people are actors, that is, that only individuals can have intentional causal powers. Against such a view, it can be argued that the decisions of social actors – and it is the decisions of such actors that shape much of the social, economic, and political terrain in (post)modern society – are not simply aggregations of the decisions of individuals

(Hindess, 1986a: 124). This relates to the concept 'emergence' which was discussed in Chapter 3; emergent properties arise not only within social structure but also, with regard to agency, within social actors as decision-making entities with causal powers that are not reducible to individuals (Harré, 1981: 142, 148, 150). Social actors such as public bureaucracies are characterized by formal institutionalized mechanisms of resource attraction and allocation, decision-making and so on, as well as formal networks of positions/roles and informal patterns of norms and of influence and communication that are 'more than' individual human actors; and these characteristics result in a form of agency that is different to individual human agency. For example, it was observed in the Introduction that organizations as social actors are capable of engaging in decisions and actions – as when a trade union decides to 'go on strike', or a political party or a government department commits itself to a particular line of action – that, though individuals influence the organization's decision-making, and some more so than others, are not reducible to the attributes, decisions or actions of individuals (Holzner, 1978; Clegg, 1989: 187–8; Hindess, 1990: 25–9). A postulate which specifies that there are supra-individual entities (social actors in my terminology) that exhibit emergent properties including, in particular, a form of agency that is not reducible to the agency of individual actors, is, as almost any investigation of the history of sociological thought will reveal, in some sense not new to sociology: see, for example, MacIver and Page (1950/1964: 14–15). But it is a postulate that, as the present and earlier discussion is intended to indicate, has not been adequately handled in sociology nor in other social sciences.

Social ('organizational') actors are in varying degrees internally differentiated (Clegg, 1989: 189, 198) and sometimes organizational action (or public policy) is a relatively indeterminate, uncertain outcome of internal processes involving deliberation and perhaps conflict, bargaining, and negotiation among individual actors and among the various groups that comprise the organization. Conceptual and empirical difficulties that attend such apparently simple questions as whether social networks (or policy networks) exhibit agency, or whether, say, the European Union is a 'political system' (Peters, 1994: 10–11), or an aggregation of individual and social actors, or else a social actor *per se* (Sibeon, 1997: 61–5), are indications that the sociology of agency and of agency–structure is underdeveloped and offers relatively few reliable guidelines for the purposes of practical social analysis. Certainly it would seem that 'modern' sociology has some way to go in developing a satisfactory conceptual framework for handling questions of agency–structure; and structuralism, poststructuralism, discourse theory, postmodernism, and some areas of cultural studies have tended to duck the issue of agency and of agency–structure altogether, by 'decentring the subject' and by reducing both structure and agency to an effect of discourse (for example, see Shillings's (2001: 340–1) criticisms of the determinism and implicit reification in cultural studies accounts of 'the body').

Among the various elements that form the conception of action and agency outlined earlier, a case was made for what Hindess terms a '*minimal*' concept of actor. Against postmodern theory, it is not assumed that individual actors are necessarily angst-ridden or internally fragmented, with no continuity in social identity or self-identity. And against, on the other hand, some modernist conceptions it is not assumed that actors employ a holistic rationality, have an integrated or consistent set of objectives, or necessarily exhibit continuities in social or self-identity. These aspects of self, and the forms of thought actors employ for deliberating and acting upon the situations in which they are involved, are treated as empirical questions for investigation in each instance; they are not matters that can legitimately be decided in advance of empirical enquiry on the basis of some reductionist or essentialist theory. Nor, therefore, are actors seen as 'cultural dopes'; conversely, there is no reason to agree with Giddens's (1984) presumption that actors are characterized by 'knowledgeability'. To repeat: these are empirical questions – not matters for a priori theoretical predetermination. It was also observed earlier that agency–structure is not co-terminous with micro–macro. In Chapter 2 it was argued that micro is not synonymous with agency, nor is macro the same thing as structure; some actors (such as organizations) are not micro-entities, and structure (the 'conditions-of-action') may be macro or micro. As well, one of the central arguments in Chapter 3 was that, *contra* Elias, there are no good reasons for collapsing a distinction between individual(s) and society or for implying the existence of a 'direct link' between action and structure; here there is a parallel with Giddens's idea of a duality of action and structure, an idea that, it was suggested earlier, should be rejected in favour of a dualism of structure and action. Unlike duality, it was argued, dualism allows us to examine the interplay over time between pre-existing structure and action and to ascertain the relative importance of each in any given situation. Structure, it was suggested, conditions action to a greater or lesser extent, but does not wholly determine action (Archer, 1995; 2000). Relatedly, it was argued that Mouzelis's (1995) distinction between positional, dispositional, and situational dimensions of social action is a heuristically useful analytical tool, particularly when it is modified in the directions that were briefly indicated in Chapter 4.

Implicit throughout much of the earlier discussion of agency, is the equally important matter of *non-agency*.[5] If, as I argue, an actor is an entity that, in principle, has the means of formulating and taking decisions and of acting upon some of them, then there are other kinds of entities that, notwithstanding numerous claims to the contrary, cannot be said to possess intentional causal powers and which, therefore, cannot be said to be actors.[6] Agency is not synonymous with the occurrence of social effects. Countless phenomena that have social effects (such as a shaping or conditioning influence upon agency) are not actors and should be regarded as components of structure, not as forms of agency. All sorts of phenomena have social consequences – this is true of, say, magazines, rain, the HIV virus, the River Nile, motor cars, the Internet, and the Moon – but to say these phenomena are agents simply by virtue of their having social effects is to engage in reification (which I regard as the attribution of agency to entities that are not actors in the strict sense that actor is defined above), to mystify both the idea of agency and of structure, and to occlude possibilities for studying the interplay over time between them.[7] In the Introduction it was noted that, for example, Touraine, Habermas, Luhmann, Foucault, poststructuralist and actor network theorists engage in reification. Numerous other instances are to be found in social science literature. For example, reification is evident in Offe's (1984) account of modern capitalism, an account in which agency is attributed to sub-systems as analytical categories, causing Keane and Held (1984: 258) to comment: 'the only remaining agents in [Offe's] anonymous world appear to be Madame Economic Sub-system and Messieurs Political-Administrative and Legitimation Sub-systems!'. For reasons that should by now be clear, there are, I suggest, also problems with Law's (1991a) conception of agency, which is heavily influenced by structuralism, poststructuralism, and actor network theory. According to Law (1991b: 173–4), 'an agent is a structured set of relations with a series of (power) effects … . Thus, unlike Hindess, my primary definition of agency refers to relations and their power-relevant effects, rather than to strategies and intentions.' To claim, as Law does, that 'social relations' are agents (or actors) is to engage in reification; for how can 'social relations' formulate, take and act upon decisions? I cannot agree, either, with Callon's use of poststructuralism and actor network theory; he goes as far as claiming that, for instance, scallops (1986: 204) and the Chernobyl nuclear plant (1991: 142) are actors. Claims of this kind are to be found in other areas of theorizing relating to science, a case in point being Pickering's (2001) notion of 'posthuman agency' which attributes agency to machines and physical objects.[8] Such claims are also to be found in some of the more 'mainstream' areas of sociological literature. For example, Clegg (1989: 200) contends that computer systems and accounting systems display agency, and that 'Agency may be vested in non-human entities as diverse as machines, germs … and natural disasters. These … may be agents under the appropriate conditions' (ibid.: 188). Such views are misplaced, and should be rejected. Nor, despite claims to the contrary by, for example, Touraine (1981: 31–2, 77–8), Scott (1990: 6) and Munck (1995: 677–8), are social movements actors/agents: their time–space boundaries are – subject to a qualification that I will return to in a moment – highly indeterminate and they are not entities equipped with mechanisms for 'internal' deliberation and action involving the formulation and taking of decisions and their implementation. It is perhaps not inconceivable that some very small professional or 'ad hoc' movements (Tilley, 1994: 18) might under certain circumstances be actors in the sense described earlier; but the larger 'communitarian' movements (ibid.: 18) such as the womens movement, cannot legitimately be regarded as actors. In the case of, for example, ecological concerns, there are individual human actors such as environmental activists, professional researchers and academic consultants, government officials and so on, as well as social ('organizational') actors such as central government departments, Greenpeace, and Friends of the Earth; but 'the Green movement' as such can 'do' nothing – it is not an actor. This is not to say that social movements – comprised of discourses, networks, and actors that may interrelate to a greater or lesser extent – are unimportant; it is to say only that they should be regarded by social researchers as part of the conditions-of-action ('structure') within which actors operate, rather than as instances of the operation of agency. Also of significance to practical social analysis, and indeed to politics, governance and public policy, is the observation that taxonomic collectivities (Harré 1981; Harré and Bhaskar 2001) such as 'society', 'the middle class', 'women', 'men', 'black people', 'white people' and so on, are not actors. Therefore they can bear no causal responsibility for existing social conditions, among which are included forms of inequality, and nor are they entities (actors) that can formulate, take and act upon decisions intended to reproduce or modify those conditions (Hindess, 1986a). It follows, on the view taken here, that models of governance, public policy, and political practice based on reified notions of causal responsibility for and capacity to intentionally act upon social conditions, are likely to be self-defeating (Sibeon, 1997; 1999c).

Social structure

My ontologically flexible and *minimal* concept of structure, like the previously discussed minimal concept of actor/agent, carries relatively little ontological baggage, leaving it to empirical enquiry to do 'most of the work' in discovering, describing or explaining, for any particular social sphere or context, the precise nature and effects of structure. But of course, the use of 'minimal' concepts in conjunction with a flexible social ontology that is framed by critique of the four 'cardinal sins', does not mean that 'anything goes' nor that social phenomena are allowed to escape definition: on the view taken here, social structure – to put it at its simplest – refers to temporally enduring or temporally and spatially extensive circumstances, whether enabling or constraining, within which actors operate. I regard social structure as mutable but more or less persistent conditions-of-action (or 'social conditions') which in varying degrees influence, though do not wholly determine, the operation of agency in any given spatio-temporal context(s). And structure and action are, I have argued, different kinds of phenomena: in short, structure and action should be understood as a dualism, not a duality.

In Chapter 2, 'social structure'[9] was defined as temporally and very often spatially extensive social conditions that to a greater or lesser extent influence actors' forms of thought, decisions and actions. Structure,[10] it was observed, includes (but *contra* methodological individualism, is not reducible to) 'other' actors and their actions (there is agency-in-structure, just as there is structure-in-agency); discourses; social institutions; recurrent practices, and resource and power distributions ('power' is discussed later in the present chapter). Structure also includes social systems/social networks, defined as more or less patterned relations – at macro-, mezo- or micro-levels of social process (see Chapter 6) – between actors and between social institutions and positions/roles (that is, in my conceptual scheme as distinct from Parsonian frameworks which regard positions/roles as the defining characteristic of social systems, it is argued that social systems/social networks consist of both institutional/system integration and figurational/social integration elements). It is not, therefore, suggested here that social structures and social systems are the same thing; the former includes, as well as social systems or social networks (I use these terms interchangeably), a diversity of other phenomena, including configurations of action and social situations that are considerably 'looser' than those associated with social systems/networks. Structure, it was also argued earlier, can be a macro-phenomenon (that is, social conditions – including distributions of actors, actor–actor relations, discourses, social practices, patterns of role–role relations, and power configurations – that stretch widely across time–space), or structure can be a micro-phenomenon; micro-structure consists of local ramifications of macro-structure, or purely local ('idiosyncratic') but relatively enduring conditions-of-action. The various levels – micro, mezo and macro – at which social structure exists, are relatively independent: in my approach there is no 'upwards conflation' – that is, there is no assumption, as in methodological individualism and methodological situationalism, that micro-events determine the macro-social sphere and that the latter therefore has no independence from the former; nor is there any commitment to the 'downward conflation' associated with methodological collectivist theories which imply that the micro-realm has no relative autonomy from the macro-social sphere. Any connections between levels of social process are contingent empirical outcomes of dialectical, diachronic links between agency, structure, and social chance (this last concept, which for the moment may be taken as a reference to indeterminacy and fortuity, will be returned to shortly). A related premise is that, though *relatively* autonomous of social action and interaction, structure nevertheless in some sense is activity-dependent. An important point here is that, as Layder (1997) and other critics of duality theory have rightly argued, there is no 'direct link' between action and structure; but nor, as we saw in Chapter 4, is Archer's alternative and strongly dualistic view of activity dependence entirely satisfactory (in that chapter it was observed that having endorsed the maxim 'no people: no society', Archer then contradictorily implies – and here she pushes her rejection of 'upwards conflation' too far – that some current structures are entirely independent of current activities).

Another theme that was developed earlier is that social conditions ('structure') are always potentially indeterminate and shifting, and that if and when particular segments of the social become stabilized across time–space (for example, as a consequence of recursive or 'pathdependency' tendencies as described in Chapter 3), this is a relatively contingent and – in principle – reversible outcome; the conditions-of-action ('structure') are not historically predetermined nor a necessary effect of some putative systemic exigency or prime mover. But nor should crude structural conceptions of 'rigid' system determination and predictability be replaced by equally crude postulates (such as those associated with postmodern theory) which portray the social as endless flux and purely random change. As Callon and Latour have observed, 'There is no chaos, but no rigid system either' (1981: 282). A conception of social structure – and its relation to agency/activities – which in some respects is similar to my own, is set out by Tom Burns:

> Human agents – individuals as well as organized groups, organizations ... are subject to material, political and cultural constraints on their actions. At the same time, they are active, often creative forces, shaping and re-shaping social structures and institutions and their material circumstances. They thereby change, intentionally and unintentionally (often enough through mistakes and failures), the conditions of their own activities and transactions. (1986: 9)

Notice that one of Burns's underlying assumptions is that the social fabric is to some extent unintended, fluid and unpredictable; it is this unplanned, contingent dimension of the social – and importantly, its differentiation from and its relation to agency and to structure – that underpins the attempt below to construct an adequate conception of *social chance*.

Social chance

The idea of social chance – a concept employed here to refer to certain categories of unforeseen happenings – subsumes though goes further than 'unintended consequences', at least in the terms that the latter tends to be used. Boudon (1986: 173) observes: 'In the social sciences, chance is generally thought to be a very unwelcome guest, ubiquitous but studiously concealed, ignored and even denied the right to exist by virtually everyone.' Boudon has a point. Despite Weber's (1949) interest in chance,[11] most of the classical theorists tended to regard chance as a residual analytical category. The neglect of social chance in classical theory is carried over into modern sociology; even today, despite, as will be noted shortly, a number of examples of serious efforts to theorize chance, greater attention is given to agency and to structure. Some theorists, such as Mannheim (1950: 3) acknowledged the existence of chance but argued that sociology's proper focus of enquiry is the study of social order, not chance. Others, in ways that are reminiscent of Montesquieu's notion of 'apparent chance', have taken the view that so-called chance events are invariably complex, hidden manifestations of social structure. In 1734 Montesquieu (1965: 165) argued that seemingly chance happenings are actually reflections of an underlying, determinate social structure, and he discussed chance in these terms: 'It is not chance that rules the world ... There are general causes ... All accidents are controlled by these causes.' A modern and reductionist application of the idea of 'apparent chance' is Althusser's notion of overdetermination and structural (or metonymic) causality – the presumption here is that a determinate social structure ultimately dictates the course of social life. Various other examples exist where social chance has been seen not as *fortuity*, but as an as yet imperfectly understood expression of underlying social laws or structural regularities, or as an expression of complex interconnected causal factors (as distinct from fortuitous conjunctions of causally unrelated phenomena). What appears to be fortuitous is, it is held, merely an appearance based on ignorance of the complexity of social systems, and once a more complete understanding of the underlying ('deep') structural generators of apparent 'chance' has been achieved, chance as such (fortuity) will vanish. There are, as will be made clearer in a moment, good reasons for rejecting such approaches: *social chance is not sociological ignorance of, or incomplete knowledge of, 'complex' structural causation.* It is true that causally related elements of social structure may sometimes have more or less hidden and unforeseen effects on the course of social life (for example, by reconfiguring patterns of interests in unexpected ways) and it may well be that 'apparent chance' features in some social situations; what is not legitimate, however, is the tendency – among writers as diverse as Montesquieu and

Althusser – to regard *all* instances of social chance as 'apparent chance' (that is, to regard all such instances as hidden expressions of a determinate social order, and not as fortuitous happenings). It may also be the case (though this is under-researched) that under certain conditions some structural forms – such as the fragmented, multi-level and processual anatomy of the European Union (Sibeon, 1999b; Cram *et al.*, 1999) – are more likely to generate chance outcomes than other structural forms. But this last possibility, which refers to structure, does not, of course, of itself remove the ontological status of social chance as a phenomenon that exists in its own right; the intention in this part of the chapter is to show that social chance is partly shaped by and partly shapes structure and agency, but is not reducible to either of them.

Boudon's observation concerning the reluctance of social scientists to countenance the idea of social chance (that is, a reluctance to treat chance not as a residual analytical category but as having an important explanatory part to play in social science), requires a certain amount of qualification. First, some social scientists – notably political scientists and historians – have tended to be more attuned to the idiographic and the indeterminate than sociologists (on this see Abrams, 1982, and Sztompka, 1991; 1993). Second, in social theory and sociology – despite a general disinclination to move beyond the notions of structure and agency – it is possible to find a number of theorists who, though they share little else in common, accord a fairly high degree of explanatory significance to social chance. As well as Weber, Boudon, Abrams and Sztompka to whom I have referred, such theorists include, for example, Elias (1978), Popper (1957: 14, 146–7), Giddens (1984), Unger (1987a; 1987b; 1997), Foucault (1972: 28, 231), Stones (1996), and to some extent, actor network theorists such as Callon (1986; 1991), Latour (1986; 1987; 1991), and Law and Hassard (1999).[12] Relevant conceptual and empirical work is also to be found in the writings of political scientists such as Marsh (1995; 1998) and Rhodes (1997) and in the work of public policy academics such as James (1997), Parsons (1995) and Wilsford (1994). A synthetic re-working of these sources and of a useful paper by Smith, M. (1993) leads to my heuristic model of social chance as 'unforeseen happenings' that are of two main types. First, fortuitous conjunctions of discrete events and/or of discrete sequences of action, social patterns or trends (the latter may be very long term, examples being industrialization and secularization); here, use of the term fortuitous (or 'accidental') signifies conjunctions of causally unrelated phenomena. Second, unforeseen conjunctions of action, consisting of two sub-types: unforeseen outcomes of intersubjectivity and interaction, including, at the mezo- or inter-organizational level of social process, the equivalent of intersubjectivity, an example being the relational, emergent nature of social action in inter-organizational policy networks (Kickert *et al.*, 1997a; 1997b); and the unforeseen aggregated outcomes of actions under 'non-intersubjective' conditions (Boudon, 1986), as when myriad individual decisions and actions result in unforeseen environmental pollution. Concerning the second main type of social chance, relating to actors' intentions and the outcomes of action, *agency causation* is of two principal kinds – the first being where intended outcomes are achieved, the second where foreseen unintended outcomes occur (if my action is designed to secure a particular outcome (x) but I foresee that another outcome (y) may unintentionally result from my action, then if (y) occurs as a result of my action this is an instance of agency causation – I could have acted differently in the light of my foresight – and not chance causation). *Chance causation*, I have argued, refers to unforeseen happenings in the terms set out above. *Structural causation* refers to situations where relatively enduring social conditions ('structure') as distinct from agency and social chance, heavily prefigure events or social patterns, an instance being those situations that display highly recursive (self-reproducing) structural tendencies (see the discussion of recursion in Chapter 3) as in the case of, for example, certain kinds of policy networks (Marsh and Smith, 2000). While there are theoretical and methodological reasons for insisting on an analytical distinction between agency, structural, and chance causation, it seems likely – as will be observed shortly – that most real-life situations are a mixture of these three constituent elements of the social.

Arising from the above, the following observations are worthy of note. First, chance causation can contribute to the transformation or reproduction of social structure (too many writers associate it only with the former). Second, chance happenings can occur at different levels of the social (Roth and Schluchter, 1979) – whether micro or mezo (see Chapter 7), or macro as in the case of, for example, large-scale unforeseen events precipitated by the break-up of an empire or of a political federation such as the former USSR. Whether chance happenings (or indeed, happenings of any kind) at one level of social process have consequences for other levels, and if so, the nature of those consequences, are empirical matters that in most cases cannot be predicted with any certainty in advance of empirical enquiry. Third, some instances of social chance are less consequential than others. Some chance outcomes whether at micro-, mezo- or macro-levels may perish whereas others – in ways that usually entail an *interplay* between agency, structure, and social chance – become extensive across time and/or space and thereby become elements of social structure. In the case of events that may be described as instances of macro-chance (for example, the unforeseen occurrence of spatially widespread political protest following the re-drawing of a national boundary), any such events, should they also become temporally extensive, cease to be instances of macro-chance and for analytical purposes should be regarded as having become elements of macro-structure. Fourth, to insist that social chance as a concept has an important explanatory part to play in social analysis, as distinct from a view of chance as a residual category, is not, of course, to ignore the importance of structure nor to suppose on a priori grounds that the social world is endlessly indeterminate. Whether any particular social scenario – at micro- or macro-levels of social process – is relatively stable or else in a state of flux, is a matter for empirical investigation: the flexible social ontology described earlier as an ontology that is allied to concept development drawing upon critique of the four 'cardinal sins', leads to the view that illicit theoretical dichotomies between 'complete statis' and 'complete flux' should be rejected in favour of a postulate which specifies that social life is always potentially open to change and variability across time and social space, the extent to which stability and continuity, or else discontinuity and change, actually occurs being treated as an empirical variable. Society, that is to say, is always potentially indeterminate, though some segments of the social fabric may become stabilized – for long or short periods – in what is otherwise unstable and shifting terrain. Any such stabilization is not a necessary effect of some macro-structural principle or system exingency, but rather, is a processual and more or less contingently sustained outcome of interaction between agency, structure, and social chance.

Interplay between agency, structure and social chance

Archer's (1995) analytical and ontological dualism refers to the idea of interplay over time between agency and structure. A more complete conception of the social, however, would insist upon the notion that agency and structure but also *social chance* may have mutually conditioning or shaping influences one upon the other; to ignore or marginalize social chance in favour of an emphasis on agency and (or 'versus') structure, is to employ a seriously incomplete social ontology. Betts (1986: 60), whose perception of structure is influenced by Giddens, puts the matter this way: 'We need to separate out three concepts: the rules and resources potentially available in given contexts (referred to here as "structure"); processes generating outcomes in the absence of conscious decision-making (referred to here as "event causation" or "fate"); and conscious human activity ("agency causation")'. As indicated in this quotation, Betts, whose approach is not identical with mine, moves some way towards my contention that social chance is a phenomenon that cannot legitimately be reduced to either structure or agency – it has, so to speak, relative autonomy from both of them.

What I particularly want to emphasize here, however, is that the relation between agency, structure, and social chance frequently takes the form of a dialectical process: each element to a greater or lesser extent influences the others diachronically. For instance, chance outcomes may modify structure which in turn may exert a predisposing effect upon agency; or social action may affect structures in ways that, intentionally or not, open them up to the operation of social chance and to a decreased likelihood of those structures becoming stabilized or institutionalized. It is not difficult to find other instances of the operation of this dialectical process. For example, predisposing conditions ('structure') may be a factor in A's exercise of agency which in turn leads to new conditions (a new 'structure') that, purely by chance, opens up opportunities for the exercise of agency by B and C whose purpose is to try to negate the effects of the action taken by A. Scenarios of this kind – or sometimes, more empirically complex ones – can occur among, for example, competitive organizational actors in policy networks (Marsh, 1998). An empirical illustration of the interweaving of agency, structure (social conditions) and social chance is Marsh's study of Thatcherism and the development of two policy areas (privatization and industrial relations). In the following extract from Marsh in which he summarizes his findings, I have inserted my own markers to indicate the presence of 'structure', 'agency', and 'chance' respectively:

> The detailed case studies indicate that Britain's continuing relative economic decline [*structure*] provided the crucial context within which both privatization and industrial relations policy were developed. However, the overall shape of the policies and, even more crucially, the detailed provisions, were strongly affected by strategic political judgements taken by politicians [*agency*]; most of them fairly short-term and concerned with the electoral consequences of actions. The Thatcher Cabinets were also responding to political events like the 'Winter of Discontent' [*chance*], over which they had no control. 'New Right' ideology played a role, but it was hardly the driving force behind policy which the analysis of ... others suggests. (1995: 595)

Diachronic interplay between structure, agency, and social chance can also occur at the micro-level. An illustration is Abram's (1982: 272) observation that for Becker and for Goffman the concept 'deviant career' unites contingency and structure via loose couplings that are predisposing but not structurally determinant:

> The individual embarks on a course of (deviant) action which in certain (contingent) circumstances is likely to evoke certain (stigmatizing) responses; the responses in turn give the individual certain problems which in certain (contingent) circumstances are likely to be solved in certain (more deviant) ways which in turn evoke responses.

The details of these illustrations need not concern us. The more general point arising from them is that it is not only the case that agency, structure, and social chance play a part in human affairs, the part played by each being a matter for empirical determination in each instance; it also is the case that agency, structure, and social chance interact dialectically and exert a shaping or conditioning influence one upon the other. Society is in some sense the product of interplay over time between these constituent elements of social life.

It can, in light of the above, be argued that investigation of diachronic interconnections between agency, structure, and social chance constitutes a large part of the subject matter of the social sciences. Cutting across these three vital elements of the social, however, is a complex, multifaceted phenomenon that so far in this discussion has not been addressed in a direct or explicit way; I refer to *power*, which together with the closely related topic of 'interests', will be the main focus of attention in the remainder of the chapter.

Power

A few years ago Barker and Roberts wrote that theoretical work on power had arrived at an impasse. In Barker and Robert's opinion, theories of power had become 'stuck' (1993: 210) between two opposed viewpoints, the first insisting that power is an attribute of individuals, the second that power is an attribute of social structures. To speak of an impasse is perhaps something of an overstatement, in so far as there are certain identifiable dimensions of the social that can usefully be incorporated into our understanding of power. In particular, there are good reasons for suggesting that power has multiple forms. Minimally, and bearing in mind the conceptual arguments developed in the earlier chapters, it seems important to acknowledge the existence of '*objective*' structural (including systemic) forms of power, together with what I call *agentic power*, defined here as the partly systemic, partly relational/emergent and potentially variable capacity of agents to shape social situations in a preferred direction. However, before proceeding to set out the details of my own conception of power, it will be helpful to first of all take stock of some fairly familiar conceptualizations that, I suggest, have heuristic analytical value.

In some areas of classical theory, power is associated with resistance. Weber (1978: 53) declared that power is 'the probability that one actor within a social relationship will be in a position to carry out his will despite resistance'; power is 'the chance for a man or a number of men to realise their own will in a social action even against the resistance of others who are participating in the action' (ibid.: 926). The association of power with resistance, and by implication with conflict, raises the question of whether it is possible to recognize the existence of power in the *absence* of observable conflict. Power and conflict and the observable exercise of power in concrete situations are, following Weber, often seen as interrelated in the sense that analysis of power, it has been argued, should be confined to investigation of concrete decisions (Dahl, 1958). In contrast, other theorists warn against confining analysis to only those occasions when power and conflict are expressed and observable: powerful groups may be able to exercise power to construct a false and manipulated consensus, and it has been claimed that 'the crucial point is that the most effective and insidious use of power is to prevent ... conflict arising in the first place' (Lukes, 1974: 23). Lukes, in his account of what he calls the first dimension of power, acknowledges that the type of power referred to by Dahl undoubtedly exists and that the study of concrete policy decisions is therefore important. In this way we can discover who politically dominated the policy agenda and who, therefore, holds the greater amount of power in, for example, the policy-making process. There is, though, a second dimension of power. Lukes observes that powerful actors can sometimes employ coercion or subterfuge to keep potentially conflictual issues *off* the decision-making agenda. This implies that the researcher who finds no evidence of struggle over concrete political or policy decisions would be wrong to assume that no power is being exercised. There is, I suggest, no reason to disagree with the view that power can exist in both of these dimensions. Lukes also argues, however, that there is a third dimension of power. This arises when dominant actors are able to shape actors' preferences in such a way that, even though there may be no experience of or expression of conflicting interests on *or* off the decision-making agenda, there may nevertheless exist a hidden form of power. Actors, in part because they are brainwashed by the power elite, exist in a condition of 'false consciousness' and they fail to understand what their 'true' or 'real' interests are. They therefore often do not, according to Lukes, perceive that their 'real' interests are under threat and they accordingly 'fail' to engage in conflict in the political decision-making arena. Thus, a notion of so-called 'objective' or 'real' interests underlies Luke's view of power. This much-criticized conception of 'objective' ('real') interests raises significant questions about the relation of agency to structure, and this is something to which I shall return later.

Weberian, Marxist, and other 'modernist' schools of thought have been challenged by approaches that draw upon the work of Foucault and of other writers who adopt a broadly poststructuralist or postmodern[13] stance towards power. As noted in Chapter 3, there is, first, some ambiguity and contradiction in Foucault's theorizing, and second, his views to some extent shifted over time. Nevertheless it is possible to identify certain ideas that are integral to the main thrust of his theoretical frame of reference. Bearing in mind the evaluation that was made of Foucault in Chapter 3, it is worth reiterating that Foucault is associated with a view of power as strategic and emergent in the sense that power is not structurally preconstituted, but rather, emerges out of social relations. It should be recalled, too, that Foucault argues that power is no one's property – it is not something that can be possessed (no actor, in other words, can be said to 'have' power). It should also be noticed that what Foucault calls 'power in general' is a 'spontaneous' rather than calculative form of power; it is contingent, precarious and reversible. This form of power is more or less the same thing as agency and social relations in general; this is why it is a form of power that is said by Foucault to be 'everywhere'. It is this conception of power that Foucault has in mind when he says we cannot legitimately ask what power is or where it comes from (Foucault, 1982: 217). Here, faced with the suggestion that we should eschew the definitional task altogether, I am tempted to say that Foucault's notion of 'power in general' is so nebulous that it is perhaps hardly surprising that he found it easy to claim that power is 'everywhere'! However, subject to the criticisms made of Foucault in Chapter 3 (criticisms which signify that some of his central concepts are in need of revision), there are grounds for taking the view that we can usefully draw upon certain elements of his conception of power. Power has a relational dimension and is never, I would argue, an entirely systemically predetermined, 'given' or fixed capacity of an agent (it was precisely such systemic views, of course, that Foucault strongly resisted – though, as will be argued later, he tended, in advocating a form of relationism, to push his rejection of systemic aspects of power too far). In other words, I would argue that actors may become more or less powerful, variation in agentic power being in part an emergent outcome of social relations and of shifts in the conditions-of-action including, for example, alterations in actors' access to and skills in deploying relevant techniques and resources.

In his later work Foucault (1991) discusses another type of power, which he calls *government*. This is a calculative form of power that is somewhat more stable and less reversible than 'power in general'. Government refers to policies and actions that affect people directly, but also to processes that operate through mechanisms of *self*-regulation and self-control. In Foucault's theoretical scheme, government refers not only to the activities of the state but, more broadly, to government of oneself (here there is an affinity with his earlier writings on 'discipline') or, say, government of a household or of a private firm. Government is not domination; government is, in large part, a process of 'action at a distance' whereby conduct is influenced by getting people to regulate their own behaviour, and by creating conditions that allow self-government to occur. Foucault's work in regard to 'action at a distance' (a term much used by his followers) is often said to be a departure from 'conventional' theory; however, the underlying assumptions about structure and agency in Foucault's writings on self-government are in some respects similar to those found in long-standing sociological uses of the concepts 'socialization' and 'internalization'.

A related aspect of Foucault's work, one which is relevant to the study of politics and the policy process, concerns power and discourse. For Foucault, the topics of social policy – social needs, rights, dependency, human welfare, and more specialized topics such as poverty, homelessness or child abuse – are not 'given' or preconstituted, but rather, are formed by political, professional, and welfare discourses that 'construct' their own topics and imbue them with particular meanings. Discourses create their subjects (actors) and their objects (phenomena to be acted upon). The socially and politically constructed nature of the objects of government and policy (for instance, images of 'the family' and of 'the economy' are respectively incorporated into family policy and economic policy) is a factor in the construction not only of the objects of policy but also of ways of acting upon those objects (for example, 'the economy' is constructed as something that, in principle, is manipulable by means of interest rates and various other policy instruments); put another way, a political or policy discourse constructs an object – crime, marriage, the welfare state or whatever – in such a way that it can be 'governed' (Miller and Rose, 1993: 79). A part of Foucault's theoretical scheme, then, centres on the idea that power is an effect of discursive practices (in politics, administration, law, medicine, psychiatry, criminal justice, and so on). Contained within these discourses are, as just noted, definitions of the objects or 'problems' that are to be targets of intervention; and discourses also specify solutions or responses – in the form of, for example, fiscal instruments, therapies, guidance, punishments or controls – to those problems. Foucault, it should be noted, insists that discourses – whether of government or administration, or professional discourses – are not expressions of structurally given ('objective') interests in the sense associated with, say, Marxist theory; here there are grounds for partly agreeing with Foucault, although it will be argued later that there is more to the question of 'objective' ('real') or 'positional' interests than he imagined. A wider point is that discourses are disseminated across time–space and Foucault argues that discursive practices are not the intentional effects of the will of any individual actors nor of the state: subject to the qualifications and criticisms made in Chapter 3, Foucault's idea that power has an 'objective' face in so far as it is secreted in discourses is, I suggest, a useful insight – providing we do not also endorse Foucault's tendency to underplay the significance of 'subjective' and agentic dimensions of power.

Foucauldian concepts relating to power, if used selectively and in modified form, can serve as a useful corrective against exclusively systemic perspectives. There is analytical justification for, in part at least, viewing power from a Foucauldian standpoint (or rather, as should be clear from the earlier discussion, for viewing power from the standpoint of a particular strand – albeit an important one – in Foucault's contrasting and not altogether consistent writings on power and social action). In opposition to theories of structural predermination, power may in part be seen as effect, not cause, of strategic success achieved during the course of social interaction (Law, 1986a: 5). In some of the early, Foucault-inspired work of Callon and Latour and others associated with actor network theory (or 'translation sociology' as it used to be called), it was argued, rightly so in my view, that not only does power have no single or prime cause, but that strategic success in the acquisition of power is always potentially reversible. It is largely because power is never wholly systemic that there are formidable strategic problems to be overcome if currently 'ascending' or 'powerful' actors are to be able to stabilize their situation for very long periods by means of *irreversibly* enrolling and 'consigning' (making durable, temporally and spatially) a large number of related ideas, policies, practices and resources (Callon and Latour, 1981: 293). Some strategically successful or 'ascending' actors may be able to achieve and sustain relatively long-lasting asymmetries in power between themselves and other actors, but any such asymmetries, if and where they occur, are contingently and/or strategically reproduced: as already noted, they are not explicable in terms of theories of first or prime causes or in terms of theories that refer to 'necessary effects' of the social totality. And sometimes, power may shift as a consequence not so much of intentional strategic action but as a consequence of interaction between agency, structure, and social chance. The more general point arising from the above is that we can, I suggest, usefully borrow elements of Foucault's ideas on power, though we should do so in critical, selective fashion that is informed by critique of the four 'cardinal sins' and by the conceptual arguments set out in the earlier chapters: power, as Foucault insisted, is indeed relational and emergent; but unfortunately, and here we have good reason to be critical of Foucault, his relationalism is capable of telling only 'half a story'.

Power has not only a relational but also a *systemic* face. We have noted that in much of Foucault's relational theorizing, power is seen as a contingent effect or *outcome* of social relations, rather than a 'prior' or structurally predetermined capacity; power, rather than being something already (pre)constituted ('stored') in social systems, social institutions and positions/roles, emerges out of networks of social relations and is a contingent *effect* of social interaction and of the operation of discourses. Latour, whose work is influenced by Foucault, claims that 'power is not something you may possess or hoard', and that power is 'an effect … never a cause' (Latour, 1986: 265). Latour is wrong; power can be hoarded or stored, and therefore power – though often an effect – can sometimes be a 'cause'. The larger (meta)theoretical picture here is that poststructural and postmodern theorists have gone too far in their almost total rejection of 'modernist' concerns with *distributions* of power. Foucault and translation theorists such as Callon (1986; 1991), Callon and Latour (1981) and Latour (1986; 1987; 1991) tend to push their relational and processual conception of power to the point of denying that power can be 'stored' in roles and in social systems and networks of social relations. Foucault in much of his theoretical work seems to ignore not only that agents 'possess' power but that some agents possess more power than others (Best and Kellner, 1991: 70), and that part of the reason for this is that certain elements of power can be stored in positions/roles, social institutions and social systems. What is required here is not an either-or theoretical opposition, but rather, a synthesis which combines (a) Foucauldian and other relational conceptions of power, with (b) an understanding that power has a systemic dimension. A synthetic approach leads to the view that agentic power nearly always has a relational, contingent and emergent dimension (that is why the position of top dogs in any institutional sphere – even the position of, say, prime minister – is sometimes only precariously sustained, or not sustained at all); yet, as Law (1991b: 170) notes, we all know that prime ministers generally have 'more power' than, for example, backbenchers. It is important, therefore, to recognize, *contra* Foucault, that there are aspects of power that – as Mouzelis (1995) would want to emphasize – can be *stored* (in social institutions, in positions/roles and in hierarchical social systems or networks), even if not always securely. As observed above, there need be no either-or dichotomy here: to acknowledge that power is partly relational is not to say elements of power cannot be stored in networks of social relations, and to say power can to some extent be stored is not to deny the possibility of contingent, relational, and emergent shifts in distributions of power. 'Objective' structural (including systemic) forms of power, and relational and agentic forms, interweave and interpenetrate, but they nevertheless are analytically distinct. Thus it is legitimate to say that an actor 'has' power (this invokes the idea of power storage), provided we *also* ask (along with Foucault and other relational theorists[14]) how that power is constituted and reproduced relationally (Law, 1991b). Therefore there are good reasons for regarding power as partly preconstituted and stored (in roles, rules, systems, social institutions, and in networks of social relations) and partly relational, emergent and contingent, with the extent to which power is 'systemic' or 'relational' being an empirical variable that may alter from one situation to another.[15]

The above leads to a view that there are multiple forms of power, including systemic power (associated with 'power storage' in discourses, social institutions, social positions/roles, and in social systems), and agentic power which refers to a capacity of agents, a capacity that is not structurally predetermined but which is partly systemic and partly relational. Systemic and agentic forms of power are ontologically distinct and relatively autonomous, though they tend to overlap, interpenetrate and influence each other. Given, however, the ontological arguments set out in previous chapters – concerning, in particular, agency–structure, micro–macro, and the relative autonomy of different levels of social process – it should be noted that powerer's multidimensionality has a multi-level aspect that has a 'hybrid', more variegated form than might, at first sight, be implied by the systemic-relational distinction to which I have just referred. Agentic power in some circumstances has a largely systemic source deriving, say, from position/role. In other circumstances agentic power may be of a relatively contingent, emergent kind that emerges during and as an effect of social interaction at the micro or mezo (for example, inter-organizational) levels of social process. Such power may interact with systemic or positional/role power of the type that is 'stored' in discourses, social institutions, and social systems/social networks. There tends, in other words, to be a two-way (dialectical) relation between systemic and relational forms of power, with each to some extent conditioning the other. Take, for example, political and policy-related discursive practices associated with the social-political and economic discourse known as 'Thatcherism'. Particularly in the 1980s, Thatcherite discourse embodied a form of power – relating to countless decisions taken by a variety of political and administrative actors involved in such matters as the 'contracting out' of certain areas of public services, the putting in place of arrangements to govern public–private partnerships, and so on – that partly shaped the conditions-of-action ('structure') within which policy actors operated and to some extent shaped agency and decision-making in many local policy settings. There is evidence to suggest, however, that the *meaning* of Thatcherism in Britain in the 1980s did not blanket the whole country uniformly but was, rather, in various ways modified, elaborated and sometimes – in some settings where circumstances made this possible – transformed or subverted (James, 1997). The wider point here is that the 'same' material (such as a political ideology, in this instance Thatcherism) is not necessarily 'the same' 'everywhere' and the material may also vary over time; the material as it 'travels' may be mediated spatially and temporally – for example, and here I employ a modified form of Rootes's (1981) conception of ideology, the material in question may in different spatio-temporal contexts acquire differing degrees of crystallization or coherence. Put another way, that which is ostensibly 'the same' phenomenon or the same social material – in the present example, the (discursive) form of 'objective' *power* embodied in the discourse of Thatcherism – travels spatially and temporally across locales (Callon and Latour, 1981; Lidz, 1981; Fararo, 1992) and in some sense the material spirals into and out of those locales (see the discussion of material diffusion in the following chapter). Thus a social material (such as 'Thatcherism') with its concomitant power effects that travel across spatio-temporal contexts will not necessarily be given identical forms of expression in every locale; as Latour (1986) put it, materials often acquire a different shape 'as they travel'. Nor, and here the micro–macro distinction is relevant, will materials necessarily gain the same form of expression within each of the relatively autonomous levels of social process that constitute society: some of the conceptual and methodological implications of the complex social ontology alluded to here – whereby social material is reproduced, elaborated or sometimes transformed as it, so to speak, moves 'horizontally' across time and space and 'vertically' between micro-, mezo- and macro-levels of society – will be discussed in Chapters 6 and 7.

The problem of interests

Debates surrounding 'power' frequently involve controversies and theoretical problems that attend the idea of 'real' (or 'objective') interests. For example, Giddens's (1984: 198–9, 318, 342) notion of 'unacknowledged interests' is, as Cohen observes, an unresolved problem in structuration theory (see Cohen, 1989: 198, 268–9). The following discussion of interests will, it is hoped, serve to help preserve the concept from misuse, while also reinforcing aspects of this chapter's underlying ontology with regard to connections between social structure, social chance, power, and agency.

One of the first and more general points to be made with regard to interests is that there are no good reasons for supposing that actors' interests are reducible to a single general (and reductionist) principle of explanation that refers, for example, to gender interests or to class interests. Reductionist theories of interests tend also to lean towards essentialism, and to entail reification and functional teleology; such theories have a tendency to presume that actors have structurally 'given' ('real' or 'objective') interests that – though the actors themselves may be unaware of the existence of such interests – inhere in those actors simply by virtue of, for instance, their memberships of taxonomic collectivities such as 'the working class', 'the middle class', 'black people', 'white people', 'women', or 'men' (Hindess, 1986b). Problems associated with the idea of 'real' interests are long-standing and it was many years ago that Child (1941: 218) asked: 'How is one to know *which* thoughts, feelings, etc., are, in point of fact, the one's rationally suited to a given class's position?'. One kind of response to questions such as Child's is Hindess's (1986b: 128): 'The notion of interests that are real or objective (unlike other interests that actors may believe themselves to have) have no explanatory significance with regard to the actions of those whose interests they are thought to be.' Hindess's argument is that interests that do not provide actors with reasons for action cannot explain the intentional behaviour of those actors (1988: 110): 'Interests have consequences only in so far as they enter actors' deliberations and contribute towards providing them with reasons for action.' These criticisms made by Hindess are part of his contention that actors' forms of thought and actors' criteria and techniques for assessing situations and for formulating goals, preferences, desires, interests and so on, are not structurally predetermined (Hindess, 1986b: 11–14). Hindess, it may be noted, is not suggesting that there are never any relatively contingent and variable connections between actors' formulation of their interests and their engagement in action, and aspects of social structure such as differences in the discourses available to actors when they formulate their interests and their reasons for action, differential access to particular means or techniques of action for giving effect to interests, and so on (Hindess, 1986b: 129); rather, what Hindess rejects are, in effect, reductionist, essentialist, and determinist theories of 'real' interests where particular interests, irrespective of whether they are acknowledged or acted upon by the actors in question, are seen as the fixed and given properties of actors simply by virtue of those actors' structural location in society. It can be argued, and here I am broadly in agreement with Hindess, that there are three sets of problems associated with the kinds of theories of 'real' interests to which I have just referred. First, there are no legitimate criteria by which academic, political or any other observers employing reductionist, essentialist, reified or teleological theories of 'real' interests can impute interests to actors who do not recognize or act upon the interests ascribed to them. Second, the closely associated doctrine of 'false consciousness', which figures in many reductionist theories as part of an attempt to explain why actors 'fail' to recognize their 'real' interests, does not provide a credible explanation of how it is that the observer is apparently unaffected by the 'false consciousness' that he ascribes to others and for whom he sometimes claims the right to speak. Third, as shown historically by, for example, Robespierre's 'reign of terror' and later the Gulags (see Fay, 1987: 213–15), potentially authoritarian and repressive implications arise (Elias, 1971: 155) when political elites claim it is necessary to reinterpret, 'speak for' and override the preferences of the masses who are said to be suffering from 'false consciousness', and that, for example, it is legitimate to act on their behalf in 'eliminating' 'class enemies' or 'enemies of the people'; these are potentially repressive aspects of reductionist and essentialist 'liberatory' theories that are condemned by, among others, postmodern theorists (Lyotard, 1986: 82; Lyotard and Thebaud, 1985: 98).[16]

In concurring with some of Hindess's and others' objections against reductionist and essentialist theories of power and 'real' interests, we encounter one of those situations where there is a danger of throwing out the baby with the bathwater. Hindess's acknowledgement that there are connections between actors' self-formulated interests and social structure can be developed in directions that he himself did not envisage. An important case in point, though surprisingly it has tended to be ignored by theorists and researchers, is Archer's concept of 'vested' or 'positional' interests. In Archer's (1995: 216) conceptual framework, structure – including 'situational logics', positions/roles, and, for example, membership of particular groups, occupations or professions – tends to generate, via vested/positional interests that are attached to, say, positions/roles and to group memberships, what Archer calls 'strategic guidance' for actors, guidance that is predisposing (or 'conditioning' as she puts it) but not absolutely compelling or determinant. Archer (ibid.: 210) refers to interests that are attached to positions/roles such as landlord and tenant (other things being equal, it's in landlords' interests to maximize or increase rents, and in tenants' interests to minimize or hold steady the amount of rent paid). Similarly, it is in the interests of capitalists to make profits, in the interests of professional groups to convince others of the importance of professional knowledge and skills, and so on. Archer argues (ibid.: 209) that 'the objective distribution of costs and benefits conditions both interpretation and action'; there are vested ('positional') interests attached to, for example, positions/roles, and to act in accordance with those interests produces benefits for the actor whereas to act contrary to those interests results in the actor incurring costs. As already noted, Archer's view of interests is bound up with her notion of 'structural conditioning'. That is, structure conditions actors' forms of thought and actions by virtue of shaping the situations and positions/roles in which actors are involved – particular interests are attached to particular situations, to particular group memberships and to positions, and these structured ('positional') interests predispose (though do not compel) actors to adopt certain courses of action in pursuance of those interests (ibid.: 203–4, 254; 1998: 82).

In previous chapters qualified support was given to Archer's general theoretical framework and to her dualistic social ontology. With regard to 'positional interests' – an important concept that provides an avenue for exploring connections between structure, interests, and agency/social activities – I find myself in broad agreement with Archer, subject to three provisos. First, positional interests are regarded by Archer as 'real', that is, as real elements of social structure (given her commitment to social realism, it could hardly be otherwise). I have no quarrel with this. However, Archer, it seems to me, does not distance herself sufficiently from problematical theories of 'real' interests, of the kind referred to earlier. Her welcome criticisms of upwards, downwards, and central conflation would, I suggest, have been rather more incisive had they entailed sustained critique of reductionism, essentialism, reification, and functional teleology (the 'cardinal sins') and also engaged with the arguments surrounding agency–structure, micro–macro and time–space as set out in this and other chapters. As things stand, Archer does not do enough to place clear blue water between her concept of positional interests as objective components of social structure, and the highly suspect notions of 'real' or 'objective' interests that have rightly been criticized by Hindess and many others. For example, functional teleological accounts of 'real' ('objective') interests, accounts which accord no explanatory significance to intentional social action (nor to unintended outcomes), have no empirical explanatory value and should be kept entirely separate from the idea of 'positional' ('objective') interests. Teleological accounts, it will be recalled from the Introduction, involve illicit theoretical efforts to 'work backwards' in an attempt to explain a cause of something in terms of its effects. Betts (1986: 51) notes that teleological explanation 'both locates the powerful and discovers their "interests" by examining outcomes … this is logically false for we cannot, in the absence of intentional planning, discover causes by examining effects'. This is not to suggest that regularized, patterned features of current social contexts never benefit some actors more than others, but it does not automatically follow that the actors who benefit most created or were able to create the current context, still less that they created it in order to achieve their interests. The general point being made here is, then, that Archer might have developed her formulation of 'objective' positional interests in ways that remove any possibility of confusion with the problematical theories of 'objective' ('real') interests that were referred to earlier. Second, Archer speaks of structural conditioning rather than structural determination of actors' forms of thought and activities (such that, in her terms, actors have an element of choice in deciding whether to act on the basis of their positional interests, or to act otherwise and incur costs). Nevertheless she tends to play down the element of creativity that actors bring to the interpretations that they make of the various elements – including positional interests – that comprise social settings, and she also underplays actors' volition, capacity for innovation, and creativity in selecting and deploying means of action. This is probably a reflection of Archer's general neglect of, for example, symbolic interactionist and phenomenological approaches; this failure in much of her writing is only partly compensated for by her more recent focus on agency (Archer, 2000). For all Archer's references to structural conditioning of agency rather than structural determination, an impression is given of a rather mechanical relation of structure (including positional interests) to agency and to social activities. Third, and closely related to the points just made, Archer's concept of positional interests does not give sufficient emphasis to the *relational* – as distinct from systemic – dimension of social activity, power, and interests. It is not necessarily incompatible with the idea of positional interests to recognize that interests and their formulation by actors are very often multiple, viscous and emergent. For one thing, actors usually have a range of differing role involvements and, more often than not, they are involved in multiple networks of social relations such that their positional interests in one network may conflict with their positional interests in another; in the real world, social activity is often bound up with cross-cutting, conflicting or contradictory sets of positional interests. Also, and leaving aside for a moment the question of actors' cross-cutting social locations and conflicting positional interests, there is in general a good case for suggesting that interests, like power, nearly always have a relational component. In politico-administrative systems, for example, interests are not only partly relational, fluid and emergent; they may also become less demarcated. A case in point is the blurring of the state–civil society distinction arising from interaction, negotiation and compromise among state and non-state actors who are joint participants in policy networks (M.J. Smith, 1993: 11): 'Interests are not predetermined but develop within the context of social and economic arrangements between groups and state actors. Therefore, both the interests of the state and of groups develop within the context of networks. Often, they cannot be clearly defined as state interests or group interests.' There are grounds for suggesting that positional interests sometimes blur as a result of negotiation, adjustment and compromise, and in some situations it is difficult to say precisely whose or which positional interests are being put into effect (indeed, it is consistent with Archer's general theoretical framework to suppose that, in some scenarios, negotiated outcomes mean that no-one's positional interests are satisfied); it is often the case that what an actor (for example, a political or policy actor) will want to do, be able to do, and decide to do (these are three separate things) are at least partly fluid and emergent during processes of interaction in a range of settings. Notice, also, that an approach to the study of relational aspects of (positional) interests can usefully draw upon 'translation sociology', which emphasizes strategic agency and processes by which actors 'enrol' or 'translate' other actors. In translation sociology – which by the late 1990s was more commonly described as actor network theory (Law and Hassard, 1999) – power, interests, intentions, social conditions, and relationships are seen as strategically and relationally constituted. For example, getting other actors (individual as well as social actors) to want what the strategic actor wants them to want, is a process of *enrolment* through which other actors' 'positions, desires, what they will want ... is channelled' (Callon and Latour, 1981: 289). Enrolment is a process that figures strongly in Callon's (1986; 1991) translation sociology and in Foucauldian theorizing on governmentality (Miller and Rose, 1988; 1993; Rose and Miller, 1992). A policy-related manifestation of the process of enrolment (or 'translation') is when a strategic actor gets a range of other actors to commit financial and other resources to a particular programme: once this happens, the resultant network of actors have been 'translated' in that they themselves come to have a vested ('positional') interest in the continuation (and perhaps the expansion) of the programme to which they have committed themselves. It is in this and other ways that new networks of power, interests, and social relations are constituted and 'consigned' (institutionalized), sometimes by chance or through unexpected shifts and unplanned alignments in social relations and in the relevant conditions of action, and sometimes intentionally and strategically.

To criticize those who neglect or underemphasize the shifting, relational face of power, interests, and social activity, need not, of course, be an attempt to downgrade the significance of the systemic dimension of the social. A central ontological postulate developed in earlier chapters is that structure (social contexts/or the 'conditions-of-action') and social action, are relatively autonomous: there typically is an indirect, loosely dialectical ('two-way') relation between pre-existing social contexts (including positional interests attached to positions/roles, group memberships, or sometimes to particular social situations) on the one hand, and social action on the other. (A useful version of this (meta)theoretical postulate is Layder's (1997) conception of social reality comprised of subjective domains (psychobiography and situated activity) and objective domains (social settings and contextual resources); the four domains are relatively autonomous – none of them wholly determines the others, and each has distinct properties and effects of its own – but, although relatively independent, they in a more or less loose fashion interpenetrate and influence each other). Viewed in these terms, which rest upon a dualism, not duality, of structure and action, it is possible to avoid unresolved problems associated with, for example, Giddens's concept of 'unacknowledged interests' (Giddens, 1984: 198–9, 318, 342; Cohen, 1989: 198–9). Difficulties associated with explicit or tacit use of reductionist, essentialist, and teleological notions of 'real' ('objective') interests, are circumvented. In sum, it is legitimate to argue, in systemic terms, that 'objective' 'positional' interests are attached to positions/roles, group memberships, and to certain social situations or contexts. Positional interests condition, but do not determine social action. Objective positional interests, it was noted earlier, may be shifting, multiple, and conflicting or contradictory, but even where they are not, there is nearly always some leeway for actors to interpret and act upon positional interests in a variety of ways, or to act in ways that are contrary to particular sets of positional interests. Configurations of social involvements and positional interests are usually not clear-cut in so far as, for example, we sometimes have to forsake one set of possible interests or rewards in order to satisfy a different set of interests, needs, or desires. The conception of interests that is proposed in this chapter is, as stated previously, a part of a wider social onto-logy. There is no 'direct link' between structure and action, but there is a loosely dialectical link. That is, there is a mutually influencing relation between pre-existing social structure (including positional interests), activi-ties, and the subsequent reproduction or elaboration of structure, and there-fore, of positional interests. In effect, what we have here is a manifestation of a more general ontological mechanism whereby agency spirals into and out of social contexts which indirectly condition and are indirectly condi-tioned by agency; in the process, patterns of agency as well as the shape of social contexts (including systemic elements of power, social action, and interests) are reproduced or elaborated.

Summary

This chapter amplified in some detail a number of previous observations con-cerning agency–structure and micro–macro, and also broadened the scope of the earlier analysis by looking at the idea of 'social chance' and by critically examining notions of 'power' and 'interests'.

Agency and social action

A non-reified and 'minimal' definition of actor, associated with an under-standing that agency refers to a conditioned though not structurally deter-mined capacity to formulate, take, and act upon decisions, applies to individual human actors – and also to social ('organizational') actors as enti-ties that have a capacity to exercise a form of agency that is emergent and not reducible to the attributes and actions of individuals. Reification, as well as the other 'cardinal sins', continues to affect many fields of social analysis. An anti-reified conception of social action is important in, for example, analysis of governance and politics and studies of the policy process.

•

Social structure, though often said to be a key concept in sociology and social theory, tends – like agency – to be a 'received notion': uses of the term are highly variable and very often ambiguous. In the (meta)theoretical framework that informs this book, an explicitly 'minimal' and ontologically flexible definition of structure is employed: it is argued that social structure refers to the temporally enduring or temporally and spatially extensive conditions-of-action (whether enabling or constraining) within which actors operate; that structure exists at relatively autonomous levels (micro, mezo and macro) of social process, each requiring investigation in terms that avoid upwards or downwards conflation; and that the relation of structure to action is, as argued earlier, a dualism and not a duality.

Social chance

There has been a tendency among social scientists to treat 'social chance' as a residual analytical category, and to assume that chance outcomes are only apparent chance rather than instances of real chance. Social chance is unforeseen fortuitous conjunctions of causally unrelated phenomena, including conjunctions of action (whether intersubjective or non-intersubjective) and of sequences of action.

●

It is meaningful to speak of agency causation, structural causation, and chance causation. Social life is the outcome of an interplay over time between agency, structure, and social chance; each of these elements influences the others, this being a dialectic that may be found at micro-, mezo- or macro-levels of the social; the question of which element – agency, structure, or chance – has the greater significance within any particular spatio-temporal context is a matter for empirical investigation, and not something that can be theoretically predetermined in advance of empirical enquiry.

Power

The (meta)theoretical precepts developed in earlier chapters lead to a view that power exists in more than one form; in particular, there are objective structural (including systemic) forms of power, and agentic power, a term which I use to refer to the partly systemic and partly relational and potentially variable capacity of agents to shape events in a preferred direction.

●

Weber's work on power has heuristic analytical value, as does Lukes's well-known typology that describes 'three dimensions of power'. Foucauldian writing is somewhat ambiguous and contradictory, although much of Foucault's work may – with a certain amount of re-working based on critique of the four 'cardinal sins' – be regarded as a helpful contribution to our understanding of some of the dynamics of power. A major criticism, however, centres on Foucault's tendency to over-emphasize relational dimensions at the expense of the systemic: power is often partly relational, but also partly systemic in so far as power may be 'stored' in social systems, positions/ roles and social institutions, and these forms of power may interrelate in various ways.

•

The topic of 'interests' is associated with debates about the nature of power. The notion of 'real' ('objective') interests has tended to be deployed in ways that rest upon reductionist, essentialist, reified, and teleological theories. However, there are empirically contingent connections between agency, interests, and aspects of social structure (including positions/roles and social settings or situations); in order to explore such connections, there are good reasons for employing a modified version of Archer's concept of 'positional interests'.

Notes

1 Recent interest in aspects of agency, subjectivity and the body (or embodiment) is to be welcomed: see, for example, the work of Archer (2000), McNay (2000), Elliott (2001) and Pettit (2001). My own approach to agency differs from the work of these writers in three main respects. First, I employ a tightly drawn, explicitly non-reified and 'minimal' concept of actor that borrows from Hindess and Harré. Second, I argue that as well as individual human actors, there are social ('organizational') actors and that the idea that there are social actors does not entail reification. Third, and more generally, my approach to agency and subjectivity is influenced by the concepts and postulates developed in this book with reference to, in particular, agency–structure, social chance, micro–macro, and time–space.

2 A concern with the question of causal responsibility for social outcomes – a responsibility that, I have argued, cannot legitimately be laid at the door of such entities as social movements, social classes, natural phenomena or machines, taxonomic collectivities such as 'men', or analytical categories such as 'global capitalism' – is implicit in many discussions of 'the risk society'. Consider the British experience, in the period after 1996, of BSE ('Mad Cow Disease') and its devastating effects on human victims (a scenario for which farmers, veterinary science and practice, the British government, abattoir managers and employees, meat wholesalers and the European Union have respectively been 'blamed'); and the *Exxon Valdez* oil spill – which led to a dispute over whether causal responsibility for the event lay primarily with the captain of the ship, the oil company, or with governments that failed to establish proper 'clean-up' measures for minimizing the environmental effects of maritime oil spillages (see Ungar, 2001: 281–2).

The question of whether any particular *individual* human actors can reasonably be held responsible for their actions and for outcomes of action is, of course, central to many legal processes and to the workings of criminal justice and also welfare systems. In terms of legal responsibility, the issue of whether *social* ('organizational') actors can be said to have responsibility for outcomes was raised in debate, which came to the fore in Britain in 2001, surrounding the question of 'corporate responsibility' for rail crashes and derailments which resulted in a number of deaths during 2000–1.

3 A separate matter which should not be overlooked is whether computers or computer systems are actors in the sense that I employ the term to refer to entities that, in principle, are capable of formulating, taking and acting upon decisions. For example, inside many aircraft there are 'automatic pilots', and in all major airports air traffic control systems are computerized. In the field of medicine, software is available for assisting in the diagnosis of illness. Industrial application of robotics, in car manufacturing, for example, is highly advanced. And so on. In each of these cases, however, computerized decision-making and manipulation of the environment are dependent on hardware that is made and maintained by humans, and upon software where the data employed in electronic decision-making is ultimately 'bounded' by parameters that are determined and monitored by human programmers. In terms of the machine calculations done by computers and their capacity to 'act' upon the world there are, then, significant differences between (a) computerized systems; and (b) the concept of agency exercised by individual and social actors in the sense that I employ these terms. This is not to deny the possibility that advances in computing hardware, software and bio-engineering might in future prompt some revision of the anti-reified conception of actor (agent) to which I have just referred.

There is a related matter to consider. Actors may, of course, employ forms of thought that in part rely upon electronically processed data. However, such data – which in effect are a form of discourse available to actors – should be regarded as an element of structure/the conditions-of-action, rather than as a form of agency. Moreover, in real life the forms of thought that actors employ are highly diverse – they rarely come from one source only, such as electronic data – and they tend to combine and overlap.

4 Mouzelis makes reference to 'macro' actors (1991: 48, 107), a term he uses interchangeably with what he calls 'collective' actors (ibid.: 48, 57). According to Mouzelis (ibid.: 47, 77, 107), collective actors may be organizations but also powerful individuals such as religious or political leaders; elsewhere (ibid.: 78, 107) he refers to these as 'mega' actors. He also suggests, in a move that slides towards reification, that social movements are macro-actors (1993a: 677).

This is a confusing terminology that is underscored by Mouzelis's claim that 'weak' individual actors (for example, shopfloor workers in a factory) are micro-actors and that 'strong' or powerful individuals (for example, top executives) are 'macro' actors (Mouzelis 1991: 45). For reasons discussed in the earlier chapters I suggest it is better to employ the concepts micro and macro in terms that, contextualized by critique of the four 'cardinal sins', are broadly consistent with their conventional usage in the social sciences. Terminological confusion, this time accompanied by theoretical contradiction, also arises when, having previously said that organizations *are* ('macro') actors (or 'collective' or 'mega' actors; see above), Mouzelis (1991: 97) claims that organizations are *not* actors: he says, wrongly so in my view, that organizations are not entities that can formulate goals and that to suppose that they can is to engage in reification; for Mouzelis (ibid.: 97) organizations are 'not … supra-individual entities, but configurations … [of] … interacting individuals'. While I agree with Mouzelis (1991: 33) – and with Giddens (1993: 7) – that it is erroneous to conflate micro with agency and macro with structure, I cannot go along with Mouzelis's curious notion that 'face-to-face interactions do not necessarily entail micro-processes' (1991: 33) nor his confusing terminology whereby 'weak' actors are said to be micro-actors and 'powerful' ones are described as macro-actors. Apart from the points I have just made (and see the discussion of Mouzelis in Chapter 4), it should also be observed that Mouzelis has a hierarchical and rather mechanical conception of power (see 1991: 75, 83, 90–1, 168): it can be argued that actors' 'power' tends in part to be an emergent, relational phenomenon that arises out of interaction; power is not exclusively a 'given' attribute of particular actors or of institutional arrangements or hierarchies (see the discussion of power in the present chapter).

5 Here it is worth clarifying one aspect of non-agency that relates to the distinction between individual human actors, and social actors (for example, committees and other micro-groups such as households, and organizations). Taxonomic collectivities (Harré, 1981: 139, 140, 147–8) such as social classes or 'women', are not actors – they do not, in principle, have access to means of formulating, taking and acting upon decisions. Implicit in the arguments set out in this and the earlier chapters is an understanding that an individual's membership of a taxonomic collectivity such as 'black people', 'white people', 'the middle class', and so on, does not determine the forms of thought and actions of that actor nor of any other individual members of the collectivity in question. With regard to membership of a taxonomic collectivity, no-one can be a member of only one. Moreover, the salience of any particular membership for an individual tends to vary situationally and over time. It is undoubtedly true that collectivity membership may sometimes predispose some actors to think and act in particular ways or to formulate a sense of having particular interests; but any such predispositions, if and when they occur, are not structurally predetermined; rather, they are structurally 'conditioned'. This relates to the concept 'positional interests', which is discussed later in the chapter.

6 Unlike Law (1994: 58–60), whose theoretical framework is a mixture of structuralism and poststructuralism, I consider it necessary to formulate a clear analytical distinction between agency/non-agency and agency and structure. Law incorrectly assumes that the agency–structure distinction is redundant by virtue of agency being empirically variable, contingent, and relational. Agency does indeed often exhibit these characteristics, but this is all the more reason for having a clear analytical distinction between agency and structure. And unlike Lewis (2002), though I am grateful for his appreciative analysis of my approach to agency–structure, I am inclined to qualify the claim – by critical realists and others – that structure can be said to have causal powers: my argument is that structure cannot be said to exhibit agency since structure has no *intentional* causal powers, but nowhere do I argue that structure can not be causally efficacious in the sense of conditioning agency and social action. Indeed, as noted later in the chapter, we can legitimately go so far as to speak of structural causation (alongside agency causation and chance causation), but this is not to say structure is or can be an agent with intentional causal powers.

It should also be observed that it is not being suggested in this chapter that the concept actor (and hence, agency) always has empirically clear-cut referents. Let me give an example. The status of actor may be *intermittent*. For instance, Pahl and Wallace (1985) assume households are capable of developing strategies (they have in mind household work strategies in relation to the labour market). Notice that this presumes households are actors. Sometimes a household undoubtedly will be an actor in the terms described earlier. But if for whatever reason – for example, the development of major conflict among family members – a particular household at some point in time happens to lose the means of collectively formulating, taking, and acting upon decisions, then that household will cease to be a social actor (or a a 'supra-individual' in Harré's terminology); this state of affairs may be permanent – or it may be that the members get together again, in which case the household once more becomes a social actor. A more macro-example of intermittent actor status, relates to governance and the policy process. Mayntz is interested in

> policy areas that are structured as "aree di movimento" (in the termino-logy of Melucci, 1984), i.e. extensive networks consisting of some institu-tions (such as service centres), small informal groups and loose interweavings of personal acquaintances fostered by meeting in certain places. Such networks oscillate between latency and activism and they will organize themselves to become collective actors only occasionally and will fall apart again afterwards. (1993: 19)

Here Mayntz makes a significant observation concerning the intermittent nature of agency and of the status of actor, albeit at the cost of skirting close to reification (in her paper she ignores that not all networks are actors).

Law's (1994) dismissal of the agency–structure distinction, referred to above, is entirely misconceived. It is precisely the empirical complexity of agency, and some-times, its intermittency, that highlights the importance of employing an unambigu-ous and non-reified concept of actor, and of having a clear analytical distinction between actor/agency and structure.

7 The conception of agency outlined here is not a form of epistemological ideal-ism nor an attempt to exaggerate the significance of agency at the expense of struc-ture. This relates to three ontological propositions that underscore the arguments set out in this and earlier chapters. First, when actors formulate reasons for action, they do so in terms of the discourses available to them (Hindess, 1986a), and discourses, it may be noted, are elements of structure that are differentially distributed: some discourses may be unavailable to some actors; it is simply not the case that actors can change at will the discourses that they employ (differential distributions of dis-courses across social contexts and positions, processes of socialization and internali-zation, as well as strategic factors and 'opportunity costs' tend to mitigate against any such possibility). Second, both the formulation and the implementation of any par-ticular line of action are in general conditioned not only by discourses but by many other elements of the social conditions/conditions-of-action ('social structure') in which actors are involved. Third, the concept 'unintended consequences' is an indi-cation that actors' definitions of the situation are not always successfully imposed upon the world to 'become' social structure. Society, as Elias, Archer and many others have observed, is the unintended, unplanned outcome of countless decisions and actions: or more precisely, society is the outcome of dialectical links between agency, structure and social chance, links which unfold diachronically (that is, over time).

8 *Reification* is strongly evident in recent work, influenced by semiotics and cultural studies, pertaining to what has come to be called the '*materialization of agency*'. For instance, Cooper (2001: 25–6) defines agency as a set of *relations* between people and physical objects such as spoons, cups, chairs, cars, roads, and bridges. Theorizing of this sort can have no useful part to play in social analysis, since it is a form of theorizing

that mystifies agency and structure, and obscures the possibility of investigating their interrelation. In similar vein to Cooper, Rose (2001), having lauded Latour's studies of science, argues that 'agency ... [is] ... the ability of all things in the Universe to act and more importantly to interact and to influence each other' (2001: 46). Even atomic nuclei are said to be agents, and 'There are as many agencies as there are objects' (ibid.: 51). This form of reification leads Rose to the view (a bizarre one, in my opinion) that not only people but also physical objects have agential powers and that they therefore may be held to be 'guilty' if these powers lead to noxious outcomes. He writes that 'objects as active agents are coming under increasing judicial scrutiny and litigation often with such legal individuals as corporations as co-defendants (*sic*!): Prozac (a serotonin re-uptake inhibitor), silicon (breast implants), autos (that explode or burn on impact).' My argument is not that nature and physical objects are somehow unimportant or that they are not interwoven with social life, but rather, that they are part of the conditions-of-action (structure) and not a form of agency: nature and physical objects condition agency, but are not themselves agency.

9 Lopez and Scott (2000) distinguish three dimensions of structure (institutional, relational, and embodied) that are relatively though not totally independent of each other. Their thesis is that which of these predominates is, in principle, something that may vary from one situation to another – no single dimension of structure has universal or automatic primacy. *Institutional* structure, which was given special emphasis in Talcott Parsons's structural-functional perspective, consists of cultural/normative patterns (including social institutions) that shape positions/roles, actors' forms of thought, and social relations. In Lopez and Scott's classification, *relational* structure, a notion that features in the writings of, for example, Simmel, Elias, and Radcliffe-Brown, consists of 'actual' social relations, including interdependencies among actors, and positional or 'role' performances. Here, it is worth noting, the authors make reference to a particular conception of 'actual' that excludes idiosyncrasies in individuals' behaviour and that instead employs inferences abstracted from general types of relationships such as mother–daughter or employer–employee (in contrast, in my approach the term 'actual' social relations includes strandardized or recurrent activities and relations, but also idiosyncratic relations and practices). *Embodied* structure, a concept which Lopez and Scott ascribe to Giddens, Foucault, and Bourdieu, is bound up with a view that structure both shapes activity and is activity-dependent; bearing in mind the two other dimensions of structure, embodied structure refers to an understanding that 'relational and institutional structures are grounded in the situated responses that people make on the basis of the knowledge available to them' (Lopez and Scott, 2000: 90).

10 Lopez and Scott observe that the concept 'structure' has, in general, been treated by sociologists in cursory fashion:

> Social structure has always been one of the central concepts in sociological theory and analysis. Indeed, it has now become something of a commonplace to see the major disputes of contemporary sociology as organized around the dualism of 'structure' and 'action' ... [but] social structure is usually treated as a taken-for-granted concept that is not in need of any explicit definition or discussion. Actual uses of the concept ... are strikingly nebulous and diverse ... it is all too easy for sociologists to be talking at cross-purposes because they rely on different, and generally implicit, conceptions of social structure ... This [is a] peculiar situation – one of the discipline's central concepts is so misunderstood. (2000: 1)

In sociology and other social sciences there has been a tendency to tacitly presume that structure is a recurring pattern among the elements that constitute social wholes. Any such vague use of the term, as Lopez and Scott note, leaves too many questions unanswered – we are not told what the elements are (for example, are they people, roles, or social institutions?), nor what the expression 'pattern' actually means (is it recurrent behaviour?; is it 'on the surface' or a 'deep' phenomenon hidden from the view of participants?); nor are we told what the mechanisms are by which the pattern is reproduced across time and space.

I should like to make a couple of additional observations. First, conventional uses of the term structure as recurrent pattern are in some respects closer to my conception of social system than to my concept of social structure. Second, for the reasons given in this chapter, the minimal concept of structure that I employ as part of a flexible social ontology is – though relatively empirically 'open-ended' – not vague or unspecific in the sense referred to by Lopez and Scott: my minimal concept of structure refers to more or less enduring conditions-of-action at macro- and/or micro-levels of social process; the concept is *intended* to be ontologically and therefore empirically relatively malleable and 'open', and rather than being employed in a tacit, untheorized kind of way, is formulated on the basis of systematic critique and explicit (meta)theoretical reasoning.

11 Although Weber's understanding of social chance is somewhat ambiguously stated by him, he was clearly aware – as in his substantive work on the rise of capitalism – of the significance of conjunctural interactions. Weber's conception of social chance is described by Kalberg (1994a: 576–7) in these terms: 'At times kaleidoscopic alterations take place that lead to a dynamic fusing of heretofore separately unfolding patterns of action-orientations. Often fully unforeseen events are called forth.'

12 This is not to say each of these authors has an entirely satisfactory approach to the idea of social chance. Giddens (1984), for example, despite his numerous formal statements about actors' creativity and the significance of conjunctions of events, unintended consequences and contingency, tends to speak of large time–space processes in a way that – even though he makes protestations to the contrary – seems deterministic and evolutionary (see Stones, 1996: 110–15). In Foucault's case, as observed in Chapter 3, some parts of his work hint at contingency and time–space variability, but other parts have holistic and deterministic overtones.

13 Postmodern conceptions of power are frequently bound up with arguments surrounding the idea of 'resistance' or 'oppositional politics'. As noted in Chapter 1, postmodernists such as Lyotard (1986) display incredulity towards the 'grand narratives' – such as liberalism or Marxism – associated with modernity. Habermas (1981) in an early essay on postmodernism concluded that postmodern thought entails conservative politics. This is refuted by some postmodernists, including Lyotard, who argue that a postmodern politics of resistance – associated with critical reflection that is not based on a single, holistic metanarrative – is possible; such politics would reflect the multiple, fragmented, and cross-cutting affiliations, differences, and allegiances that characterize the postmodern condition. Postmodern and poststructuralist theorists' emphasis on the indeterminacy of meanings is a factor in, for example, Laclau and Mouffe's (1985; 1987) argument that what some call 'postmodern politics' – a struggle over definitions and meaning – is likely to become increasingly important. Postmodern theorists' scepticism towards attempts to unify society around some large-scale plan or blueprint – in highly diverse postmodern

society, attempts by a centralized state to impose unity and order will lead, in Lyotard's view, to totalitarianism – is echoed in Fox and Miller's (1995) text on 'postmodern public administration'; the argument here is that any political or policy-related contracts or consensus must be 'local' and provisional. Postmodern theorists' emphasis on diversity and anti-essentialism is, though many aspects of postmodern epistemology and ontology are questionable (see Chapter 1), in certain respects congruent with features of contemporary politico-administrative processes. There is, for example, a resonance between aspects of postmodern theory and recent conceptual and empirical work on governance (Pierre and Peters, 2000; Sibeon, 2000; Hay, 2002).

However, aside from the general criticisms made of postmodern theory in Chapter 1, there is a strand in postmodern politics of emancipation that should be explicitly resisted. In my opinion, we should be highly sceptical of postmodern emancipatory claims which suppose that 'it is politics rather than knowledge which is of concern' (Yeatman, 1994: 106) or that 'strategic essentialism' is justified (see the Introduction, note 5), or which endorse Seidman's (1992: 60) postmodern strategic anti-essentialism (this is discussed in Chapter 1, note 3).

14 Foucauldianism and relationalism are not, of course, synonymous, since relational dimensions of the social are recognized in a variety of theoretical approaches. For example, a policy-related and empirically documented political science endorsement of the idea that power distributions as well as actors' formulation of their interests are in part a shifting outcome of social relations and interaction in policy networks, is developed in an excellent book by M.J. Smith (1993).

15 There is a sense in which Foucault moves beyond relationism and acknowlededges, to some degree, the existence of an 'objective' dimension of power and power storage – that is, his notion of power as an effect of discourse implies power is secreted or 'held' within discourses, and to this extent he moves some way towards the synthetic approach to power that I advocate. However, problems remain. Foucault's approach, on the one hand, is not sufficiently systems-oriented (he has very little to say about the objective aspects of social systems), but on the other, he is not sufficiently agency-oriented. Concerning the latter, his later work, in attempting to redress the neglect of agency in his earlier writings, refers to individual actors in a way that fails to incorporate an explicitly non-reified definition of actor, and which acknowledges subjectivity but ignores intersubjectivity as a crucial mediating factor in the relation of individual agency to structure; see Best and Keller (1991: 66) and Layder (1994: 110–13).

16 See note 13 above.

6

Spatial Dimensions of the Social

A central theme in the previous chapters has been that substantive theories and explanatory schemes unavoidably employ metatheoretical constructs and ontological assumptions concerning agency–structure, social chance, and micro–macro, and that any such constructs should therefore be defined and employed explicitly, rather than tacitly or unreflectively. The intention in the following pages is to develop a linked set of (meta)theoretical concepts and postulates which refer to dimensions of the social that in previous chapters were touched upon only briefly and indirectly. In terms that continue to draw upon critique of the four deficient forms of theoretical-methodological reasoning that were identified in the Introduction, it is intended to focus on social space (and to a lesser extent, time) and upon a set of related conceptualizations that refer to social networks/social systems, 'materials', and material-diffusion.

Time–space: a note on the temporal dimension

Comparatively slow progress has been made by social scientists in developing meta-conceptualizations relating to a post-postmodern ontology of time–space. The most that can be attempted within the confines of this chapter is an abridged account of some of the implications of 'time' and 'space' for current efforts to renew sociological theory. Since the bulk of the chapter will refer to social space – a dimension of social reality that, arguably, has been even more neglected by social theorists than time (Soja, 1989) – it is appropriate to first acknowledge the *temporal* properties of social life. Time is multifaceted and it has been observed, for example by Adam (1990; 1995) that there exist heterogeneous temporalities, each of which merit scrutiny by social theorists. Such scrutiny, incidentally, can have important empirical and practical applications; for example, Greca's (2000) study of disparate organizational time-codes refers to the governance of inter-organizational relations.[1] Among the classical theorists it is probably Durkheim who is most closely associated with theoretical work on time. Durkheim (1965) argued that time is not given by nature.[2] Nor, for Durkheim is time something that is fashioned by individuals. Rather, time is 'social time', that is, an objective, abstract, and general category – a social institution – that is to be found at the level of society itself; therefore, the meaning of time may vary from one society to another. Elias (1984), for example, argued that time is not a universal, uniform flow that is extra-social, but is, rather, something that differs from culture to culture. The cultural relativity of time – as distinct from a view of time as an unvarying, non-social and 'natural essence' – may be illustrated (see Urry, 1995: 4–5) in terms of, on the one hand, Weber's (1932: 158) reference to the Protestant ethic as a system of thought that decries idleness and frivolous pursuits that 'waste' time, and on the other, Evans-Pritchard's (1940) anthropological account of the Nuer people who have no concept of time as something that can be 'wasted' or 'saved' and who conceive of time as something that is inextricably bound up with ecological cycles. In the type of society that Weber had in mind, that is, modern industrial society, it is 'clock-time' – a concept of an abstract, objective, and divisible measurement of something called time – that tends to predominate; indeed, as Simmel observed (see Urry, 2000a: 417), modern urban life would be inconceivable without the temporal integration of activities afforded by impersonal, general temporality built around clock-time.

In modern sociology, temporality is a variable factor among competing paradigms. As Clegg (1989: 212) remarks: 'Different theoretical perspectives diverge on the temporality within which the conceptualization of action is conceived.' The two most obviously contrasting examples are ethnomethodology, which focuses on the immediate temporal context of action, and institutional analysis which investigates processes that may stretch across decades or perhaps centuries (ibid.). As should be evident from the earlier chapters, the approach adopted in this book focuses upon the *durée* of day-to-day life as well as the *longue durée*, these being regarded as interconnected time-frames rather than as entirely separated entities. But *how* these differing time-frames relate to each other is a controversial matter that is bound up with the debate – discussed in Chapters 2 and 3 – of a duality versus dualism of structure and action. Cohen (1989: 77) observes:

> If social patterns are embedded in the reality of social activity, then a concern for time and space becomes difficult to avoid. Social conduct, after all, is always situated in specific settings, and it takes time to engage even in the most fleeting practices, let alone sustained sequences and series of interactions.

The context of Cohen's remark is his account of structuration theory and Giddens's concept of a duality of structure. In Giddens's theoretical framework, structure and agency are, so to speak, manifested instantaneously, within the moment of instantiation and each successive moment of instantiation (a similar, 'duality' conception of a simultaneity of structure and action is also to be found in the work of Bourdieu). In contrast, as observed in Chapter 4, Archer's (1995) commitment to dualism insists on a temporal separation between structure and action (structure precedes and conditions action, which in turn reproduces or elaborates structure).

Layder's theory of social domains, which was discussed in Chapter 4 where it was suggested his theoretical framework has considerable merit, makes explicit reference to temporality. His approach to temporality is in my opinion a potentially highly fruitful one that merits closer attention than has been accorded to it by contemporary writers. Two of the domains identified by Layder – psychobiography and situated activity – constitute the subjective dimension of society, with two others (social settings, and contextual resources) comprising the objective dimension. Layder (1997: 2) observes: 'The domains are related to each other not only as "layers" of social life within the same time unit, but also as stretched-out over time and space.' Interconnections of objective and subjective aspects of reality, and of agency and structure, are complex conjunctions of time–space where the relatively short time-frames of face-to-face activity (situated activity) meet the extended time-frames of long-standing institutional conditions that extend from the past into the present; here, it is worth emphasizing, there is a temporal separation of structure and action and it is Layder's commitment to a dualism (not duality) of structure and action that underpins his understanding of conjunctions of 'long' and 'short' time-frames (Layder, 1998b: 88). Layder argues (1997: 248) that phenomenology, symbolic interactionism, and structuration theory obscure complexities surrounding time, since theories which focus almost exclusively on an ontology of 'being and doing' give an exaggerated emphasis to the continuous production and reproduction of society via activity or 'instantiation', and thereby conflate and obscure the intersection of two quite different time-frames (institutional time, and the time-frame of situated activities); therefore in Layder's theoretical scheme, these time-frames are seen as melding together though without there being any decomposition of their distinct but interconnected properties.

Theoretical and empirical aspects of the idea of spatiality

Soja (1989), a social geographer, argues that social science academics have concentrated more on time than space. Soja's claim has some substance. It can, I think, be legitimately argued that in the social sciences spatiality (Agnew et al., 1996; Benko and Strohmayer, 1997; Peet, 1998) has been even more neglected than temporality – or at least, it is the case that much theoretical and empirical attention has been given to the study of social change and social stability and to temporal continuities and/or discontinuities in the form taken by social phenomena, and to the more general idea of history as an unfolding over time of concrete events or of social trends or patterns. The neglect of spatiality in sociology has not gone unnoticed, and it has been observed by some that Simmelian-type interests in social space have declined over a period of years (Frisby, 1992: 98–117). As Harrison White (1992: 130) put it, 'social science has shied away from locality', causing Dickens (1990: 2) to re-assert the importance of spatiality: 'there ... [should not] ... be any aspatial sociology'. It should, however, be acknowledged that there has been a certain amount of relatively recent interest in aspects of spatiality. First, in the recent past a re-appraisal of the significance of locale, contingency, and spatial variation has taken place in the field of historical sociology and in studies of social change: this is evident in, for example, the writing of Abrams (1982), Boudon (1986), Mann (1986), Unger (1987a; 1997), and Sztompka (1991; 1993). Second, in the period from the mid-1980s in British sociology there has been a certain amount of renewed interest in community studies (this is noted in Bulmer, 1985; 1986), and in efforts to make connections between community studies conceptualizations and theoretical constructions of the idea of place (Duncan, 1989; Day and Murdoch, 1993). Third, in policy-related empirical work there has in the past few years been increasing awareness of not only national variations (Bryant and Makrzycki, 1994) but also regional and local variations in responses to trans-national and to some extent global economic, political and social change (Cooke, 1989; Harloe et al., 1990; Urry, 1995). The idea of public policy diversity across localities is illustrated by, for instance, Gyford (1991: 32–4) with reference to local government, and in Meethan and Thompson's (1993) study of spatial variation in community care policy. As in sociology, there is in political science some evidence of recent interest in spatiality with particular reference to governance and the policy process. Among political scientists there are, for example, signs of increased attention being given to data which indicate that national (and transnational) socio-economic and political patterns of change have not impacted upon localities in a uniform way. This is an important theme in Duncan and Goodwin's (1988) *The Local State and*

Uneven Development. The authors comment: 'Post-war consensus, constructed around a fairly uniform geography as well as a uniform society, has given way to diversity and disjuncture. Places, as well as people and social groups, have become less alike and there is a greater disparity between various parts of the country' (1988: 275–6). Fourth, postmodern thought emphasizes the idea of spatial variation. However, it will be clear from the critique set out in Chapter 1 that no support is given here to postmodern 'reassertion' of space over time (Lash and Friedman, 1992: 10); the so-called postmodern 'privileging' of spatiality over temporality (1992: 1–2) seems to erroneously assume that a concern with spatiality is synonymous with ('postmodern') discontinuity and supposedly unconnected 'local narratives'. A more adequate approach to these matters would regard questions relating to continuities/ discontinuities across space (and time) as empirical matters that require investigation. Fifth and as will be briefly noted in the following section of the chapter, Foucauldian studies of governance and networks incorporate a focus on spatial dimensions of the social. Finally, there has been a growth of interest in spatial aspects of the ways in which global and local phenomena intersect (Smith, M.P., 2001). Of importance here is the need to avoid either-or dichotomies that in a priori fashion emphasize localism and heterogeneity *or* globalism and homogenizing tendencies; for reasons that will become apparent in this and the following chapter, the social is not reducible to either of these reductionisms.

Some of the credit for bringing the idea of spatiality (and time–space) into sociology and social theory, must undoubtedly go to Giddens. Some years ago he had argued (1979: 201): 'At first sight nothing seems more banal and uninstructive than to assert that social activity occurs in time and space. But neither time nor space has been incorporated into the centre of social theory.' Giddens's (1984: 376) emphasis on locales and their interconnections is part of the theory of structuration, in terms of which social action is viewed as 'the structuring of social relations across time and space'. His references to, in his terminology, locales (ibid.: 375), regionalization (ibid.: 376), system and time–space distanciation (ibid.: 377) refer to an *intertwining* of physical and social dimensions of reality, and as Harrison White (1992: 130) observes, 'To meld social with geographic concepts is very hard ... Localities are intersections between physical space and social networks.' Bearing in mind the discussion of micro–macro in Chapter 2 and the associated idea that each level of social process has relative autonomy, locale can in some sense be thought of as a *bridging concept* that spans micro-, mezo- and macro-dimensions of the social. Sites, or settings as many sociologists prefer to call them, are particular time–space locations of face-to-face interaction (situations of co-presence, in Giddens's language). This means that, for example, the medical training school that currently exists at a particular university is, for analytical purposes, a site or setting but 'medical training' is not. A somewhat similar point is made by Lave in her study of the practices of shoppers. Lave (1986) defines supermarkets (plural) as an *arena*, that is, a general type or category of institutional setting. In Lave's terminology, a setting (a supermarket) is a singular, actually experienced place, as distinct from an arena (supermarkets) which is an institutional category ('a type of place'). Shoppers can walk into a setting (a supermarket) and directly experience it: they cannot do this in respect of the arena, because the arena consists of many places (supermarkets) scattered through time and space. To anticipate a point that will be developed more fully in the next chapter, sites and arenas are linked in various ways, and this has important methodological implications. To study only an arena as an institutional category (for example, 'medical training') without making some reference to data that describe the internal, relatively autonomous properties of at least some relevant local sites, is to run the danger of failing to check empirically for the existence of possible situational specificity within particular sites (for example, within particular medical schools). Because no structural predetermination is involved, some local events may be relatively site-specific, or be part of empirically significant patterns of variation across sites within the particular institutional sphere ('arena') in question. Conversely, as the following chapter will demonstrate in methodological terms, an exclusive preoccupation with micro-situational analysis is too narrow an approach, by virtue of its failure to analyze emergent properties of time–space links *across* sites and the relationship(s) of sites to arenas and to wider (macro) social, economic and political conditions that stretch spatially and temporally away from any particular sites, agents, or activities.

Networks, materials and material diffusion

A number of theorists and researchers, including Scott (1988: 109) have argued that network analysis should be regarded not as a specialized technique or sub-field of sociology, but rather, as sociology's theoretical and methodological foundation stone: 'the roots of ... [network analysis] ... are as old as sociology itself. This perspective, centred on the image of the intertwining of social relations, offers not so much a specialized method as a formulation of the fundamental concepts of the sociological enterprise.' Network analysis, Scott observes (ibid.), is concerned with links between actors: the intersection of chains of action and their consequences; and the emergent structural properties of networks of social relations. A concern with networks raises a number of important ontological questions; some of these are examined in the following part of the chapter. First, however, it will assist the later discussion if we briefly identify a concept ('social materials') that is closely bound up with this chapter's focus upon social networks (or social systems). Borrowing in part from Callon (1991: 143), Callon and Latour (1981: 284) and Latour (1986), I employ the term *materials* in a very general way to include a wide variety of discourses (for example, religious, technical, professional or political discourses or any combination of these), laws, rules, some types of resources, written materials, and public policies, together with value expressions, social practices and typifications of the kind ordinarily associated with the routines of everyday life.[3] In the following pages an attempt is made to demonstrate that an important dimension of time–space centres on the proposition that much of the stuff of social life consists of 'materials', and that social science has neglected the significance of what Callon terms the *travel* or 'passage' of materials across spatio-temporal contexts. While the notion that some materials 'travel' may at first sight seem curious (or else obvious), the idea of diffusion is hardly unknown in social science (see Braithwaite, 1994), though it refers to dimensions of the social that – if they are to be better understood – require that social analysis be informed by new theoretical and methodological orientations to time–space. Some implications of the idea that certain materials travel, will be explored later; a prior task – given that it is often within and between networks that materials flow – is to provide an outline of this chapter's conception of social networks.

Social networks/social systems

As argued in Chapters 2 and 5, it seems best to use the concept social structure to refer – as part of a flexible, realist social ontology – to relatively enduring social conditions (or 'the conditions-of-action') denoted in very broad terms (in this respect, my concept of structure is similar to Archer's (1995)):[4] structure, which may be defined as *the circumstances in which an agent(s) operates*, includes, for example, discourses, power configurations, social systems/social networks, social institutions and roles, and 'other actors' (in regard to the last of these, to repeat an earlier observation, there is agency-in-structure just as there is structure-in-agency). Thus, in my terminology, social systems or social networks (I use these terms interchangeably) are elements of structure, but structure itself is a wider category than system(s). Social networks/social systems are comprised of phenomena – including more or less patterned relations between actors and between or within social institutions and between social positions and roles – that may exist at micro-, mezo- or macro-levels of social process; as will be evident from part of this statement, social networks/systems, as I conceive of them, exhibit both institutional/system integration and figurational/social integration properties.[5] In light of these remarks and the earlier critique of the four 'cardinal sins', it follows that the approach described here departs from what can be broadly described as the structuralist paradigm of network analysis as represented in the writings of, for example, Wellman (1983), Rosenthal *et al.*, (1985) and Harrison White (1992); these authors, though their approaches to network analysis are not identical, have in common an objectivist perspective that is determinist and neglectful of the significance of agency (see the useful discussion in Emirbayer and Goodwin, 1994).

Limitations of space prevent my exploring at length other details of the ontology that informs this chapter's approach to social networks/social systems; briefly stated, they are as follows. First, it is important to recognize that, to use Giddens's (1984: 377) apt expression, there are 'degrees of systemness'. There sometimes exist tightly coupled social systems/networks but relatively 'loose' configurations of action – which might entail, for example, sporadic or irregular actor–actor interaction, somewhat tenuous role–role connections, and an only partially consensual or interrelated set of values – may exhibit an at least minimal degree of social patterning or coherence and therefore possess certain network-like characteristics. Another way of putting this is to say that social networks/social systems vary in the degree of integration, unitaryness or homogeneity that they exhibit: an interesting parallel is political scientists' distinction between two contrasting types of policy network (namely, policy communities and issue networks).[6] Second, recursion (discussed in Chapter 3) tends to be associated with – though is not confined to – social systems/networks. Here recursion refers to social channelling and self-generating reproductive tendencies, though not in the reified sense associated with Luhman's (1982: 265) theory of recursion in 'autopoietic' social systems, a theory which portrays systems as actors or agents. Third, arising from the preceding point, it is worth recalling the definition of actor (or agent) set out in previous chapters where it was argued that an actor is an entity that, in principle, is capable of formulating and taking decisions and of acting upon at least some of them. While there may be occasions where networks are actors (for example, a small consortium of firms with a collective decision-making mechanism), it is best to adopt a non-reified rule of thumb which specifies that, more often than not, social systems/networks are part of the conditions of action ('structure') within which actors operate, rather than actors themselves. Thus, for example, Law's universalizing claim – derived from his attempted synthesis of structuralism, poststructuralism, and actor network theory – that social networks as 'structured sets of relations' are actors (Law, 1991b: 172, 173–4), is an instance of reification and should therefore be resisted: likewise we should leave aside Habermas's (1987: 159–60) assumption that social systems are agents, and also reject Castells's

(2000) reification of networks.[7] Fourth, concerning the above references to 'degrees of systemness', and to recursion, it is likely that the durability of the materials that circulate within a social network/social system is related to network architecture. Other things being equal, institutionalized materials circulating within tightly coupled networks are more difficult to disturb or change than materials in looser material network configurations that have low levels of 'irreversibilization' (Callon, 1991: 149). For example, M. J. Smith (1993), a political scientist, observes that within a policy network, particularly if it happens to be a tightly coupled policy community, 'standard operating procedures' (institutionalized procedures and rules) tend to shape events and limit the number of options open to policy actors, and in most circumstances the existence of standard operating procedures in a policy network tends in the direction of recursion and material(s) and network reproduction. Fifth, social networks have emergent properties (the concept 'emergence' was discussed in Chapter 3). In this connection it is worth taking note of Knoke and Kuklinski's (1991: 174–5) observations on emergent properties in industrial and medical social systems:

Relational measures capture emergent properties of social systems that cannot be measured by simply aggregating the attributes of individual members. Furthermore, such emergent properties may significantly affect both system performance and the behaviour of network members. For example, the structure of informal friendships and antagonisms in formal work groups can affect both group and individual productivity rates in ways not predictable from such personal attributes as age, experience, intelligence, and the like. As another example, the structure of communication among medical practitioners can shape the rate of diffusion of medical innovations in a local community and can determine which physicians are likely to be early or late adopters. (1991: 174–5)

It should be clear from the preceding remarks that to recognize the existence of emergent properties in social systems is not to endorse reification; emergence need not, as I have already observed, entail the equivalent of Luhmann's (1982: 265) self-referential systems which, says Luhmann, are able to reflect and have consciousness of themselves as systems and are also able to take decisions. Sixth, neither the coming into existence nor the reproduction or elaboration of a social network/social system – whether at the micro-, mezo- or macro-level of the social – can legitimately be explained in terms of any single, reductionist principle of explanation. Social systems/networks are not, for example, the expression of some structural principle or exigency of the kind associated with theories that are premised upon methodological collectivism, and nor, on the other hand, can systems/networks be accounted for in terms that draw upon methodological individualism: the coming into being of a social network/system and its subsequent development, or indeed, its demise, are relatively unpredictable outcomes of diachronic interconnections between structure, agency, and social chance.[8]

Materials and their diffusion

Underpinned by the arguments set out in the Introduction's critical references to the four 'cardinal sins', my synthetic approach to material diffusion draws critically and selectively on contrasting theoretical sources, none of which are entirely satisfactory but each of which contain significant analytical insights. These include actor network theory and Law's (1986a) view that the time–space mobility and durability of materials are relational and contingent outcomes of social processes; Giddens's (1984; 1993) work on time–space, and Cohen's (1989) use of the concept 'circuits of reproduction' in an interesting though not wholly successful attempt to remedy explanatory deficit in Giddens's theory of structuration; Lidz's (1981) transformational theory; Fararo's (1992) 'generative structuralism'; Buckner's (1978) empirically grounded phenomenological insights into the nature of those social scenarios where, as materials move from one context to another, their transformation tends to be predictable and routinized; and Foucauldian writing on governmentality, including Miller and Rose's thesis (1993: 84) which suggests a vital part of the process of governance is the time–space dissemination of discourses resulting in the emergence of policy networks.

Although there exist phenomena that to a large extent are specific to particular individuals or to a particular local setting, many materials are trans-situational – that is to say, such materials 'flow' across locales in a temporal and also spatial sense. Indeed, to take up but one aspect of the point that has just been made, Callon (1986) and Callon and Latour (1981) argue that actors have no structurally predetermined 'size' and that power is an effect of success in strategically 'consigning' (or institutionalizing) material and propelling the consigned materials across spatio-temporal contexts to a widening 'enrolled' audience, so that the material becomes 'what everybody is saying' (Callon and Latour, 1981: 298); for these authors, power is success in making consigned material spatially and temporally more *mobile* and more *durable* than other, competing materials. A flexible social ontology of the kind argued for earlier would suggest that the question of 'what happens' to material as it travels through time and from one locale to another – and it may be that, say, laws, rules of engineering as applied to bridge-building, and mathematical equations have, other things being equal, higher thematization thresholds (Schwartz, 1973) than, say, folklore, poetry, or psychotherapists' forms of knowledge – is an important empirical question; does the material retain its shape as it travels, or is it transformed (Lidz, 1981), and if the latter, what factors pertaining to media, contexts, and the dialectics of agency, structure, and social chance are involved in its transformation? Is the material fragmented – for example, is a new professional code applied in a hundred and one different ways in local settings? – or is transformation itself patterned or directional? These are empirical questions: but some theorists prejudge them, a case in point being Latour's (1986: 267) sociology of translation which presumes that materials move along actor-chains and that since different actors, says Latour, typically have differing values, priorities, interests, and objectives, they 'act upon' the material in different ways with the result that the material is endlessly transformed during the course of its passage across locales (indeed for Latour, the expression 'it' is inappropriate since the material in question is continuously transformed during its travel and is never for long 'the same' material). Latour errs; on a priori *theoretical* grounds he treats material transformation as natural, and material transmission as abnormal or unusual. These, to repeat, are *empirical* questions. What is important, however, about Latour's performative conception of the social is that in anti-reductionist and non-teleological fashion he challenges the notion that if some materials travel far in unchanged form that this is because of a gigantic initial impetus provided by an all-powerful originating source, such as 'the interests of capitalism', 'patriarchy' or 'globalization'. With regard to 'prime mover' or 'initial impetus' theories of material diffusion, Latour's comparison of the social with a rugby match is in some ways appropriate: we cannot assume that the *first* throw or kick of the ball (or of social material) has any more significance than the fourth, fortieth or four hundredth; when material is passed from actor to actor and from one locale to another, the shape (or 'content') of the material is largely a function of what actors *do* with the material when it comes their way, rather than a function of its initial impetus. However, the wider point that I should like to make here is that once reductionist, essentialist, reified, and teleological theories are put aside – this means, for example, forsaking reductionist notions that materials are epiphenomenal reflections of 'deep' structure or of the 'objective' interests of taxonomic collectivities – it becomes clearer that empirical investigation of the construction, reproduction or elaboration of materials, their contents and contexts, and actors' strategies and use of media (oral, written, electronic) for disseminating and acting upon materials, are important topics of empirical enquiry *in their own right*. Put another way, materials are neither created by nor propelled across time–space by a putative 'deep' structure nor are they somehow held in place – or dislodged or fragmented, as the case may be – by an omnipotent or omnipresent 'grand architect', for no such architect exists; hence the origins and nature of materials and their relative mobility and durability across time and space are factors that should always be regarded as unknown prior to their empirical investigation.

An interesting approach to social network analysis and material dissemination processes is Fararo's (1992: 320) 'generative structuralism'. There are problems in Fararo's overall theoretical position: his perspective, which relies on mathematical modelling of network and system processes, is prone to the reification of social systems. However, the processual elements in his theoretical scheme (ibid.: 48) are worth retaining. Providing that they are, so to speak, detached from his own paradigmatic contextualization of them, his metatheoretical formulations on material dissemination within and across social networks can usefully be incorporated into sociological analysis. One of Fararo's interests (ibid.: 261) is 'the process of flow or spread of something through a network'. This is associated with his proposition that *social structure* can be defined as 'a social network within which various diffusion processes may occur' (ibid.: 266). In Fararo's theoretical scheme (ibid.: 274) it is 'social relations that function as the linkages along which the cultural object can flow and be inhibited or not in its spread through a population'. For Fararo, as indicated in the following extracts from his work, diffusion is very closely associated with processes of institutionalization:

> Diffusion processes, which can be understood as processes in networks, are more important for general sociology than is often recognized. Institutionalization, in the sense of a scheme of typifications (and corresponding interaction generators), can be construed as diffusion from local subnetwork to local subnetwork using paths of integrative ties. (ibid.: 340)

> A theoretical model of the local process by which the institution is adopted or not would be possible but the main structural interest would lie in the global process by which it is spread throughout the network of local embodiments so as to ultimately constitute an institutional procedure in the social system of which each local network is a part. (ibid.: 274)

> Global integration means connectivity, the extent to which paths of ties permit information, attitudes, and other entities – including emerging typification schemes constituting aspects of institutions – to diffuse widely through the system. (ibid.: 306–7)

Depending on the nature of the particular analytical task in hand, the term *materials* as discussed earlier can refer to general cultural meanings which circulate on a widespread basis across a nation–state (Harrison White, 1992: 5, 294), or from one nation–state to another (Braithwaite, 1994); or for some analytical purposes the term can refer to specialized materials of the kind that tend to be largely concentrated within a particular institutional domain such as an academic, administrative, or professional community. These matters are taken up in Miller and Rose's (1993) useful extension of Foucault's work. In effect, Miller and Rose's thesis is that contingently reproduced materials play a vital part in processes of governance (1993: 81), including the time–space dissemination of discourses which result in the emergence of policy networks (ibid.: 84). It is important to recognize that in the case of, for example, governance processes, some policy materials, or aspects of materials, may remain unaltered as the material moves across time–space, whereas other materials, or aspects of them, may be modified or transformed during their passage across spatio-temporal contexts. And some materials perish, perhaps at the same time as new materials are created. That these are often interwoven and *overlapping* processes has an empirical importance that is recognized by some policy researchers. For example, in his study of the historical development of urban regeneration policy in England, Stewart (1994: 136) observes: 'Successive stages of urban policy are not totally discrete; each successive stage incorporates elements of earlier policy cultures. Equally, however, each new stage adds its own distinctive dimension.' The more general point arising from Stewart's study is that configuration of the flow of materials across time–space, and also the relative durabilities of different kinds of materials in any particular locales, are very often empirically complex and variegated.

In light of the theoretical arguments developed in earlier chapters, it is worth reiterating that analysis of the construction and diffusion of materials is not reducible to explanations of the kind associated with methodological individualism (for example, rational choice theory). But nor can methodological collectivism – as embodied in theories that are based on, for example, Marxism, teleological functionalism, structuralism, and radical feminism – offer any suitable methods of social analysis. As I have already observed more than once, reified and methodological collectivist forms of interpretation have no empirical explanatory value. The creation, diffusion/reproduction or transformation of materials are not structurally predetermined processes; materials are not reflections of any 'deep' cultural logic, or of structural imperatives. There is no single or primary structural mechanism or principle (the economy, gender interests, systemic needs, globalization, 'risk', 'trust' or whatever) that predetermines social life. The properties of social materials, of their spatio-temporal contexts and of media or channels of diffusion are not, in other words, reducible to any single general principle of explanation. To suppose otherwise is reductionist, and to attempt to combine reductionisms is to engage in 'compounded reductionism'. Nor, I have argued, should essentialist or teleological forms of theorizing be allowed to have any part to play in the analysis of those dimensions of the social that have been highlighted in this chapter. And we have seen that to attribute agency to entities that are not actors in the terms set out earlier, is to engage in a fourth 'cardinal sin', namely reification. So as to avoid these four defective modes of theoretical-methodological reasoning and to sustain an ontologically flexible ('open') orientation to social analysis, close investigation of processes involved in the construction of social materials and investigation of their contents and contexts and of actors' forms of thought, intentions, strategies, and use of media (whether oral, written or electronic) for disseminating and in various ways acting upon materials, should always be regarded as empirical questions – they are not, in other words, matters that can legitimately be theoretically predetermined in advance of empirical enquiry.

Summary

Time–space is an expression that refers to significant but neglected dimensions of the social. Though primarily concerned with spatiality, the chapter opened with some observations on temporality. Durkheim, Elias and others have argued that time is 'social time', as distinct from a natural essence. The question of how differing time-frames – including those associated with the macro-social order and those with the micro-social – interweave is a complex matter that relates to, for example, the debate of duality versus dualism (in structuration theory and Bourdieu's writings, structure and action are not temporally separated, but rather, are manifested instantaneously, within the moment of instantiation), and that also relates to Layder's (meta)theory of social domains where connections between objective and subjective domains entail some intermingling of two quite different sets of time-frames, namely those associated with (macro) institutional time and those with (micro) situated activity.

•

In social theory and the social sciences, the spatial dimension of society has received even less attention than the temporal. A number of approaches have focused on spatiality, sometimes in terms that refer to indeterminacy and to spatial variation (this is true of, for example, some recent work on governance and the policy process). In general, however, spatiality is a neglected area of study and much remains to be done in developing a post-postmodern (meta)theoretical and methodological framework that addresses social space in terms that steer clear of the four 'cardinal sins'.

•

Locale can be thought of as a bridging concept that spans micro-, mezo- and macro-levels of the social: some local events may be specific to the location in question, others may be connected to the macro-social order – it is therefore necessary to examine the internal properties of local sites as well as the emergent properties of temporal and spatial linkages across sites.

●

The concepts networks (or systems), materials, and material-diffusion have major importance with regard to the design of empirical studies concerned with investigation of the properties of time–space. Networks/systems are more or less patterned relations between actors and between, for example, positions/roles (that is, on the view taken here, networks/systems exhibit both figurational/social integration and institutional/system integration properties) and it is partly, though not exclusively, within networks that materials 'flow'. The term materials, as used in this book, refers to, for example, discourses, social practices, and typifications where these phenomena are inspected in terms of their tendency to 'travel' across spatio-temporal contexts. The question of 'what happens' to materials as they move across time and space should be regarded as a crucial focus within social analysis, and this is why the chapter identified a number of conceptual and methodological themes that relate to new ways of thinking about material diffusion and, more widely, that relate to the development of methods that are suited to the investigation of time–space in the terms set out in this chapter.

Notes

1 Rainer Greca's (2000) is an empirical study of inter-organizational co-governance in Munich; the study refers to a range of public, voluntary, and private organizations involved in the planning and provision of social services. His data identifies time–space factors that can help or hinder inter-organizational co-operation; Greca observed that different categories of organizations involved in social services tend to have varying time codes and also varying spatial orientations. In terms of the latter, some organizations in his study had a 'city-wide' orientation, others a 'district' and, in some cases, a 'local' orientation. In regard to time codes, some social work organizations operated on the basis of 'organizational time' (for example, youth centres tended to be open from 3 p.m. to 9 p.m. and centres for the elderly from 10 a.m. to 8 p.m.); some organizations employed a time code that Greca describes as 'standard business time' (which refers, usually, to the hours 9 a.m. to 5 p.m.); others operated on the basis of 'flexible time' (these organizations invested time in co-operation activities as and when they perceived a necessity to do so, in the form of either routine contacts or urgent meetings); some traditional self-help groups were unusual in that they operated a 'private time' code, where the working day is planned by individuals around the demands of the work situation and their own families. Greca documents how these variations in time codes and spatial orientations affected co-governing and inter-organizational co-operation.

As well as its empirical relation to aspects of the theoretical constructions of time–space discussed in this chapter, Greca's study has, it may be noted, a practical significance that relates to (post)modern 'governance' which entails the co-management of inter-organizational policy networks that are comprised of a variety of governmental, quasi- and non-governmental actors (Kickert *et al.*, 1997a; Rhodes, 1997; Marsh, 1998; Pierre and Stoker, 2000; Richards and Smith, 2002; Kooiman, 2003).

2 Barbara Adam (1990; 1995) suggests that conventional social science distinctions – as in the work of Durkheim, Sorokin, and Merton – between 'natural' and 'social' time rest on an oversimplified view of 'natural' time: the latter, she argues, is highly variable, as instanced by, for example, Einstein's thesis that time is relative to the sphere or system in which the observer is located

3 In my theoretical framework, materials are a part of social structure (see Chapter 2). As employed in this book, a distinction between 'structure' and 'materials' relates to the methodological procedure known as *perspectivism* (that is, for analytical purposes inspecting the same phenomenon from different perspectives): for example, Mouzelis (1997: 114) describes Lockwood's distinction between system- and social-integration forms of enquiry as a distinction which allows us to examine different aspects of 'the same' phenomenon (such as, say, a classroom). As Stones (1996: 23) notes, perspectivism – in the form described here – is not incompatible with social realism.

In terms of the topics discussed in this chapter, some phenomena (discourses, for instance) may be regarded both as elements of structure (the 'conditions-of-action'/'social conditions'), and as 'materials': the latter term is employed whenever analysis focuses upon the *flow* of, in this instance, discourses across spatio-temporal contexts and upon attendant matters to do with, for example, the degree of mobility and durability of materials *during* the course of their 'travel' (Callon, 1986; Law, 1986a; Fararo, 1992).

4 As Parker (2000: 110) puts it: 'For Archer, structure includes anything which pre-exists agency, has durability and relative autonomy, is causally efficacious and may be elaborated in interaction.'

5 Stated another (and formal) way, in my theoretical framework a social network (or system) is an assemblage of actors, positions/roles, locales, and materials that exhibit a degree of patterned interconnectedness and continuity across time and/or social space, and where the network is sufficiently self-contained to be distinguishable from other networks and from the larger social environment in which it is located.

6 For example, M.J. Smith (1993), drawing on the work of other political scientists, distinguishes policy communities from issue networks. Policy communities (an example being post-war British agricultural policy) tend to have a relatively small number of state and non-state actors and these have a fairly stable and continuing relationship with each other; and a fairly high degree of consensus regarding policy objectives and the means adopted in regard to those objectives. In contrast, *issue networks* are a far looser, less integrated type of policy network (an example being policy in relation to abortion). Here there tends to be a large number of state and non-state actors with a 'shifting population' of participants entering and leaving the network (rather than a small number of actors who have regular contact with each other); and while occasionally some agreement may exist over values and policy, there tends in general to be a significant level of conflict over values, policy objectives, and the means to be adopted for the achievement of objectives. This distinction is a useful one providing it is employed as a continuum rather than a dichotomy; and providing it is not

associated with theories of structural predetermination – in principle, a policy community may become an issue network, and vice versa (see Sibeon, 1997: 41).

7 Castells's emphasis on social networks and flows is in many respects to be welcomed; however, he has an unfortunate tendency to reify networks and imbue them with agency. He argues, for example, that networks have 'tasks' and 'goals' and that networks can 're-arrange' themselves and 'communicate' with each other (see Castells, 2000: 15–16).

8 Like Castells's, Urry's work on networks (for example, 2000b; 2000c) is a welcome recognition of the importance of the idea that what I call 'materials' – Urry describes them as 'fluids' – flow across networks. But again like Castells's, his perspective is flawed in certain crucial respects. Urry argues that people, images, money, information, and objects flow across, in particular, transnational networks; that a new 'post-societal' sociology is necessary (the concept 'society' is, says Urry, tied to the notion of nation–states and since Urry believes the latter are – in the globalization era – no longer of much significance, the concept 'society' should be abandoned; henceforth, says Urry, 'the social' should refer not to 'society' but to networks and the flow of fluids across national borders); and Urry considers that the concepts 'agency' and 'structure' and therefore contemporary sociological debates of agency–structure and of dualism and/or duality of structure and action, are largely redundant – in part for the reason that the proper focus of sociological enquiry (global networks and fluids, rather than 'society') are, according to Urry, 'inhuman hybrids', composed of people and physical objects or 'actants'. While we should welcome Urry's emphasis on networks and what he calls 'mobilities', his approach is open to the following criticisms. First, his argument that we should cease to employ the term 'society', is ill-founded: 'society' refers to social relations and processes that occur within and across nation–states – including emergent postnational phenomena – and to do away with such a useful concept seems wholly unnecessary (indeed, what other suitable concept could we put in its place?). In, for example, recent work on multi-level governance and public policy, use of the expression *postnational governance* (Sibeon, 1999b) is a way of denoting that in Europe there are supranational (European Union), transnational (this being Urry's preoccupation), national, and subnational (for example, local government) 'levels' of the policy process, each of these levels or spheres being relatively (though not totally) autonomous (see the discussion of Archer and upwards/downwards conflation in Chapter 4): to acknowledge postnational dimensions of the social does not erase 'societal' processes within and across states, processes which involve diachronic linkages between structure, agency, and social chance (Sibeon, 2000). To adopt Urry's prescription that we should reduce 'the social' to transnational networks and mobilities would be to exaggerate globalizing tendencies (the nation–state 'still matters': see, for instance, Hirst and Thompson, 1999, and Scholte, 2000), and it would also be, as just noted, to ignore important postnational aspects of the dialectics of agency, structure, and social chance (see Chapter 5). Second, oncerning an aspect of the point that I have just made, Urry's dismissal of contemporary theoretical debate of agency–structure and of duality/dualism (for example, Urry, 2000b: 194–6), is unjustified. It is true that contemporary theory and empirical enquiry pay insufficient attention to networks and material diffusion, and tend also – to take up another of Urry's points – to overlook the relation of the social to physical objects (see Dant, 1999), but these, bearing in mind the discussion in the earlier chapters, are not valid reasons for abandoning 'agency' and 'structure' as

concepts. Indeed, as I have tried to show in various places throughout this book, meta-conceptual assumptions centred upon agency and structure are unavoidable: for example, and here we glimpse Urry's lack of interest in recent sociological theoretical debate of agency–structure, he mistakenly believes that current theoretical sociology – itself an umbrella term that, with regard to agency–structure, masks important differences between, for example, Giddens, Archer, Mouzelis, and Layder – promulgates the simplistic notion that 'if social systems change, this is seen to result from agency' (Urry, 2000b: 196). This is an inaccurate characterization of recent debates in theoretical sociology, and nor, as the discussion in previous chapters has indicated, is it the case that contemporary sociological debate of agency–structure and social chance ignores what Urry calls 'emergent, unintended and non-linear consequences' (2000b: 195).

In sum, Urry's 'post-societal' sociology, which he claims is a sociology for the twenty-first century (2000c), is to be applauded in so far as it focuses on the neglected topic of networks and 'mobilities' but Urry exaggerates the extent to which the nation–state is in decline in the face of globalizing tendencies; he wrongly reduces 'the social' to transnational networks and flows; and he unjustifiably dismisses important debates – to do with agency, structure, social chance, time–space and micro–macro – that lie at the heart of recent theoretical work in sociology and in some other social sciences such as social geography, political science, and public policy/administrative science.

7

Towards an Integrated Metatheoretical and Methodological Framework

One of this book's underlying themes – that society has ontological depth and is in some sense 'layered' – features in the work of major contemporary sociological theorists such as Mouzelis (1995), Archer (1995; 2000), and Layder (1997). What is at issue here and in the earlier chapters is the ontological proposition that the social world is not a unitary, 'flat' terrain. Society consists of micro-, mezo- and macro-levels of social process, each of which – though they overlap and indirectly influence each other – have a relatively independent existence in the sense that each exhibits distinct properties and effects of its own that are not reducible to (that is, cannot be explained in terms of) the properties of other levels.[1] In Chapter 2, for example, criticisms were made of Giddens's and others' preference for removing a distinction between micro and macro and also for collapsing agency and structure into a theoretical amalgam formed of elements (micro, macro, agency and structure) that are fused together so tightly that it is impossible to separate them and therefore impossible to study the ways in which they influence each other over time; in opposition to duality theorizing it was argued that agency–structure and micro–macro should be regarded as dualisms in which each of the elements that comprise a dualism have distinct, identifiable properties.[2] A related ontological understanding that was examined in the preceding chapter, is that a part of social reality consists of material diffusion processes. When these two dimensions of the social – society is both layered and made up of spatio-temporal contexts across which materials travel – are simultaneously brought into focus, we are presented with a complex social ontology. In the 'vertical' dimension there are social domains (conceived of in terms of, for example,

Layder's (1997) four domains as discussed in Chapter 4, or in terms of micro–macro); however, micro- and macro-levels of society, as well as having a vertical dimension, are *also* a 'lateral' expanse of time and space (that is, spatio-temporal contexts across which widespread social materials flow). Later, arising from the point that I have just made, it will be observed that as a piece of social material travels temporally and spatially it may take on different forms at differing levels of social process (for example, a political ideology – such as, in Britain, Tony Blair's 'New Labour' – may be given special, distinctive meanings in some local, micro-settings, at the same time as having certain general defining features that may be common across many settings, features which have a 'macro' reality that is largely trans-situational). What is being indicated here is that any particular material may acquire different forms of expression within differing levels or spheres of time–space, and that the notion that social reality is layered has important conceptual and methodological implications for researchers involved in investigation of the temporal and spatial travel of materials.

Before, however, taking a closer look at some of the methodological implications that arise from the multi-dimensional ontological processes to which I have just referred, it will first of all be necessary to extend some of the ideas set out in earlier chapters concerning micro–macro. In doing so, and throughout the rest of the chapter, it is intended, as in earlier chapters, to make illustrative reference to governance and the policy process; this will provide the reader with concrete illustrations of necessarily abstract metatheoretical arguments, and also reflects an epistemological commitment to a conception of metatheory and theory as forms of social scientific understanding that, in principle, may shape and be shaped by empirical studies.

Micro-, mezo- and macro-levels of social reality

Like most other social science theoreticians, I use the term micro–macro as a form of shorthand that makes no explicit reference to an 'intermediate' (or 'mezo') layer of social process: this is largely a matter of terminological convenience – the expression 'micro-mezo-macro' has a somewhat clumsy ring to it. Later, it will be argued that, ontologically speaking, the mezo-social is a significant social domain that is neither micro or macro. But for a moment, let us continue to leave the mezo-domain aside and refer to 'micro–macro' as an analytical distinction that indicates differences in the size or scale of social phenomena; as defined in Chapter 2, the expression *micro–macro* refers to differences in the units of and scale of analyses concerned with the investigation of varying extensions of time–space. That is, the expression 'micro' refers to small stretches of time and of space, whereas the macro is to do with large temporal and spatial extensions. In previous chapters it was argued, against quite widespread tacit assumptions to the contrary, that micro is not the same thing as agency and nor is macro synonymous with structure (on the one hand, I have argued some forms of agency are exercised by social ('organizational') actors that are not micro-entities, and on the other, that social structure (the conditions-of-action) is comprised of macro- but also micro-phenomena). It was also suggested earlier that both micro-analysis and macro-analysis can refer to institutional and/or figurational dynamics. Micro-analysis entails investigation of meanings, positions/roles, networks/social systems, and actor–actor relations in small-scale settings where interaction takes the form of what Giddens calls 'co-presence',[3] whereas macro-analysis is the study of large time–space extensions of actors, materials, and social conditions ('macro-structure') including large social systems/social networks.

As used here, the expression micro–macro, viewed in terms of differences in the size or scale of social phenomena, refers not to any clear dividing line or dichotomy but to a *continuum* with micro and macro as polar opposites, and with mezo located somewhere around the mid-point of the continuum. The macro end of the continuum includes system-integration/institutional and social-integration/figurational aspects of large-scale phenomena such as nation–states or transnational structures; the mezo includes organizations, inter-organizational networks and other intermediate time–space extensions of actors, materials and practices; the micro refers to individual psychobiography (the 'self'), to figurational dynamics associated with inter-subjectivity and face-to-face relations among actors, and to institutional phenomena such as role–role relations in situations of co-presence. As implied earlier with reference to an ontological conception of society as complex, multi-dimensional and variegated, the micro–macro continuum as employed here refers both to phenomena that have a 'lateral' dimension which refers to differing expanses of time and space, and a 'vertical' dimension – to do with micro-, mezo- and macro-levels of social reality – that refers to ontological depth and to the 'layered' nature of the social. In effect, then, micro-, mezo- and macro-domains, though rarely explicitly stated in these terms, are *both* 'vertical' layerings of society and 'lateral' spreads of actors, locales, and materials across varying extensions – from small to large-scale – of time and of space. This multifaceted ontological formulation is one that post-postmodern sociological theory and method has barely got to grips with and, as Layder observes, it is a formulation that 'it is not possible to represent properly in diagrammatic form' (1997: 77). Layder is speaking here, in somewhat embryonic terms which remain to be developed in future work, of a complex social ontology that simultaneously refers to vertical and lateral dimensions of society, and to conjunctions of different time-frames and of differing extensions of space; to which should be added, I have argued, the important notion of material-flows as discussed in the previous chapter.

Micro

As already indicated, micro-analysis in my theoretical schema is a broader analytical category than in many others: it is a category that includes individual psychobiography together with small-scale institutional/system integration and figurational/social integration forms of analysis. The last of these – as exemplified in symbolic interactionist studies – is widely associated with micro-social research, and it is the figurational element that I shall concentrate upon here.[4] In light of the discussion of micro–macro in Chapter 2 and given that the purpose of the present chapter is to draw together some of the earlier arguments concerning (meta)theory (and method), the intention in what follows is to restate in summary form those aspects of the micro-social domain that relate to the book's overall (meta)theoretical and methodological frame of reference.

Of course, in arguing here and in the earlier chapters for recognition of the importance of the micro-social, no attempt is made to advocate methodological situationalism (for example, Collins 1981; 1983; 1988) which attempts to reduce the macro- to the micro-social – that is, the macro-sphere is erroneously said to be no more than countless micro-episodes. In opposition to methodological situationalism it is argued that insights derived from, for instance, macro-structural and discourse theories, some of which share points in common with Durkheimian sociology, have a legitimate part to play in social analysis. For example, Alexander and Smith (1993), whose paper has as its context the recent growth of interest in cultural sociology,[5] examine American political discourse on civil society. The authors claim there is an underlying structure to discourse pertaining to the idea of American civil society; their method is to construct – in a manner that is reminiscent of Lévi-Strauss's (1963; 1974) structuralism – a series of binary oppositions ('equality' versus 'hierarchy', 'rule-regulated' versus 'arbitrary', 'law' versus 'power', and so on) that contrast democratic and counter-democratic practices, relations, and institutions. Alexander and Smith are concerned to uncover internal logics, formal grammars and the autonomy of cultural codes or of discourses. This type of autonomizing approach to the study of discourse is a perfectly legitimate heuristic research tool *if* it is used as an ideal-type that, unlike the way in which ideal-type models are often employed (Holmwood, 1996: 119), is in principle open to empirical sources of revision; in addition, I would argue, ideal-type constructs should be located within an analytical framework of the kind outlined in this book. For example, the point was made earlier that there are good reasons why researchers should remain open to the empirical possibility that ostensibly trans-situational cultural codes – such as discourse on American civil society – that are assumed to be more or less invariant across large ('macro') intervals of time and space may be given particular or 'discrepant' meaning(s) by actors within one or more local sites. In addition to the possible emergence of 'new' meanings and practices during the course of local social interaction, actors' use of transformative concepts (Lidz, 1981) may conceivably result in quite extensive local re-working or modification of putative macro-cultural discourse(s). The matters under discussion here, however, relate not only to cultural materials such as discourses, but also to roles. Among post-war writers associated with symbolic interactionism, Blumer was a major critic of Parsonian sociology and of other paradigms that, as he saw it, involved a macro-structural predetermination of behaviour allied to determinist usages of the concept *role*. For Blumer interaction is not a relation between roles but between *people*, who are not straightforwardly 'role-players' (other than in settings involving highly ritualistic relations such as the role of priest in a religious ceremony); people, in short, for the most part are relatively non-determined beings who improvise and creatively interpret the situations in which they are involved (Blumer, 1969: 65).

The idea that the realm of the micro-social is a significant part of social reality is not, as Thrift (1994) rightly observes, threatened by the existence of (post)modern conditions such as the seemingly ever-enlargening social forces associated with globalization. Giddens (1990), for example, refers to a globalized re-ordering of time–space. But his conceptions (1991b: 21) of small-scale locale and of globalization, are not antithetical; rather, globalization is the 'largest' expression of time–space distanciation. The more general point to be made here is that we should avoid crude either-or dichotomies that emphasize localism and particularity *or* globalizing and homogenizing tendencies: the connections that develop between local micro-domains and larger-scale forces are likely to be variable and complex (M.P. Smith, 2001) and social science should be concerned with the study of time–space in such a way that both material continuities and discontinuities are kept in focus.

Mezo

Some years ago in a text on micro-, mezo- and macro-levels of welfare policy interventions, Mullen and Dumpson referred to spatial differences in the 'size' of the problems to which public welfare services are addressed:

> *Micro*system problems ... are those in which the determining forces seem to be within the boundaries of either an individual or a small group ... *Mezo*system problems are those in which the determining forces seem directly to involve not only ... individuals and small groups ... but geographic localities such as neighbourhoods and communities ... *Macro*system problems are those in which the critical determining factors extend beyond given individuals, groups, or localities and ... occur on the broadest level of social organization involving large geographically scattered populations. (1972: 11–12)

This quotation, though its authors – whose main concerns are practical aspects of social policies – are not as theoretically explicit as they might have been, serves to amplify my and Layder's earlier observation that the ('vertical') levels – micro, mezo, and macro – of society are also spatial (and temporal) extensions of varying scale and where time and space can be said to exist in the 'lateral' dimension. Further, Mullen and Dumpson contend that social problems which occur at one level may overlap with problems at another level, but that the levels themselves are relatively independent of each other and that problems experienced at one level cannot be assumed to be a product of or mirror-reflection of conditions or events that occur at another level. In many other areas of social science we find that the concept 'mezo' is employed in a style that is roughly equivalent to Mullen and Dumpson's. In political science, for example, Goverde *et al.* discuss differing 'circuits of power' that, though they may interrelate, are respectively embedded at micro-, mezo- and macro-levels of the social: in defining these levels, Goverde *et al.* observe (2000: 32) that 'the ... mezo level represents a structured *intermediate* level of social, economic and/or political organization lying somewhere between the macro-(large-scale) and the micro-(small-scale) levels, partly separate and autonomous but also linking the two' (original italics).

It is sometimes said that mezo-analysis is primarily concerned with organizations and, in particular, with inter-organizational networks (see, for example, Webb, 1991: 237). This may be so to some extent (many studies that describe themselves as mezo-level analyses are concerned with inter-organizational networks; see M.J. Smith, 1993: 7, 233); but like a number of other theorists I prefer to employ the concept *mezo* in a broad sense that includes but is not restricted to inter-organizational processes. The term is employed here to refer to 'intermediate' time–space configurations of actors, social relations and practices, materials and structures – including social systems/social networks – that are larger than micro spatio-temporal contexts (defined as settings of face-to-face interaction), but smaller than macro expanses of actors, materials and structures that may stretch (temporally) across intervals of years, decades or even centuries and extend (spatially) across, say, a nation–state or perhaps across a number of nation–states. Stones (1998: 293) refers to micro, mezo and macro as 'levels of sociological analysis (a focus on either small, medium or large-scale phenomena)'. As Stones points out, and has argued at length elsewhere (1996), it is possible to examine a set of widespread social practices at each of these levels (1998: 294): 'That is, one could look at a few local (micro) practices, at a greater number of those practices spread over a larger geographical region (mezo) or a very large number of them spread out over an even greater geographic expanse (macro).' Here Stones, like many other theorists, is *implicitly* referring to the micro–mezo–macro distinction as having both 'vertical' and 'lateral' (or 'horizontal') dimensions. It is desirable that social science theory in future should endeavour to treat these ontological issues in a rather more explicit fashion. A strength, however, of Stones's (1996; 1998) reference to society as having ontological depth in terms of differing extensions of time–space is his emphasis upon what might be called a 'zooming' approach in the study of widespread social practices:[6] at the micro- and mezo-levels the researcher can pay close empirical attention to local details, while at the macro-level – using such methods as historical and contemporary documentary analysis, and social surveys – it is possible to look at the dynamics of the spatially and temporally larger picture, some aspects of which are discussed in the next section of the chapter.

In earlier chapters I referred illustratively to policy network analysis, this being an important example of a form of social enquiry that political scientists and governance researchers tend to identify as a mezo-level mode of enquiry. The concept 'policy networks' refers not to co-presence encounters (such as informal relations among a group of shopfloor workers) nor to macroscopic variables (such as a nation–state's political culture or national system of government), but to, usually, a handful of state and non-state organizational actors – government departments, professional associations, private firms, interest groups, and so on – engaged in inter-organizational interaction centred upon 'joint' policy making and policy implementation within a policy sector such as education, health, or criminal justice. In policy network analysis it is argued that inter-organizational networks constitute a mezo-social order (a policy network) which has distinct emergent properties and effects of its own (for example, network membership may modify participating organizations' power and interests and their decisions and actions), properties and effects which are not reducible to micro-happenings nor to the macro-social order. That having been said, it is also worth noting – when it comes to conceptualization of and empirical investigation of connections between levels – that policy network analysis, though in principle well equipped to study systemic, recursive and also relational/emergent components of agency, interests, and power in the governance process (Sibeon, 2000), has a tendency to neglect the important matter of linkages between mezo- and relevant micro- and macro-social domains: this partly (meta)theoretical, partly methodological question of connections between levels of society and therefore across different expanses of time and space, is something that will be returned to later in the chapter.

Macro

Consistent with the theoretical arguments put forward in earlier chapters, macro-analysis may be defined as the study of institutional and-or figurational aspects of extensive time–space dispersions of individual and social ('organizational') actors, and of large expanses of materials and of social conditions ('structure') including large social systems/social networks. Macro-structure[7] includes, for instance, extensive temporal and spatial distributions of actors, discourses, institutionalized practices, and large-scale social systems such as formal constitutional or governmental systems or sustained inter-governmental or postnational networks of interactions. Macro-social conditions (macro-structure), defined in the terms just indicated – that is, as social conditions that stretch widely across time and space – are not a unitary phenomenon, nor do they have a single 'cause'; to assume otherwise is, as was pointed out in Chapter 2, to engage in essentialist and reductionist theorizing. The macro-social is contingently produced, reproduced or elaborated/transformed: here, agency, structure, and social chance play a part, the part played by each being an empirical question. But while the relative weighting or influence of each may vary from one time or place to another, all three elements – agency, structure, chance – will almost certainly have figured diachronically in the constitution of current macro-social phenomena. There is no question here of siding either with those who, on the basis of some theory of structural predetermination, focus primarily on social stability and those, on the other hand, who assume society is an almost endlessly indeterminate process of flux. In Chapter 1 it was noted that postmodern theorists have tended to exaggerate the nature and scale of social discontinuities across time and space (Best and Kellner, 1991). Postmodern theorists have largely ignored the cautionary advice of Aron (1967: 27) and others concerning the importance of avoiding an either-or dichotomy centred on *social statis* or *social dynamics*. This relates to themes explored in earlier chapters; building upon critique of the four theoretical and methodological 'cardinal sins', it was argued social analysis should proceed on the basis of an understanding that the extent to which any particular materials – such as discourses, value preferences, institutionalized practices, conventions, interpretative schemes, and typifications – are spatially and temporally mobile and durable, is a matter for empirical assessment and not something that can legitimately be theoretically predetermined.[8]

A sense of the processual, contingent, and heterogeneous nature of the macro-social is conveyed quite well in Harrison White's (1992: 311) observation that 'there is no mechanism for locking space-times into some unified totality'. Harrison White is surely correct: there is no structural machinery for creating and sustaining a unified social totality and nor is there an omnipresent, omnipotent 'grand architect' with powers to structure the social world across time and space in a preferred direction. Of significance here is the anti-reductionism of Roberto Unger (1987a; 1987b; 1987c; 1997), a Brazilian political scientist and political activist whose specialism is critical legal studies. Though Unger often writes from a political science standpoint, he is versed in other disciplines and argues for an integrated social scientific approach to the study of society. He rejects what he calls 'deep-structure theories' (exemplars of which are, he suggests, the work of Marx and also Durkheim, and Weber to some extent); he rejects such theories for the reason that they tend to rely on a single explanatory principle – such as 'capitalism' or 'the division of labour' – and to depict society as an effect of deep-seated imperatives, logics, or developmental laws. As well as avoiding what he describes as the 'structure fetishism' of, say, Marxist or Durkheimian theories of society, Unger also rejects 'institutional fetishism', by which he means that it is erroneous to suppose that existing institutional arrangements are the embodiment of abstract institutional concepts such as property rights, a market economy, or representative democracy (Unger, 1987a: 200–1): instead, says Unger, institutional arrangements, whether in, for example, capitalist societies or in communist societies such as the former Soviet Union, are a contingent outcome of historical accidents and conjunctions – in other words, the macro-social is not the expression of a deep logic based on a putative social, political, or economic necessity (Unger, 1997: x–xi). Unger frequently uses the expression 'formative contexts', which for our purposes can be roughly equated with the macro-social order or 'society'. The core of his argument is that formative contexts – though seemingly resilient in so far as many if not most actors tend to mistakenly regard them as necessary, natural or inevitable – are not actually 'necessary' at all, but are precariously sustained by actors' reproductive practices; formative contexts, then, are not the outcome of natural or social laws or of some 'deep' structural script or logic, nor are they the product of a single blueprint developed by some particular actor(s). Rather, it is argued – and here Unger's social ontology in some respects parallels my own – that formative contexts emerge out of earlier relatively uncoordinated events, decisions, forms of thought, technological developments, conflict-resolving compromises, strategic alliances, attempts at problem-solving, and so on (Unger, 1997).

In making reference to this book's flexible and processual social ontology, however, an earlier observation should be kept in mind: there is no invariant either-or (stability *or* flux) involved in the constitution of society, and in some circumstances the macro-social, or at least some segments of the macro-social, may become relatively stable, institutionalized and to some extent homogeneous across large stretches of space and time. Where this happens, the influence of the macro-social upon mezo- and micro-domains is often easier to discern than where the macro is heterogeneous and in a state of relative flux. Numerous examples of the influence of the macro are available in the disciplines of political science and public policy. For example, M.J. Smith (1993) observes that it is possible to develop a few cautious generalizations concerning the emergence of different types of policy networks. He cites empirical evidence which suggests, for instance, that integrated policy communities – as distinct from loose issue-networks – are more likely to occur in a relatively centralized political system (such as the UK) than in a 'fragmented', decentralized system like the USA (1993: 138–9, 234), although there are exceptions to this general tendency. Another illustration, this time relating to European styles of governance, is Flynn and Strehl's (1996: 4) empirically based observation that, within European nation–states, a number of macro-social phenomena shape national public sectors; these macro-phenomena include, for example, constitutional arrangements, national political cultures, public attitudes towards state services, and the news media.

A previously mentioned ontological and methodological postulate relates to the present discussion. This concerns upwards conflation, as in methodological individualism and methodological situationalism which illicitly attempt to reduce the macro-social to the actions of individuals in the former case and to 'situations' (contexts of co-presence) in the latter. Randall Collins's methodological situationalism (for example, 1981; 1983; 1988) was briefly referred to at the beginning of the chapter; it is worth citing his work as a reminder of the inadequacies of upward conflationist accounts of the macro-social. Collins believes macro-phenomena are made up of aggregations and repetitions of many similar micro-episodes; in his model, the macroscopic social world is 'nothing more than large numbers of micro-encounters repeated (or sometimes changing) over time and actors' space' (Collins, 1987: 195). As critics have pointed out, Collins's theoretical account of the macro-social is seriously flawed. His conception of 'horizontal' and 'vertical' inter-situational linkages is unconvincing (Mouzelis, 1991: 82–8) and cannot adequately account for power differentials among actors (ibid.: 87–8) nor for the 'layered' characteristics of social organization (ibid.: 87) associated with a stratified social ontology. At the same time, Collins's framework prevents him from properly dealing with the question of 'lateral' connections across space and time. Underlying the limitations of Collins's framework is, as one critic has put it, the problem that Collins 'denies that trans-situational rules of conduct contribute to the constitution of persistent modes of social activity' (Cohen, 1987: 294). Knorr-Cetina (1981: 28) puts the matter this way: methodological situationalism's aggregation hypothesis conspicuously fails to address 'the *interrelation* between situated social events ... the *linkage* between the happenings of diverse micro-situations'. These observations, and the arguments set out in earlier chapters, serve to indicate that it is erroneous to suppose that macro-phenomena are no more than – or can be reduced to – aggregates of micro-interactional episodes. Collins's micro-translation of the macroscopic social order is, on the one hand, incapable of providing an adequate account of emergent and configurational/interactive properties of social systems and of material diffusion and distribution patterns that are 'larger' than micro-situations; and on the other, is incapable of adequately accounting for the influence of macroscopic variables upon mezo- and micro-levels of social process. These metatheoretical/ontological observations have, as we shall see in the following section, a number of important methodological implications.

Levels and spheres of social process: some metatheoretical and methodological considerations

Earlier, explicit reference was made to the idea of a stratified (or 'depth') social ontology. The existence of relatively autonomous, distinct properties and effects of the different 'layers' that constitute social reality is a reason for resisting the central conflationist tendency of those theorists – such as Giddens, Elias and Foucault – who collapse the micro–macro distinction and thereby portray society as a 'flat', seamless web of social relations with no distinction between micro-, mezo- and macro-phenomena; for central conflationists the idea of making any such distinctions does not make sense. In contrast, other theorists, myself included, argue that the micro-social and macro-social orders should be analysed as interpenetrative but relatively independent levels of reality, each with their own properties (such as varying patterns and scales of 'emergence', differing time-frames, and different spatializations). We should not, in other words, try to explain the characteristics of one level *in terms of another*. It is important to avoid downward conflation, which 'rests on the a priori assumption that the lower levels of analysis point to phenomena which have no dynamics of their own, and can therefore be entirely explained in terms of regularities grasped at higher levels' (Mouzelis, 1991: 138). We have also noted that neither is it the case, as upward conflationists assume, that happenings which occur at 'higher' (mezo or macro) levels of social process are no more than – and can therefore be explained in terms of – events that happen at 'lower', localized or micro-levels; theories and methodologies – notably those associated with methodological individualism and methodological situationalism – that are based upon upwards conflation invariably obscure the significance of the emergent properties of mezo- and macro-social domains, and fail to adequately get to grips with the idea of temporal and trans-situational material diffusion.

It is worth highlighting some other methodologically relevant features of the social ontology described above. It was clarified earlier that to say that micro-, mezo- and macro-layers of social reality each have a relatively independent existence is not, of course, to deny that empirically significant connections between them may develop over time and that each level may influence and be influenced by the others, a crucial proviso here being that explanation of such connections should, I have argued, employ concepts and theories developed in tandem with critique of reductionism, essentialism, reification, and functional teleology. A related clarification is, in effect, contained in the above remarks on conflation. That is, just as it can be argued – against Berger and Luckmann, Giddens, Bourdieu, Foucault, and Habermas – that there is no 'direct link' between action and structure, so also can it be argued that there is no direct link between micro-, mezo- and macro-social domains; in terms of the social ontology referred to earlier it is to be expected on (meta)theoretical grounds (though this postulate, as stated in Chapter 1, should always remain open to empirical sources of revision) that connections between these domains will tend to be relatively 'loose' and 'indirect', that is, a change in one domain will not necessarily be followed by a matching change in another. A further methodological consideration is that in the real world the different levels of social process, though analytically distinct, may interweave such that, in research practice, it is empirically difficult to disaggregate them. An example is to be found in studies of European governance where, in the European Union and across EU member states, the four main layers or spheres of governance (supranational, transnational, national, subnational) sometimes mingle together. In the European Union, the 'European' and the 'national' spheres of governance in many policy sectors – including highly Europeanized ones such as agriculture, telecommunications, competition, and external trade – overlap and interpenetrate to such an extent that the boundary between them is at times indistinct (Meny *et al.*, 1996: 16; Sibeon, 2000: 303).

The ontological premises referred to above, including their anti-reductionist and non-teleological form, have time–space dimensions that in some respects are akin to those mentioned by Duster:

All social action can be conceived as local in the sense that it must occur in settings bound by local time and local space and the local constitutive expectancies of social exchange. It may ramify and serve as a future point of reference for many other local scenes, both temporally and spatially ... But the question of whether ... [a particular] ... local scene has some future historic import is a problematic matter for empirical assessment. (1981: 114)

The empirical assessment called for by Duster is always required, because there is no structurally 'necessary' or given hierarchy of sites with some always having total dominance over others (Hindess, 1986a: 122) (see the discussion of power in Chapter 5). One way of putting this, and here I draw upon the language of actor network theory, is to say that actors have no exclusively structural or systemically determined capacity to enrol other actors 'irreversibly' or to *consign* (institutionalize) material and successfully propel it spatially and temporally across locales to a widening 'enrolled' audience (Law and Hassard, 1999). In more general terms, it has been argued by Fararo (1992: 349) that a concept of material diffusion solves, in principle, Giddens's 'reconstructed social order' problem (Fararo 1992: 275) which is to do with how separate contexts and entities become connected temporally and spatially. What these remarks point to – theoretically and methodologically speaking – is the complex relation of material-diffusion processes (see Chapter 6) to notions of locale and time–space.[9] One of the empirical complexities involved here is that 'the same' material (a political, administrative, or professional discourse, for example) may, as briefly noted earlier, be given different forms of expression at different levels of social process and in different spatio-temporal contexts. Again, Duster's observations are worthy of note, though he himself does not directly relate them to the ontological themes under discussion here. Duster's methodologically multi-layered approach is evident in his study of American medical screening programmes for inherited disorders. His research objective was to examine empirically the ways in which the phenomenon under investigation are manifest at different levels of social process:

Three levels of entry are (1) direct observation of behaviour in the local setting in which it routinely occurs, the grounding for the 'micro' base of the study; (2) observation and analysis of the administrative, bureaucratic, or organizational unit(s) that are interposed between the local scene, and (3) the 'macro' trend, rates, or perhaps law, or federal social policy development. (Duster, 1981: 133)

This relates to a more general thesis which specifies that 'the same' material may be modified or even transformed at different levels – micro, mezo, macro – of social reality, which is also to say that the material may be given different expression (in a 'lateral' sense) in a range of spatio-temporal contexts scattered across variable expanses of space and time. However, this thesis, though not often conceptualized in the particular form described here, is in some sense hardly novel, as the following examples will show. Rootes's (1981) sociology of knowledge leads him to point out that world-views (or in his analysis, political ideologies) may be 'mediated' at different levels of crystallization, explicitness, and internal conceptual consistency; day-to-day professional practice, for example in psychiatry, health or welfare settings may indirectly contribute to the reproduction of a holistic political ideology even though the exigencies of practice may mean that the ideology, at the level of everyday local practice, is less crystallized, less explicit, and less internally conceptually consistent than in other settings (for example, academic seminars or political conferences). Also of interest is Berger and Luckmann's (1971) and Bernardes's (1985) thesis that ideologies and theories in modern society frequently embody 'multiple realities' and a plurality of 'contradictory' meanings; and Levitas's (1976) work on the ways in which adoption and rejection of belief systems or ideas may, in some instances, rest less upon logical consistency than upon emotional consistency or (as in the case of 'cognitive dissonance') upon a positive orientation towards the source of an idea. Of significance, too, is the notion that theories, perspectives and ideologies have 'publics' (the mass media, professional bodies, politicians, consumer groups, governments, and so on) to which ideologies have to 'relate' in a variety of ways. An insightful review of the range of types of relationships that may develop between ideologies and their 'publics' is provided by Bouchier (1977) who examines empirically the ways in which ideologies for their survival may require pragmatic flexibility and plasticity in relating to the sometimes conflicting demands of different 'publics'. Also relevant here is Layder's multi-dimensional conception of power. He argues (1997: 13, 250–1) that power – concerning, let us say, gender roles or social class – takes many forms. It is 'objective' (external to any particular individual's subjectivity or activities) and embodied in discourse, as Foucault argued, but it is also 'subjective' (and intersubjective): power wends its way across the micro-, mezo- and macro-domains that constitute social life – for Layder, as noted earlier, these are psychobiography, situated activity, social settings, and contextual resources – and is given a different mode of expression within each domain. Power, in other words, has relatively independent, distinct and domain-specific modes of existence, although forms of power, like the domains themselves, may also be interpenetrative and overlapping, with more or less loose or indirect links between the differing forms of power that exist in each domain.

Some important theoretical and methodological implications of the above will be returned to in a moment. A more general (meta)theoretical observation, and here it may be helpful to re-state a number of ontological postulates that were referred to earlier, is that society is 'vertically' layered into micro-, mezo- and macro-levels of social process and that such layering is one and the same thing as 'lateral' distributions of actors, locales, materials and social systems/social networks across extensions of time–space that range from the small-scale (micro) to the large (macro). (Although, as noted earlier, this postulate is rarely put in quite this way, it is regularly deployed across a range of social science disciplines, very often tacitly and therefore in conceptually and methodologically underdeveloped fashion.) The idea of material diffusion, including the important question of whether certain materials retain their shape or else are elaborated (or perhaps go out of existence) *during* the course of their travel across time–space, relates to the empirical question, referred to above, of whether any particular material (including material associated with 'power') is manifest in perhaps differing forms at each of the levels of social process – micro, mezo, and macro – that constitute society; or whether, to put this another way, the material in question manifests itself in different forms within a range of locales and within differing time-frames (the latter being a reference to a distinction between, in particular, institutional time, and the time-frame of situated activity). An issue here is the importance of studying the travel of material *across* spatio-temporal contexts (tracking it as it moves; see Callon and Latour, 1981) while also investigating 'what happens' to the material *within* a range of contexts scattered across time and space. In any particular instance we might want to know, for example, whether the material is transformed – given special meaning – in some locales, whether local transformations are idiosyncratic or part of a larger transformative pattern (Lidz, 1981), and whether and if so in what form local transformations are transmitted to other spatio-temporal contexts. Any such micro- and mezo-happenings cannot, once downward conflation is abandoned, be predicted on the basis of – cannot be be 'read off' from – a knowledge of the macro-social order. Equally, once upward conflation (such as methodological individualism and methodological situationalism) is rejected, we cannot discover the nature of the macro-social by using micro-situational methodology: we cannot, for example, know the macro-social by undertaking a series of co-ordinated ethnographies (that is, the co-ordination of a number of micro-situational studies – using such methods as participant observation – conducted at a number of locations). The reason for this was broached earlier. As Knorr-Cetina (1981) and others have observed, micro-situational research premised on the principles and methods of symbolic interactionism is neither theoretically nor methodologically equipped for examining the emergent properties of mezo- and macro-social phenomena nor for investigating linkages between sites across time and space; and in terms of my framework, it is clear that micro-social research is ill equipped for investigating the travel of materials *across* spatio-temporal contexts (though it to some extent is equipped for investigating the handling of material *within* contexts). In, for example, the field of public policy, micro-situational methodology is a necessary tool for studying local emergent policy meanings that may be specific to the locale in question, and for investigating local handling of trans-situational materials that the researcher believes may be relatively common to a large number of sites (Haimes, 1993; Lidz, 1981: 226–7). But as just noted, micro-situational analysis has its limitations. In large part, emergent properties – at micro-, mezo- (for example, inter-organizational) and macro-levels – require analysis and investigation *at the level of social process at which they occur*: this is not to ignore that layered ('vertical') domains may influence each other, but it is to insist that domains are relatively independent and that this has implications for methodology. Of relevance here, as we have seen, are material dissemina-tion processes as described in Chapter 6, where it was suggested that for analytical purposes we should take seriously the commonplace observation that materials – using this term in a broad sense to include, for example, generalized forms of thought, the contents of written media, and practice conventions – flow spatially and temporally across locales. That some mate-rial changes in form *as it travels*, is undisputable. Reflecting on the struc-ture and form of scientific knowledge, Fleck, a practising microbiologist, observes that 'knowledge changes unpredictably and ideas alter *in the process of their communication*' (Fleck, 1979, quoted in Jacobs, 1987: 269, my italics). If this happens to knowledge in the physical sciences, which tend to be regarded as having an epistemologically relatively 'firm' knowl-edge mandate, it is perhaps even more to be expected in the case of other types of materials (such as those with high aesthetic or normative content). It was argued in Chapter 6 that the form and effects of any particular mate-rials, including the extent of their *mobility* and *durability* across time and space, are contingent outcomes of social processes involving diachronic links between agency, structure, and social chance; the materials are not given by nature and nor are they necessary effects of the social totality. In order to track the movement of material across time–space, and to investi-gate its handling – including its reproduction or elaboration – *within and across* sites, micro-situational method is a necessary but not a sufficient research tool. What is required in light of the stratified social ontology described earlier, is a multi-method and multi-level research strategy in which, to repeat, micro-, mezo- and macro-social domains are analysed as interpenetrative and mutually influencing but empirically distinct layers of social reality, each with distinct properties (in particular, differing time-frames, forms of emergence and spatializations) that require investigation on the basis of a selective use of methods – participant observation, historical documentary analysis, social surveys, and so forth – appropriate to the domain in question and to the immediate task in hand. As noted earlier, one advantage of a methodological orientation of this kind is that it focuses attention on the need to investigate, among other types of phenomena, those instances where 'the same' material may be manifest in different forms at each level of social process, that is to say, given somewhat differing forms of expression across varying extensions of time and space.

One particularly interesting and important attempt to construct a multi-level research strategy, is Layder's (1993; 1997; 1998b).[10] His research strategy has a certain amount of affinity with my own. As outlined in Chapter 4, Layder's stratified social ontology is a modification and elaboration of the previously described distinction between micro-, mezo- and macro-domains. Layder (1997) identifies four social domains, or 'layerings' as he sometimes calls them. These are *psychobiography*, the largely unique, asocial components of self and behaviour; *situated activity*, which refers to face-to-face interaction and intersubjectivity in situations of co-presence; *social settings*, that is, the locations in which situated activity occurs; and *contextual resources*, consisting of macro-distributions and ownerships of resources (relating, in particular, to social class, gender, and ethnic divisions) and widespread cultural meanings, discourses, and social practices. As already noted, Layder argues that each domain has relative autonomy but that the domains overlap and influence each other, and that any connections that develop between them are likely to be relatively 'loose' with no 'direct links' between micro, mezo and macro, or in Layder's terms, between the four social domains listed above. The first two domains (psychobiography and situated activity) constitute the *subjective* dimension of society, the other two – social settings and contextual resources – being the *objective* dimension. An attractive feature of Layder's methodological orientation is that, on the one hand, due attention is given to the relative autonomy of each level or layer of the social, which implies that researchers should avoid attempts to explain phenomena that exist at one level exclusively in terms of phenomena that exist at another (the familiar problems of upwards and downwards conflation): on the other hand, an overly rigid Durkheimian[11] insistence on explanation of what Durkheim called 'social facts' (macro-phenomena) in terms of *other* (macro) social facts is avoided in so far as it is recognized that, while it may well be that phenomena at one level have crucial implications for other phenomena at that level, it is also the case that each level or domain may to a greater or lesser extent influence the other domains. For example, while micro-occurrences cannot determine the macro-social order order (nor vice versa), they are indirectly linked and there are always likely to be at least some 'loose' couplings between the micro- and macro-social orders, or sometimes rather closer or 'tighter' couplings.

Although the concerns of this book are primarily ontological, there is good reason to suppose that epistemology – as is evident in Layder's framework – cannot be entirely separated from ontology; our conception of what, in general terms, the social world is like (that is, our conception of the sorts of things that constitute the social) is distinct from but has implications for our understanding of the kinds of knowledge of that world that might be sought. Layder is committed to the idea of *epistemological pluralism*; in his case this is not epistemological anarchy or the adoption of a cavalier 'anything goes' position – his is a principled epistemological pluralism that is derived from his (ontological) conception of four domains, two of which, as we have seen, constitute the subjective sphere of social life, and two the objective. His argument, like mine, is that instead of an either-or standpoint concerning research methods and their epistemological underpinning (for example, quantitative 'versus' qualitative methods or objectivist 'versus' grounded theory approaches) sociology and other social sciences should selectively employ methods appropriate to the task in hand, and especially, appropriate to investigation of each sphere or domain; epistemological precepts and methods that are suitable for investigating one domain may be wholly unsuitable for investigation of another. The methods and supporting epistemological principles appropriate to the task of investigating, say, the psychobiographical domain, will necessarily have to be supplanted by other methods when it comes to the study of 'objective' domains such as social settings or contextual resources. In Layder's social realism the world is indeed 'real', but is a highly variegated social reality consisting of subjective, intersubjective, and objective-systemic phenomena that interact and overlap. The social world, in other words, is multidimensional and cannot be reductively accounted for in terms of any single explanatory principle such as 'subjectivity'/'individualism', 'intersubjectivity'/'interaction', 'habitus', 'figurations', or 'social systems' or 'structures', nor in terms of any single epistemological rubric or single method of enquiry. Layder's nicely articulated plea is for epistemological pluralism incorporating objective and subjective epistemologies and for flexible methodological approaches that are capable of coming to terms with the distinct, differing properties of each domain, and with the mutual influences between domains; hence it is necessary to employ – depending on the nature of the research task at hand – humanist/phenomenological/interpretative epistemologies and methods, as well as 'objective' epistemology and method. Layder's (1993; 1997; 1998a; 1998b) (meta)theoretical and methodological framework involves an analytical movement from actors' perspectives to the 'external' perspective of an 'independent observer' (Habermas, 1987) as one shifts from the psychobiographic and situated activity domains to the more encompassing domains of social settings and contextual resources. In the psychobiographic and situated activity domains, which together constitute the subjective dimension of society, actors' standpoints and perspectives are given analytical priority (this refers to the criterion of 'subjective adequacy'), whereas at the systemic levels of 'objective' social reality – the domains described by Layder as social settings and contextual resources – it is appropriate to emphasize an 'external' observer's perspective.[12] In regard to the latter it should be noted, bearing in mind the existence of both subjective and objective domains, that this is not a case of a 'superior' or 'more accurate' external perspective being substituted for 'inferior' or 'distorted' subjective perspectives held by lay people; that is, the more encompassing domains *are* objective and they are not analytically graspable in terms of any *particular* participant's meaning or motives, nor in terms of any particular local activities.

For reasons that are implicit (and very often explicit) in each of the previous chapters, I find myself in broad agreement with most of Layder's epistemological and ontological arguments. However, there are some differences of emphasis in our respective approaches. I prefer to refer to agency, structure, and social chance, and to micro-, mezo- and macro-domains in the form that I have discussed them; these concepts as I have defined them are, I believe, appropriate descriptors of multidimensional and stratified social reality that – though I concur with much of what he says about that reality – Layder prefers to describe as psychobiography, situated activity, social settings, and contextual resources. Other differences that were noted in Chapter 4, are as follows. I employ a a 'tighter', more explicitly anti-reified concept of actor than Layder, and I am critical of Layder's tendency (for example, 1994: 4–5) to emphasize individual human actors at the expense of social ('organizational') actors; Layder neglects material diffusion processes, these being crucial elements in the constitution of society; and while, in principle, his formulations clearly acknowledge the objective dimension of social life, his main writings to date have tended to emphasize the subjective dimension (currently in British theoretical sociology the work of Mouzelis and Archer is in some respects more useful than Layder's as sources of conceptual and methodological insights for investigating macroscopic phenomena and the objective dimensions of the social). None the less, Layder's metatheoretical and methodological framework is, in my opinion, a highly promising contribution to the reconstruction of sociological metatheory and methodology 'after postmodernism'; certainly, it can be argued that his framework deserves closer and more systematic attention by social scientists than has so far been accorded to it.

Finally, it is not, of course, suggested here that *all* empirical studies should necessarily encompass and give equal attention to the micro-, mezo- and macro-domains (or to Layder's modified and elaborated versions of these social domains). As Layder observes, in practice it is likely that researchers – for any number of reasons to do with academic specialisms, resources available for research, and so on – will focus primarily on one or two domains; this form of 'methodological bracketing'[13] is acceptable, providing the underlying premises of domain theory – especially those concerned with the relatively autonomous but intertwining nature of social domains – are constantly borne in mind (Layder 1997: 76; 1998a: 101). An in some ways parallel approach to research is to be found in Berger's large-scale theoretical scheme which synthesizes micro- and macro-perspectives. The Bergerian micro–macro synthesis explicitly acknowledges that separate empirical studies may usefully be undertaken at micro- and macro-levels respectively, and that such studies may be complementary (Berger and Luckmann, 1971: 208), although there is, it is argued, a strong case for also carrying out work that involves explicit analytical integration of data produced by separate micro- and macro-level studies. Thus this chapter's arguments in favour of a multi-level and multidimensional research strategy and for the epistemological pluralism that is allied to it, embody a holistic but flexible conception of empirical studies which may legitimately range from rather grand empirical syntheses to smaller-scale, specialist studies focused on perhaps only one or two of the domains that constitute the social.

Summary

This chapter brought together key concepts and postulates that have featured throughout the book, and argued for an integrated (meta)theoretical and methodological framework that is epistemologically and methodologically pliable. As in earlier chapters, (meta)theoretical material was illustrated with reference to empirical and policy-related topics; this reflects commitment to an epistemological understanding that metatheoretical postulates should shape and be shaped by empirical studies (or more precisely, by a reciprocity between substantive theory and empirical data: see Chapter 1).

●

The idea of ontological depth is not unidimensional. Micro-, mezo-, and macro-domains are both vertical layerings of society and lateral spreads of actors, locales, and materials across varying extensions – from small to large-scale – of time and space. We are referring here to a complex social ontology.

●

In terms of the approach developed in this book, both micro-analysis and macro-analysis can focus on institutional and/or figurational dynamics, where the micro–macro distinction refers in part to differences in the units of and scale of analyses concerned with empirical investigation of varying stretches of time–space: these statements apply equally to mezo-level analysis.

•

Structure may be defined as – in the case of macro-structure – institutional and figurational aspects of extensive time–space dispersions of actors, locales, materials, and social conditions that include social systems/social networks. Although relatively autonomous from agency and from social chance, structure is the outcome of diachronic linkages between agency, structure, and social chance. For reasons identified in earlier chapters, the methods employed for investigating structure and agency should avoid upward and downward conflation; there are no direct links between action and structure nor between micro-, mezo- and macro-social domains. As well, we have observed that materials 'travel' temporally and spatially (though the relative durability and mobility of materials may vary). An implication of the social ontology referred to here is that, for example, the 'same' material (such as, let us say, a political or administrative discourse) may sometimes be given different forms of expression at different levels of social process and in different spatio-temporal contexts; and that social analysts should employ methods flexibly, based on epistemological and methodological pluralism of a kind that acknowledges the existence of objective and subjective domains viewed in terms of the heuristic, ontologically flexible (meta)theoretical concepts and postulates set out in this book, these being meta-concepts and meta-postulates that, as observed earlier, are in principle open to theoretical and empirical sources of revision.

Notes

1 Here no reference is made to the epistemological question of whether it is legitimate to claim that some concepts and conceptual distinctions – including micro–macro – may be analytically indispensable, yet have no real empirical referents: this is taken up in the concluding chapter.

2 In Chapter 3 it was argued that despite its undoubted contribution to the development of sociological theory, Bergerian sociology has a tendency to overemphasize the subjective dimension of reality at the expense of the objective, and, in duality fashion, to collapse distinctions between action and structure and micro and macro while at the same time endorsing dualism as part of a contradictory endorsement of both 'upwards' and 'downwards' conflation. Elias, it was argued, often wrongly implied that there is a 'direct link' between individual activities and society and between micro and macro, an implication that also figures strongly in Giddens's theory of structuration. And we saw that Foucault is associated with unfortunate tendencies to dissolve distinctions between agency and structure and micro and macro, and to largely ignore the significance of intersubjectivity. Foucault

also, it was argued, fails to acknowledge discontinuities between macro-cognitive and micro-behavioural dimensions of the social, and he displays strong traces of reification and functional teleology in some of his theorizing.

Nor are more recent sociological theorists' treatments of micro–macro entirely satisfactory: for example, it was observed in Chapter 2 that Mouzelis errs in refusing to associate 'micro' with co-presence, and that Archer has a curious notion of micro–macro such that, say, a nation–state is for some analytical purposes defined by her as a micro-entity. Though I employ strands of Mouzelis's and Archer's work and regard their overall contributions to the development of contemporary sociological theory as important, my approach to micro–macro and to the notion of a layered social ontology is in some respects closer to Layder's (1997) than to theirs.

3 Interaction implies two-way communication as distinct from the one-way process of communication associated with, for example, the impact of the contents of a book, newspaper, or electronic journal upon readers. Electronically mediated relations (involving, say, telephone, e-mail or the Internet) exhibit some of the characteristics of interaction associated with situations of co-presence, but there are also some obvious differences; for instance, in the former case the participants do not, in the communication process, share the same physical setting nor – as with e-mail or texting – do they necessarily share the same temporality. This means, for example, that two-way electronic communication, though in some sense a micro-phenomenon, has macro-connotations in so far as interactants may be dispersed across some interval of time–space. It is possible to discover in the literature some suggestive observations concerning the continuing significance of co-presence alongside compression of time and space in a global age (for example, Giddens, 1984, and M.P. Smith, 2001; Thompson, 1995), and concerning cyberspace interaction (for example, Fox and Roberts, 1999; Star, 1995), but it remains the case that in the social sciences considerably more work – theoretical, methodological, and empirical – remains to be done in making connections between (a) spatio-temporal dimensions of electronically mediated forms of communication, and (b) the micro–macro distinction.

4 The figurational, intersubjective/interactional element has long provided the distinctive thrust of micro-social research (Meltzer et al., 1975; Charon, 1995): but in acknowledging this I also want – for reasons set out in earlier chapters –- to establish the proposition that conventional understanding of the micro-social order should be revised and broadened so as to explicitly focus not only on interaction/intersubjectivity but also subjectivity/psychobiography, small-scale institutional dynamics (for example, role–role relations), and connections – investigated empirically within small-scale spatio-temporal contexts – between these relatively autonomous elements.

In turn, the micro-social order comprised of the 'internal' elements to which I have just referred, is a relatively independent domain that to a greater or lesser extent is connected in contingent, empirically discoverable ways to the mezo- and macro-social orders.

5 Here it is worth noticing – leaving aside Alexander and Smith's (1993) overly 'structuralist' orientation to cultural analysis – that the recent resurgence of interest in cultural sociology (for example, P. Smith, 2001; Spillman, 2002) is likely, if anything, to strengthen social scientific interest in the meaning-making, culturally reproductive and/or meaning-elaboration significance of the micro-social order and its relation to macro-structural phenomena.

Cultural sociology is not the same thing as cultural studies; while the distinction – as with the distinction between sociological and social theory – is far from clear-cut, cultural studies is interdisciplinary (spread across a range of humanities, including English), tends to draw implicitly on Marxist, structuralist, and postmodern theory and to employ *ad hoc* methods, whereas cultural sociology tends to explicitly draw on classical and contemporary sociological perspectives – ranging from Marx, Durkheim, Weber, to Bourdieu and Foucault – and to employ systematic methodologies (see Edles, 2002: 14–15). Cultural studies' aestheticization of social life and displacement of the social in favour of textual analysis and intertextuality, are criticized in Rojek and Turner's (2000) critique of the cultural turn. For Rojek and Turner, cultural studies is part of a trend toward 'decorative sociology', a trend that lacks a developed empirical research agenda and which undertakes little serious historical and comparative work. Rojek and Turner also point to a tendency among a number of cultural studies writers to adopt, with reference to such topics as race, gender, colonialism and various forms of conflict or 'social exclusion', a condemnatory 'we know best' and 'moral high ground' attitude that exudes what Rojek and Turner describe as 'moral arrogance, intellectual narrowness and over-confidence' (2000: 634). A not dissimilar assessment is Turner and O'Neill's (2001: 10) comment that social theory has become almost identical with 'cultural theory' and

> has become a ragbag for almost any set of observations on modern society. There is no sense of an effective distinction between opinion and theory … There has been a tendency for cultural theory to re-orient sociology away from the study of specifically social institutions to a vague reflection on cultural phenomena from chocolate bars to Bach's concertos.

6 However, having in somewhat conventional fashion suggested micro–mezo–macro should be defined in terms of their differing spatial extensions, Stones (1998: 304), rather confusingly, seems to also approve of Mouzelis's unusual conception of macro-action as associated with 'powerful' actors and micro with 'weak' actors. In Chapter 2 I showed why, on this issue, Mouzelis's terminology is unhelpful and his analysis flawed.

7 In my theoretical scheme, structure ('social conditions' or 'the conditions of action') consists of both macro- and micro-phenomena (many writers have a tendency to associate social structure with macro, and agency with micro), hence my differentiation between macro-structure and micro-structure.

8 It is perhaps appropriate to reiterate that the conception of the macro-social referred to here is in some ways a departure from existing theorizing, in other ways not. My partly systemic, partly relational approach to the macro-social is one element within a stratified and processual social ontology informed by concept development that entails critical synthesis of a range of theoretical positions, as well as critique of what I call the four 'cardinal sins' which are to be found in many areas of theoretical and methodological reasoning: but while my approach to the macro-social may be distinctive in certain respects, it is clear that the approach in some ways resonates with others in so far as, for example, other theorists, though not necessarily in terms that I would wholly support, have in various ways drawn attention to contingent, processual dimensions of the macro-social (for instance, Boudon 1986; Skocpol, 1984; Mann, 1986; Sztompka, 1991; 1993; Stones, 1996. Another example is the work of Roberto Unger, which is discussed in this chapter).

9 On the question of the relation of material diffusion processes to spatio-temporal contexts, Cohen's observation – which can be kept separate from his commitment to a duality of action and structure – is broadly congruent with my position:

> Systemic relations are maintained and reproduced as ... [the] ... results of social conduct are transmitted or transported to other agents who may be situated in the same spatio-temporal setting, or who may be situated in another systemic locale across some interval of time–space. These agents, in turn, may engage in further transformations of the outcomes of activities which have been transmitted/transported to them. Each transformation in some way changes the content of events and/or material objects. (1989: 127)

This quotation serves to highlight a remarkably neglected dimension within sociological theory and research. It is noticeable – Cohen being an example of this – that the occasional passing reference in the literature to what I call material-diffusion tends to be tacit and theoretically and methodologically underdeveloped.

10 Other attempts to formulate an integrated, multi-level research strategy include Geertz's (1979) notion of 'dialectical tacking' between micro and macro; this involves the use of multiple methodologies and the combining of micro-ethnographic data with reconstruction of historical data so as to bring different spatial and temporal levels of social process into focus simultaneously: and Reed's (1985) multi-method, holistic research framework which consists of four main elements – described by him as cognitive mapping, interpretative understanding, structural analysis, and historical reconstruction.

11 Here I employ the adjective 'Durkheimian' as a convenient and conventional shorthand. However, it has been argued by some – though I do not have the space to enter this debate here – that Durkheim's principle that social facts must be explained in terms of other social facts (for our purposes this means that macro-phenomena must be explained in terms of *other* macro phenomena), has been misconstrued and that Durkheim has a more nuanced social ontology than he is generally given credit for; see, for example, the sympathetic reading of Durkheim set out in Stedman Jones (2001).

12 But as Layder (1997) himself observes, in so far as social domains interpenetrate and overlap, so also – if concepts are to represent social reality as accurately as possible – must there be some allowance for interpenetration among the concepts (and epistemological and methodological criteria) that are used to describe and investigate those domains: this means, for example, that an element of actors' subjectivity and intersubjectivity (that is, actors' perspectives) should be allowed to infuse investigation of 'objective' domains (though with objective methodology remaining central), and that while 'subjective' methodologies should be given primacy when investigating the subjective sphere of social life (psychobiography and situated activity), an element of 'objective' methodology should not be excluded. Thus assessment of the adequacy of 'objective' concepts/methods must partly refer to the extent to which they can be linked to 'subjective' concepts and methodologies, and likewise subjective concepts/methods should have a capacity to link to and overlap with objective ones. This also, it may be noted, relates to a version of the idea of 'methodological bracketing': we are speaking here of a matter of emphasis (not an either-or) – where objective domains are the focus of enquiry, attention should centre largely (though not exclusively) on 'objective' concepts and methods, and vice versa in the case of subjective domains.

13 See note 12 above.

Conclusion

Central to this book's approach to metatheory, substantive theory, and methodology is a relatively pliable social ontology, with concept development – relating to such concepts as agency, structure, recursion, social chance, micro–macro, social systems/networks, time–space, power, interests, and material-diffusion – that entails theoretical synthesis, and where the idea of a flexible minimal ontology is allied to critique of four 'cardinal sins' that (either singly or in combination, and often in tacit form) continue to be fairly widespread in the social sciences. I shall return shortly to the need to transcend these theoretic-methodological sins. For the moment, I should like to reiterate that a minimal and relatively 'open' social ontology is the converse of ontological and (meta)theoretical closure, where empirical phenomena are prematurely described or 'explained' – in a priori fashion – in advance of empirical enquiry. It is not metatheory or social ontology, nor indeed substantive theory but empirical enquiry that should do the bulk of the work in revealing the characteristics and significance of any particular empirical phenomena: equally, the question of which type of minimal ontology is selected as a guide to research practice, is crucial. A couple of examples will serve to clarify my assertion that an over-expanded and inflexible ontology will tend to lead to premature (meta)theoretical and ontological closure. First, consider the sub-field of organizational studies (see, for example, the useful overviews in Clegg and Hardy, 1999, and in Strati, 2000). In the 'ecological' paradigm, analysis of organizational processes rests on the notion that organizations compete for scarce resources and that some organizations thrive while others decline as a result of environmental selection of 'the fittest'; supporters of the so-called 'institutionalist' paradigm seize on the idea that social reality is made up of socially constructed meanings and practices which become institutionalized and acquire a taken-for-granted Durkheimian facticity which in turn influences actors' forms of thought and actions; advocates of the 'interpretative' paradigm insist organizations – and indeed, social life in general – must be viewed in terms of interaction and actors' creative interpretations and re-interpretations of meanings. More often than not, such 'approaches' are treated by their proponents not as heuristic models open to empirical sources of revision, nor as ways of affording a preliminary glimpse into certain selected dimensions of social reality, but rather, as overarching, single-order (meta)theories; therein lies a route to reductionism and other problems associated with inflexible social ontologies. Rather than insist organizations be viewed in terms of ecology *or* institutionalization *or* interaction, and thereby arbitrarily foreclose the possibilities for engaging in multi-dimensional and relatively 'open-ended' empirical investigation, it is better to adopt an ontologically pliant schema in the terms set out in the previous chapters and treat the degree to which meanings are institutionalized, the nature of and the factors that influence the relation of organizations to their environments, and so on, as variables whose relative significance and characteristics cannot be known in advance of empirical enquiry. As argued in the preceding chapter, there are also, I suggest, good reasons for employing a stratified social ontology in tandem with the idea of epistemological pluralism: this means, for example, that for investigating subjective domains of organizational life an emphasis upon interpretative concepts and methods is entirely appropriate, but not for investigating objective domains.

A second illustration relating to premature ontological closure, concerns investigation of governance processes in the European Union (EU). At least until quite recently, many political scientists explained the continuing existence and functioning of the EU – which in some respects is a unique hybrid not replicated anywhere else in the world – in terms of 'supranationalism' *or* 'intergovernmentalism' (see the discussion in George and Bache, 2001). Supranationalism occurs when elements of national sovereignty are transferred to a third party supranational entity (here the European Union) that is empowered to make decisions that are binding upon member states. Intergovernmentalism, in contrast, refers to a form of governance where there is no formal transfer of sovereignty and law-making rights to a supranational entity; rather, intergovernmental governance relies on negotiation, exchange, bargaining, and collaboration between 'sovereign' national governments. For some analysts the increasing importance of the EU is due to supranationalism, which implies that once 'in' a club with supranational powers such as the EU, it is hard to get out again and that the EU rules the roost; others, in the intergovernmentalist camp, are committed to explanations in which national governments are said to be relatively independent but to see advantages in choosing to continue to be a member of the European Union and in negotiating national interests within the EU framework. There is evidence that neither of these competing camps have got it right: the reality appears to be not only that supranationalism and intergovernmentalism co-exist within the European Union but that these interrelate in complex ways with – and are partly being replaced by – highly processual and contingent multi-level governance processes in Europe (Sibeon, 2001). The point of these illustrations is that premature ontological closure and a priori theoretical predetermination of empirical happenings tends, as in the above examples relating to organizational studies and to European governance, to lead to simplistic so-called 'explanations' of social and political affairs.

As well as a relatively flexible, minimal stratified social ontology, a further condition that in my opinion is necessary to the achievement of explanatory success in the social sciences was set out in the Introduction and subsequently referred to throughout the book. There is a need to transcend problems associated with what I have termed the four 'cardinal sins' of theoretical and methodological reasoning. This together with the previously described conception of society as something that is stratified into relatively autonomous layers, signifies that the social ontology referred to here is not so flexible or so minimal as to amount to an 'anything goes' stance of the kind associated with certain strands of postmodern thought; we are speaking here of an ontology that, in the sense described in Chapter 1, is relatively but not totally 'open'. As described in the Introduction, the four sins, each of which should in my view be kept firmly in mind when formulating concepts or developing theoretical propositions and methodological prescriptions, are defined as follows. *Reductionism* refers to illegitimate attempts to reduce social explanation in the first or 'last-instance' ('deferred reductionism') to a single, unifying principle of explanation or, in the case of what I call 'compounded reductionism', to a combination or synthesis of two or more reductionist principles of explanation; *essentialism* attributes homogeneity to social phenomena on a priori grounds (as distinct from uses of this term which are to do with the question of whether phenomena – social categories, for example, such as 'women' – have real essences or are socially constructed); *reification* in my use of the term refers not to any failure to recognize that society is activity-dependent ('made by people') nor to Lukácsian notions of individuals' alienation from society, but to the ascription of agency to entities that are not actors/agents, where the latter are defined as entities that, in principle, are capable of formulating and taking decisions and of acting on some of them; and, finally, *functional teleology* refers to attempts to explain causes in terms of effects, where 'effects' refers to outcomes or consequences that are regarded – in the absence of any demonstration of relevant, intentional, and successful planning by actors somewhere, sometime – as performances of 'functions' or, more generally, as the expression of a structural purpose. In the book it was argued, with the aid of numerous examples, that the four sins are quite widespread in so-called modernist theorizing and in postmodern social theory, and that critique of them goes some way towards avoiding an unfortunate tendency – on the part of too many theorists and researchers – to replicate or com- pound social sciences's explanatory failures (this will be returned to in a moment, with reference to a cumulative orientation towards the construc- tion of social scientific knowledge).

A point that is worth emphasizing here is that critique of the four 'sins', in conjunction with theoretical synthesis and a flexible social ontology of the kind referred to above, enables us in principle to 'rehabilitate' concepts which may be of dubious lineage but which nevertheless seem to be potentially of some importance, providing they can be re-worked in an appropriate fashion. And sometimes concepts – even when drawn from antithetical paradigms – can with advantage be redefined with a view to their being combined into a synthesis. The following list of examples, drawn from the earlier chapters, refers to some of the ways in which concepts or analytical distinctions may be misused, or alternatively, re-worked and re-contextualized in a fashion that enables them to be put to good analytical use. The concept *relative autonomy* as employed in the previous chapters refers primarily to the nature of the relation between micro-, mezo- and macro-levels of social reality (though it can also refer to the relation between social phenomena that exist at the same level); this usage is quite distinct from, for instance, Althusser's reductionist deployment of the concept (see the Introduction). In Chapter 5 it was argued that the problematical concept *'real' (or 'objec- tive') interests* can be rescued from misuse by means of a re-worked version of what Archer (1995) terms 'positional interests'. As in all of the examples cited here, the theoretical re-working to which I have just referred is con- sistently and self-consciously counterposed against – and is in some sense an inversion of – formulations which contain elements of reductionism, essentialism, reification, or functional teleology; this involves analytical movement from critique to conceptual reformulation which entails syn- thesis and concept development that is allied to the social ontology referred to above. In Chapter 3 problems surrounding objectivist and subjectivist approaches to the idea of *structural contradictions*, and failed attempts to combine or reconcile these approaches, were addressed by means of a cri- tique that led to an understanding of structural contradictions (or indeed, compatibilities) in terms of a particular conception of the dialectics of agency and structure. A related but rather more general construct was developed in Chapter 1 in the form of a version of the proposition that *discourses* – conceived of in terms that reject reductionist, essentialist or teleological theories of their genesis, reproduction or elaboration – spiral into and out of social contexts. The *system-* and *social-integration* distinction, it was suggested in Chapter 3, is indispensable in social analysis. However, it was also noted the distinction is employed in, for example, Marxism (see Mouzelis, 1995: 122) and in radical feminism, both of which ultimately are reductionist forms of theorizing that also contain – often in tacit or deferred ('last-instance') form – strong traces of essentialism, reification, and functional teleology. Here, as with the examples given above, we have an instance of a concept or conceptual distinction that is marred by inappropriate usage but which, when the problems posed by its misuse are addressed and transcended, is capable of being employed to good effect. Another example examined in Chapter 3 is the concept of *recursion* (or 'path dependency' in political science terminology), a concept which, once shorn of inappropriate applications – as in Luhmann's (1982, 1989) reified, essentialist and reductionist theory of recursion and autopoiesis – is an invaluable analytical tool for investigating contingently reproduced structural continuities.

There are some rather more general propositions that, it was argued in the earlier chapters, are of considerable importance to the development of sociological theory and research, and indeed, of importance to the future development of the social sciences in general. First, while there must always be room for competing perspectives, there is a case for a more cumulative orientation to conceptual development and knowledge accumulation within each of the social science disciplines: this is likely to help erode an unfortunate tendency to replicate or compound previous explanatory failures in the social sciences, and is also a way of recognizing that, as Bauman (1992c: 168) put it, 'the other side of collective amnesia in sociology is the Columbus complex'. Second, and closely related to the point just made, there is no necessary incompatibility between the development of disciplinary and interdisciplinary foci; indeed, it is the case that 'disciplinarity (in teaching and research) is logically a necessary precondition for interdisciplinary activity' (Turner and O'Neill, 2001: 5). In the Preface and again in Chapter 1 reference was made to the desirability of dialogue between scholars from different disciplines and between them and interdisciplinary researchers working across such fields as sociology, political science, economics, psychology, social geography, and public policy; to illustrate this point, reference was made in each of the chapters to material drawn from the disciplines of political science and public policy/public administration. Third, and again related to the remarks made above, it seems desirable that there should be more two-way traffic between general social theory and intellectual developments within disciplines; in Chapter 1 it was observed that social theory seems to be somewhat detached from the theoretical and methodological innovations currently taking place within and across a range of social science disciplines (including, in the examples employed in this book, those disciplines which focus on governance, politics, and the policy process). Fourth, it was argued in Chapter 1 that it is desirable that the central elements of social scientific activity – that is, metatheory (including social ontology), substantive theory, methodology, and analysis of empirical materials – should (a) be consistent with each other; and (b) should regulate each other: this epistemological frame of reference bears a certain amount of resemblance to Archer's (1995) and Layder's (1997; 1998a), these being two writers who tend to be rather more explicit on epistemological matters than some other contemporary sociological theorists. In accordance with the rubric to which I have just referred, metatheoretical and ontological constructs, I have argued, should be open to empirical sources of revision. It is important, as well, to acknowledge that, as Archer (1995: 3, 17) recognizes, consistency and mutual regulation as between metatheory, substantive theory, methodology, and empirical analysis are no 'guarantee against error', or as I prefer to put it, consistency and mutual regulation among these elements are a necessary but not a sufficient condition for explanatory success in the social sciences. This is because consistency and mutual regulation, of the kind just referred to, may be found in all manner of paradigms, including those implicated in reductionism and other problematical forms of reasoning. The additional ingredient necessary for explanatory success is, for Archer, her morphogenetic social theory, and for Layder it is his (meta)theory of social domains; in my schema it is concept formation grounded in critique of the four 'cardinal sins', allied to theoretical synthesis that is congruent with a flexible, minimal but realist social ontology.

Finally, although the concerns of this book are primarily ontological (and to some extent methodological), mention should be made of an important but little discussed epistemological divergence among contemporary theorists concerning the relation of metatheoretical and theoretical concepts (as well as models and analytical distinctions) to empirical reality. This concerns the question of whether it is necessary or desirable that concepts should refer to 'real' things. Suffice it to say that the concepts argued for in this book are held to refer to real empirical phenomena – as distinct from analytical constructs of a kind that a number of theorists claim are analytically or methodologically necessary even where the constructs do not refer to any 'actually existing' empirical reality. A few examples will serve to illustrate some major contemporary theorists' unfortunate tendency to employ concepts and analytical distinctions that are claimed to be essential for the purposes of social analysis, but to have no concrete empirical referents. Hay (2002: 127), a political science theoretician, believes a distinction between structure and agency, though 'necessary' in social analysis, is entirely analytical and not ontological. Ritzer (2001: 5, 81, 88), for undisclosed reasons, suggests that the social world is not 'really' divided into micro- and macro-levels but that, nevertheless, it is *analytically necessary* to conceive of social reality 'as if' it were stratified into these levels. In similar fashion, Mouzelis (1995: 77) says the figurational-institutional distinction is invaluable but is 'purely analytical', although he is slightly ambiguous elsewhere where he states (1995: 196) the distinction, which is derived from Lockwood (1964), does not 'faithfully reflect' social reality but is, rather, an important analytical rather than ontological dualism (1995: 196). So far as the concepts micro and macro are concerned, these are said by Mouzelis to be analytically indispensable but, he claims, they do not refer to 'two ontologically different social realities' (1995: 197). In her earlier work Archer (1988: xiv) suggested analytical dualism is a necessary heuristic but that agency–structure dualism itself is not empirically real (that is, does not exist in social reality); however, in her later work (for example, 1995) she shifts position and argues, correctly in my view, that dualism is analytically necessary and ontologically real.

Layder (1997: 102) rejects Giddens's and Mouzelis's claims that Habermas, in invoking a distinction between social integration and system integration, confuses analytical and methodological distinctions with substantive or empirical ones. Layder, unlike Giddens and Mouzelis, is adamant that concepts should have real empirical referents, and that, for example, a distinction between figurational (social integration) and institutional (system integration) spheres should be seen as both analytical *and* real:

> Surely to argue for the usefulness of an analytical or methodological distinction (such as that of social and system integration) is to suggest that there is something intrinsic to the substance of that which is being analyzed that makes it necessary in the first place – otherwise the distinction is indeed spurious. That is, if the distinction is not about something substantive in the social world then its status is merely rhetorical. (1997: 102)

I share Layder's view of this matter: the notion that a concept or distinction that is said to be analytical or methodological with no real empirical referent can also be said to be 'indispensable' for the purposes of social analysis is one that I find unconvincing, if not downright strange. A, in my view, more adequate epistemological position, relating to the flexible, realist social ontology referred to in previous chapters, suggests that reality plays a part in shaping concepts; adequate concepts reflect (even if partially or imperfectly) the nature of the reality to which they refer. In other words, social reality influences and limits what can legitimately be said about it. It is possible and in my opinion desirable that social science should adopt an intermediate position that rejects positivistic claims that 'facts speak for themselves', and that, on the other hand, rejects postmodern and other forms of relativism or idealism. Neither concepts, models, metatheories/ social ontologies, or theories should be regarded as immune from empirical sources of revision and, somewhat similarly to Archer's epistemology (1995; 1998), the approach followed in this book is predicated on the idea of a dialectical interplay among these elements and between them and empirical materials. To be sure, the social world is empirically complex and almost certainly variegated to such an extent that, as Weber (1949) argued, concepts and analytical distinctions at best are likely to be incomplete 'approximations' of social reality rather than exhaustive descriptions; and as observed in Chapters 1 and 2, academic discourse (including concepts) tends to spiral into and out of social contexts (an idea reflected in Giddens's 'double hermeneutic'). As well, perspectivism, where differing concepts are employed for inspecting different aspects of 'the same' phenomenon, is a perfectly legitimate methodological procedure (see Chapter 6, note 3). But none of these epistemological and methodological observations are valid grounds for claiming that there are concepts, models or conceptual distinctions that are analytically 'indispensable' in the absence of any empirical referents whose characteristics could, in principle, lead to revision of the concepts or models in question. It should be observed – and here we attest the continuing relevance of the classics – that Weber's metatheoretical and methodological prescriptions have a distinct bearing upon the epistemological and ontological issues to which I have just referred. Weber's realist epistemology rested on an understanding that social reality is unimaginably 'large', complex and highly differentiated, so much so that the necessary use of *concepts* to simplify and abstract from reality and thereby make it cognitively available for the purposes of analysis, will always mean that an element of distortion is present in theorists' and researchers' perception of the social world. Weber contends that there are no underlying social laws governing the empirical world, laws which positivists such as Comte and Marx presumed are discoverable in principle. In Weber's social science, reality is too complex, contingent, and multifaceted to know in its entirety. His epistemology suggests that we can never grasp social reality 'as it is', but rather, by using concepts and by employing probabilistic causal explanation (in the form 'if x then probably y') alongside explanation that incorporates a grasp of actors' subjective meanings and motives, we can hope to construct *approximations* of reality (Freund, 1968: 7–9; Turner, 1992a: 214). In effect, Weber rejects either-or formulations which on the one hand specify that, as positivists tend to claim, we eventually can in principle 'know everything' about social reality, or on the other, which insist – along the lines of idealism, relativism, and today, poststructuralism, and postmodern theory – that ultimately we are fated to 'know nothing' about the social, since there is no such thing as an ontologically prior, pre-discursive reality. It seems, as this book has tried to demonstrate, that Weber was correct in his view that there is indeed a pre-existing social reality 'out there', albeit a highly complex, processual reality that will probably never be completely known: we would do well to remember Weber's injunction that the social world is real, and as such it can be known, but only via the use of concepts and therefore only in a somewhat incomplete, probabilistic and approximate kind of way. Therefore it is better to have a comparatively modest but realizable prospectus for the social sciences, rather than assume no worthwhile social scientific knowledge is ever possible, or alternatively, that social reality is knowable in its entirety and with absolute certainty.

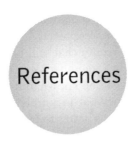

References

Abrams, P. (1981) 'The Collapse of British Sociology?' in P. Abrams, R. Deem, J. Finch, P. Rock (eds), *Practice and Progress: British Sociology 1950–1980*. London: Allen and Unwin.

Abrams, P. (1982) *Historical Sociology*. Ithaca: Cornell University Press.

Abercrombie, N. (1980) *Class, Structure and Knowledge*. Oxford: Blackwell.

Adam, B. (1990) *Time and Social Theory*. Cambridge: Polity Press.

Adam, B. (1995) *Timewatch: The Social Analysis of Time*. Cambridge: Polity Press.

Agnew, J., Livingstone, D.N. and Rogers, A. (eds) (1996) *Human Geography*. Oxford: Blackwell.

Albrow, M. (1996) *The Global Age*. Cambridge: Polity Press.

Albrow, M. (1999) *Sociology: The Basics*. London: Routledge.

Alexander, J. (1987) 'The centrality of the classics', in A. Giddens and J. Turner (eds), *Social Theory Today*. Cambridge: Polity Press.

Alexander, J. (1988) 'The new theoretical movement', in N.J. Smelser (ed.), *The Handbook of Sociology*. London: Sage.

Alexander, J. (1992) 'General theory in the postpositivistic mode: the "epistemological dilemma" and the search for present reason', in S. Seidman and D.G. Wagner (eds), *Postmodernism and Social Theory*. Cambridge, MA, and Oxford: Blackwell.

Alexander, J. and Colomy, P. (1992) 'Traditions and competition: preface to a postpositivist approach to knowledge cumulation', in G. Ritzer (ed.), *Metatheorising*. London: Sage.

Alexander, J., Giesen, B., Munch, R. and Smelser, N. (eds) (1987) *The Micro-Macro Link*. Berkeley, CA: University of California Press.

Alexander, J. and Smith, P. (1993) 'The discourse of American Civil Society: a new proposal for cultural studies', *Theory and Society*, 22: 151–207.

Althusser, L. (1965) *For Marx*. Harmondsworth: Penguin.

Althusser, L. (1971) *Lenin and Philosophy and Other Essays*. London: New Left Books.

Amin, A. and Thrift, N. (1995) 'Institutional issues for the European regions: from markets and plans to socioeconomics and powers of association', *Economy and Society*, 24 (1): 41–66.

Antonio, R.J. (1998) 'Mapping postmodern theory', in Sica, A. (ed.), *What is Social Theory? The Philosophical Debates*. Oxford: Blackwell.

Antonio, R.J. and Kellner, D. (1992) 'The limits of postmodern thought', in D. Dickens and A. Fontana (eds), *Postmodernism and Social Inquiry*. Chicago: University of Chicago Press.

Archer, M. (1982) 'Structuration versus morphogenesis: on combining structure and action', *British Journal of Sociology*, 33 (4): 445–83.

Archer, M. (1988) *Culture and Agency: The Place of Culture in Social Theory*. Cambridge: Cambridge University Press.

Archer, M. (1995) *Realist Social Theory: The Morphogenetic Approach*. Cambridge: Cambridge University Press.

Archer, M. (1996) 'Social integration and system integration: developing the distinction', *Sociology*, 30 (4): 679–99.

Archer, M. (1998) 'Social theory and the analysis of society', in T. May and M. Williams (eds), *Knowing the Social World*. Buckingham: Open University Press.

Archer, M. (2000) *Being Human: The Problem of Agency*. Cambridge: Cambridge University Press.

Aron, R. (1967) *Eighteen Lectures on Industrial Society*. London: Weidenfeld and Nicolson.

Baehr, P. (1990) 'Critical realism, cautionary realism', *Sociological Review*, 38 (4): 765–77.

Baert, P. (1998) *Social Theory in the Twentieth Century*. Cambridge: Polity Press.

Baert, P. (1989) 'Unintended consequences, (un)awareness and (re)production', paper presented at British Sociological Association Annual Conference, Plymouth.

Bagilhole, B. (1997) *Equal Opportunities and Social Policy*. London: Longman.

Barbalet, J. (1985) 'Power and resistance', *British Journal of Sociology*, 36 (4): 531–48.

Barker, R. and Roberts, H. (1993) 'The uses of the concept of power', in D. Morgan and L. Stanley (eds), *Debates in Sociology*. Manchester: University of Manchester Press.

Barnes, B. (1985) *About Science*. Oxford: Blackwell.

Barnes, B. (1995) *The Elements of Social Theory*. London: UCL Press.

Barthes, R. (1967) *Elements of Semiology*. London: Cape.

Baudrillard, J. (1983) *In the Shadow of the Silent Majorities or the End of the Social and Other Essays*. New York: Semiotext(e).

Baudrillard, J. (1988) *Selected Writings*. M. Poster (ed.), Cambridge: Polity Press.

Bauman, Z. (1979) 'The phenomenon of Norbert Elias', *Sociology*, 13 (1): 117–25.

Bauman, Z. (1987) *Legislators and Interpreters*. Oxford: Polity.

Bauman, Z. (1989) 'Hermeneutics and modern social theory', in D. Held and J.B. Thompson (eds), *Social Theory of Modern Societies: Anthony Giddens and his Critics*. Cambridge: Cambridge University Press.

Bauman, Z. (1992a) *Intimations of Postmodernity*. London: Routledge.

Bauman, Z. (1992b) 'Foreword', in F. Crispi, *Social Action and Power*. Oxford: Blackwell.

Bauman, Z. (1992c) 'Review' *The Sociological Review*, 40 (1): 168–70.

Bendix, R. (1984) *Force, Fate and Freedom: On Historical Sociology*. Berkeley, CA: University of California Press.

Benko, G. and Strohmayer, U. (eds) (1997) *Space and Social Theory: Interpreting Modernity and Postmodernity*. Oxford: Blackwell.

Bennington, J. and Harvey, J. (1999) 'Networking in Europe', in G. Stoker (ed.), *The New Management of British Local Governance*. London: Blackwell.

Benton, T. (1981) '"Objective" interests and the sociology of power', *Sociology*, 15 (2): 161–84.

Berger, P. (1966) *Invitation to Sociology: A Humanistic Perspective*. Harmondsworth: Pelican.

Berger, P. (1969) *The Social Reality of Religion*. London: Faber and Faber.

Berger, P. (1979) *Facing up to Modernity*. Harmondsworth: Penguin.

Berger, P. and Berger, B. (1978) *Sociology: A Biographical Approach*. Harmondsworth: Penguin.

Berger, P., Berger, B. and Kellner, H. (1974) *The Homeless Mind*. Harmondsworth: Penguin.

Berger, P. and Luckmann, T. (1971) *The Social Construction of Reality*. Harmondsworth: Penguin.

Bernardes, J. (1985) 'Family ideology: identification and exploration', *The Sociological Review*, 33 (2): 275–97.

Best, S. and Kellner, D. (1991) *Postmodern Theory: Critical Interrogations*. London: Macmillan.

Betts, K. (1986) 'The conditions of action, power, and the problem of interests', *Sociological Review*, 34 (1): 39–64.

Bhaskar, R. (1978) *A Realist Theory of Science*. Brighton: Harvester.

Bhaskar, R. (1979) *The Possibility of Naturalism*. Brighton: Harvester.

Bhaskar, R. (1989a) *Reclaiming Reality; A Critical Introduction to Contemporary Philosophy*. London: Verso.

Bhaskar, R. (1989b) *The Possibility of Naturalism*. London: Harvester Wheatsheaf.

Blau, P. (1963) *The Dynamics of Bureaucracy*. Chicago, IL: University of Chicago Press.

Blumer, H. (1954) 'What is wrong with social theory?', *American Sociological Review*, 19: 3–10.

Blumer, H. (1969) *Symbolic Interactionism: Perspectives and Methods*. Englewood Cliffs, NJ: Prentice Hall.

Bonnett, A. (1993) 'The formation of public professional radical consciousness: the example of anti-racism', *Sociology*, 27 (2): 281–97.

Bottomore, T. (1984) *Sociology and Socialism*. Brighton: Wheatsheaf.

Bouchier, D. (1977) 'Radical ideologies and the sociology of knowledge; a model for comparative analysis', *Sociology*, 11 (1): 25–46.

Boudon, R. (1986) *Theories of Social Change*. Cambridge: Polity Press.

Bourdieu, P. (1977) *Outline of a Theory of Practice*. Cambridge: Cambridge University Press.

Bourdieu, P. (1984) *Distinction: A Social Critique of the Judgement of Taste*. Cambridge, MA: Harvard University Press.

Bourdieu, P. (1990) *In Other Words: Essays Towards a Reflexive Sociology*. Cambridge: Polity Press.

Bourdieu, P. (1998) *Practical Reason: On the Theory of Action*. Cambridge: Polity Press.

Bradley, H. (1996) *Fractured Identities: Changing Patterns of Inequality*. Cambridge: Polity Press.

Bradshaw, A. (1976) 'A critique of Steven Lukes's *Power: A Radical View*', *Sociology*, 10 (1): 121–7.

Braithwaite, J. (1994) 'A sociology of modelling and the politics of empowerment', *British Journal of Sociology*, 45 (3): 444–79.

Brittan, A. (1973) *Meanings and Situations*. London: Routledge.

Brown, K. M. (1985) 'Turning a blind eye: racial oppression and the unintended consequences of white "non-racism"', *The Sociological Review*, 33 (4): 670–90.

Brubaker, R. (1984) *The Limits of Rationality*. London: Allen and Unwin.

Bruijn, J.A. de and Ringeling, A.B. (1997) 'Normative notes: perspectives on networks', in W. Kickert, E.H. Klijn and J.F.M. Koppenjan (eds), *Managing Complex Networks: Strategies for the Public Sector*. London: Sage.

Bryant, C. (1991) 'The dialogical model of applied sociology', in C. Bryant and D. Jary (eds), *Giddens's Theory of Structuration: A Critical Approach*. London: Routledge.

Bryant, C. (1995) *Practical Sociology: Post-Empiricism and the Reconstruction of Theory and Application*. Cambridge: Polity Press.

Bryant, C. and Jary, D. (1991) 'Intro: coming to terms with Anthony Giddens', in C. Bryant and D. Jary (eds), *Giddens's Theory of Structuration: A Critical Approach*. London: Routledge.

Bryant, C. and Makrzycki, E. (1994) 'Introduction: theorizing the changes in East-Central Europe', in C. Bryant and E. Makrzycki (eds), *The New Great Transformation? Change and Continuity in East-Central Europe*. London and New York: Routledge.

Bryson, L. (1992) *Feminist Political Theory: An Introduction*. London: Macmillan.

Buckner, H.T. (1978) 'Transformations of reality in the legal process', in T. Luckmann (ed.), *Phenomenology and Sociology*. Harmondsworth: Penguin.

Bulmer, M. (1985) 'The rejuvenation of community studies? Neighbours, networks and policy', *The Sociological Review*, 33 (3): 430–48.

Bulmer, M. (1986) *Neighbours: The Works of Philip Abrams*. Cambridge: Cambridge University Press.

Bulmer, S. (1993) 'The governance of the EU: a new institutionalist approach', *Journal of Public Policy*, 13 (4): 351–80.

Burns, T. (1986) 'Actors, transactions, and social structure', in U. Himmelstrand (ed.), *The Social Reproduction of Organization and Culture*. London: Sage.

Burns, T. (1999) 'The evolution of parliaments and societies in Europe: challenges and prospects', *European Journal of Social Theory*, 2 (2): 167–94.

Calhoun, C., Gerteis, J., Moody, J., Pfaff, S. and Virk, I. (eds) (2002) *Contemporary Sociological Theory*. Oxford: Blackwell.

Callon, M. (1986) 'Some elements of a sociology of translation: domesticiation of the scallops and the fishermen of St. Brieuc Bay', in J. Law (ed.), *Power, Action and Belief: A New Sociology of Knowledge?* London: Routledge.

Callon, M. (1991) 'Techno-economic networks and irreversibility', in J. Law (ed.), *A Sociology of Monsters: Essays on Power, Technology and Domination*. London: Routledge.

Callon, M., Courtial, J.P., Turner, W.A. and Bauin, S. (1983) 'From translation to problematic networks: an introduction to co-word analysis', *Social Science Information*, 22: 199–235.

Callon, M. and Latour, B. (1981) 'Unscrewing the big Leviathan: how actors macro-structure reality and how sociologists help them to do so', in K. Knorr-Cetina and A.V. Cicourel (eds), *Advances in Social Theory and Methodology: Towards an Integration of Micro- and Macro-Sociologies*. London: Routledge.

Callon, M. and Law, J. (1982) 'On interests and their transformation: enrolment and counter-enrolment', *Social Studies of Science*, 12: 615–25.

Camic, C. (1997) 'Classical sociological theory as a field of research', in C. Camic (ed.), *Reclaiming the Sociological Classics: The State of the Scholarship*. Oxford: Blackwell.

Campbell, C. (1998) *The Myth of Social Action*. Cambridge: Cambridge University Press.

Castells, M. (2000) 'Materials for an explanatory theory of the network society', *British Journal of Sociology*, 51 (1): 5–24.

Charles, N. (1994) 'Review' *The Sociological Review*, 42 (3): 581–4.

Charon, J.M. (1995) *Symbolic Interactionism*. Englewood Cliffs, NJ: Prentice Hall.

Child, A. (1941) 'The problem of imputation in the sociology of knowledge', *Ethics*, 51 (2): 200–19.

Cicourel, A.V. (1980) 'Language and social interaction: philosophical and empirical issues', *Sociological Inquiry*, 50: 1–30.

Cicourel, A.V. (1981) 'Notes on the integration of micro- and macro-levels of analysis' in K. Knorr-Cetina and A.V. Cicourel (eds), *Advances in Social Theory and Methodology: Towards an Integration of Micro- and Macro-Sociologies*. London: Routledge.

Clegg, S. (1989) *Frameworks of Power*. London: Sage.

Clegg, S.R. and Hardy, C. (eds) (1999) *Studying Organization: Theory and Method*. London: Sage.

Cohen, I. (1987) 'Structuration theory and social praxis', in A. Giddens and J. Turner (eds), *Social Theory Today*. Cambridge: Polity Press.

Cohen, I. (1989) *Structuration Theory: Anthony Giddens and the Constitution of Social Life*. London: Macmillan.

Cohen, P. (1968) *Modern Social Theory*. London: Heinemann.

Coleman, J.H. (1990) *The Foundations of Social Theory*. Cambridge, MA: Harvard University Press.

Collins, R. (1981) 'Micro-translation as a theory-building strategy', in K. Knorr-Cetina and A.V. Cicourel (eds), *Advances in Social Theory and Methodology: Towards an Integration of Micro- and Macro-Sociologies*. London: Routledge.

Collins, R. (1983) 'Micromethods as a basis for macrosociology', *Urban Life*, 12 (1): 184–202.

Collins, R. (1986) 'Is 1980s sociology in the doldrums?', *American Journal of Sociology*, 86 (4): 1336–56.

Collins, R. (1987) 'Interaction ritual chains, power and property; the micro macro connection as an empirically-based theoretical problem', in J. Alexander, B. Giesen, R. Munch and N. Smelser (eds), *The Macro-Micro Link*. Berkeley, CA: University of California Press.

Collins, R. (1988) 'The micro contribution to macro sociology', *Sociological Theory*, 6: 242–53.

Collins, R. (1992) 'The romanticism of agency/structure versus the analysis of micro/macro', *Current Sociology*, 40 (1): 77–97.

Cooke, P. (ed.) (1989) *Localities: The Changing Face of Britain*. London: Unwin Hyman.

Cooley, C. (1902) *Human Nature and Social Order*. New York: Charles Scribner.

Cooper, R. (2001) 'Interpreting mass: collection/dispersion', in N. Lee and R. Munro (eds), *The Consumption of Mass*. Oxford: Blackwell.

Cram, L. (1997) *Policy Making in the European Union*. London: Routledge.

Cram, L., Dinan, D. and Nugent, N. (eds) (1999) *Developments in the European Union*. London: Macmillan.

Crook, S. (1991) *Modernist Radicalism and Its Aftermath: Foundationalism and Anti-Foundationalism in Radical Social Theory*. London: Routledge.

Dahl, R. (1958) 'A critique of the ruling elite model', *American Political Science Review*, 52: 462–9.

Dahl, R. (1961) *Who Governs? Democracy and Power in an American City*. New Haven, CT: Yale University Press.

Danaher, G., Schirato, T. and Webb, J. (2000) *Understanding Foucault*. London: Sage.

Dant, T. (1999) *Material Culture in the Social World*. London: Sage.

Day, G. and Murdoch, J. (1993) 'Locality and community: coming to terms with place', *The Sociological Review*, 41 (1): 82–111.

Dean, M. (1994) *Critical and Effective Histories: Foucault's Methods and Historical Sociology*. London: Routledge.

Delanty, G. (1999) *Social Theory in a Changing World: Conceptions of Modernity*. Cambridge: Polity Press.

Delanty, G. (2000) 'The foundations of social theory: origins and trajectories', in B.S. Turner (ed.), *The Blackwell Companion to Social Theory*. Oxford: Blackwell.

Derrida, J. (1982) 'Différence', in *Margins of Philosophy*, trans. A. Bass, Hemel Hempstead: Harvester Wheatsheaf.

Derrida, J. (1996) 'Remarks on deconstruction and pragmatism', in C. Mouffe (ed.), *Deconstruction and Pragmatism*. London: Routledge.

Dickens, P. (1990) *Urban Sociology: Society, Locality and Human Nature*. London: Harvester Wheatsheaf.

DiMaggio, P. (1997) 'Epilogue: Sociology as a discipline', in K. Erikson (ed.), *Sociological Visions*. New York: Rowman and Littlefield.

Dominelli, L. (1997) *Sociology for Social Work*. London: Macmillan.

Duncan, S. (1989) 'What is locality?', in R. Peet and N. Thrift (eds), *New Models in Geography*. London: Edward Arnold.

Duncan, S. and Goodwin, M. (1988) *The Local State and Uneven Development*. Cambridge: Polity Press.

Dunning, E. and Rojek, C. (eds) (1992) *Sport and Leisure in the Civilizing Process*. London: Macmillan.

Durkheim, E. (1951) *Suicide: A Study in Sociology*. London: Routledge.

Durkheim, E. (1964) *The Division of Labour in Society*. New York: Free Press.

Durkheim, E. (1965) *The Elementary Forms of the Religious Life*. New York: Free Press.

Durkheim, E. (1982) *The Rules of Sociological Method*. London: Macmillan.

Duncan, S. (1989) 'What is locality?', in R. Peet and N. Thrifts (eds), *New Models in Geography*. London: Edward Arnold.

Duster, T. (1981) 'Intermediate steps between micro- and macro-integration: the case of screening for inherited disorders', in K. Knorr-Cetina and A.V. Cicourel (eds), *Advances in Social Theory and Methodology: Towards an Integration of Micro- and Macro-Sociologies*. London: Routledge.

Dye, T. (1998) *Understanding Public Policy*. Upper Saddle River, NJ: Prentice Hall.

Edles, L.D. (2002) *Cultural Sociology in Practice*. Oxford: Blackwell.

Eisstadt, S.N. and Helle, H.J. (1985) 'General introduction to perspectives in sociological theory', in S.N. Eisstadt and H.J. Helle (eds), *Macro-Sociological Theory*. London: Sage.

Elias, N. (1971) 'Sociology of knowledge: new perspectives, Part 1', *Sociology*, 5 (2): 149–68.

Elias, N. (1978) *What is Sociology?* London: Hutchinson.

Elias, N. (1983) *The Court Society*. Oxford: Blackwell.

Elias, N. (1984) *Über die Zeit*. Frankfurt: Suhrkampf.

Elias, N. (1991) *The Society of Individuals*. Oxford: Blackwell.

Elias, N. (1994) *The Civilizing Process*, combined edition. Oxford: Blackwell.

Elliott, A. (2001) *Concepts of the Self*. Cambridge: Polity Press.

Elster, J. (1985) *Making Sense of Marx*. Cambridge: Cambridge University Press.

Emirbayer, M. and Goodwin, J. (1994) 'Network analysis, culture, and the problem of agency', *American Journal of Sociology*, 99 (6): 1411–54.

Evans-Pritchard, E. (1940) *The Nuer*. Oxford: Oxford University Press.

Eyerman, R. and Jamison, A. (1991) *Social Movements: A Cognitive Approach*. Oxford: Polity Press.

Fararo, T.J. (1992) *The Meaning of General Theoretical Sociology: Tradition and Formalization*. Cambridge: Cambridge University Press.

Farganis, S. (1994) *Situating Feminism: From Thought to Action*. Thousand Oaks, CA, and London: Sage.

Fay, B. (1987) *Critical Social Science: Liberation and Its Limits*. Oxford: Blackwell.

Featherstone, M. (1988) 'In pursuit of the postmodern', *Theory, Culture and Society*, 5: 195–215.

Fleck, L. (1979) *Genesis and Development of a Scientific Fact*. Chicago: University of Chicago Press.

Flynn, N. and Strehl, F. (1996) 'Introduction', in N. Flynn and F. Strehl (eds), *Public Sector Management in Europe*. London: Prentice Hall.

Foucault, M. (1970) *The Order of Things: An Archaeology of the Human Sciences*. London: Tavistock.

Foucault, M. (1972) *The Archaeology of Knowledge*. New York: Pantheon Books.

Foucault, M. (1980a) *Power/Knowledge*. New York: Pantheon Books.

Foucault, M. (1980b) *The History of Sexuality*. New York: Vintage Books.

Foucault, M. (1982) 'The subject and power', in H.L. Dreyfus and P. Rabinow (eds), *Michel Foucault: Beyond Structuralism and Hermeneutics, with an Afterword by Michel Foucault*. Brighton: Harvester Wheatsheaf.

Foucault, M. (1991) 'Governmentality', in G. Burchell. (ed), *The Foucault Effect: Studies in Governmentality*. Hemel Hempstead: Harvester Wheatsheaf.

Fox, C.J. and Miller, H.T. (1995) *Postmodern Public Administration: Towards Discourse*. London: Sage.

Fox, N.J. (1991) 'Postmodernism, rationality and the evaluation of health care', *The Sociological Review*, 39 (4): 709–44.

Fox, N. and Roberts, C. (1999) 'GPs in cyberspace: the sociology of a "virtual community"', *The Sociological Review*, 47 (4): 643–71.

Franklin, J. (ed.) (1998) *The Politics of Risk Society*. Cambridge: Polity Press.

Freund, J. (1968) *The Sociology of Max Weber*. Harmondsworth: Penguin.

Friedrichs, R.W. (1972) *A Sociology of Sociology*. New York: Free Press.

Frisby, D. (1992) *Simmel and Since: Essays on George Simmel's Social Theory*. London: Routledge.

Gamble, A. (2000) 'Policy agendas in a multi-level polity', in P. Dunleavy, A. Gamble, J. Holliday and G. Peele (eds), *Developments in British Politics*. London: Macmillan.

Garfinkel, H. (1967) *Studies in Ethnomethodology*. Englewood Cliffs, NJ: Prentice Hall.

Geertz, C. (1979) 'From the native's point of view: on the nature of anthropological under- standing', in P. Rainbow and W.M. Sullivan (eds), *Interpretive Social Science: A Reader*. Berkeley, CA: University of California Press.

Gellner, E. (1993) *Postmodernism, Reason and Religion*. London and New York: Routledge.

George, S. and Bache, I. (2001) *Politics in the European Union*. Oxford: Oxford University Press.

Gibbs, J.P. (1989) *Control: Sociology's Central Notion*, Urbana, IL: University of Illinois Press.

Giddens, A. (1976) *New Rules of Sociological Method*. London: Hutchinson.

Giddens, A. (1977) *Studies in Social and Political Theory*. London: Hutchinson.

Giddens, A. (1979) *Central Problems in Social Theory: Action, Structure and Contradiction in Social Analysis*. Berkeley, CA: University of California Press.

Giddens, A. (1981) 'Agency, institution, and time-space analysis', in K. Knorr-Cetina and A.V. Cicourel (eds), *Advances in Social Theory and Methodology: Towards an Integration of Micro- and Macro-Sociologies*. London: Routledge.

Giddens, A. (1982) *Profiles and Critiques in Social Theory*. London: Macmillan.

Giddens, A. (1984) *The Constitution of Society*. Cambridge: Polity Press.

Giddens, A. (1987) *Social Theory and Modern Sociology*. Cambridge: Polity Press.

Giddens, A. (1989) 'A reply to my critics', in D. Held and J. Thompson (eds), *Social Theory and Modern Societies: Anthony Giddens and his Critics*. Cambridge: Cambridge University Press.

Giddens. A. (1990) *The Consequences of Modernity*. Cambridge: Polity Press.

Giddens, A. (1991a) 'Structuration theory: past, present and future', in C. Bryant and D. Jary (eds), *Giddens's Theory of Structuration: A Critical Appreciation*. London: Routledge.

Giddens, A. (1991b) *Modernity and Self-Identity*. Cambridge: Polity Press.

Giddens, A. (1993) *New Rules of Sociological Method*, 2nd edn. Cambridge: Polity Press.

Giddens, A. (1998) *The Third Way: The Renewal of Social Democracy*. Cambridge: Polity Press.

Giddens, A. and Turner, J.H. (1987) 'Introduction', in A. Giddens and J.H. Turner (eds), *Social Theory Today*. Cambridge: Polity Press.

Glucksmann, M. (1974) 'The structuralism of Lévi-Strauss and Althusser', in J. Rex (ed.), *Approaches to Sociology*. London: Routledge.

Goffman, E. (1983) 'The interaction order', *American Sociological Review*, 48 (3): 1–17.

Gould, H.A. (1987) *The Hindu Caste System: The Sacralization of a Social Order*. Delhi: Chanakya.

Gouldner, A. (1971) *The Coming Crisis of Western Sociology*. London: Heinemann.

Goverde, H., Cerney, P.G., Haugaard, M. and Lentner, H. (2000) 'General introduction: power in contemporary politics', in H. Goverde, P.G. Cerney, M. Haugaard, and H. Lentner (eds), *Power in Contemporary Politics: Theories, Practices, Globalizations*. London and Thousand Oaks, CA: Sage.

Greca, R. (2000) 'Institutional co-governance as a mode of co-operation between various social service carriers and providers', *Public Management: An International Journal of Research and Theory*, 2 (3): 379–95.

Gregory, D. (1989) 'Presences and absences: time-space relations and structuration theory', in D. Held and J.B. Thompson (eds), *Social Theory of Modern Societies; Anthony Giddens and His Critics*. Cambridge: Cambridge University Press.

Gregory, D., Martin, R. and Smith, G. (eds) (1994) *Human Geography: Society, Space and Social Science*. London: Macmillan.

Gregson, N. (1989) 'On the (ir)relevance of structuration theory to empirical research', in D. Held and J.B. Thompson (eds), *Social Theory of Modern Societies: Anthony Giddens and His Critics*. Cambridge: Cambridge University Press.

Gurnah, A. and Scott, A. (1992) *The Uncertain Science: Criticism of Sociological Formalism*. London: Routledge.

Gyford, J. (1991) *Citizens, Consumers and Councils: Local Government and the Public*. London: Macmillan.

Haas, P. (1992) 'Introduction: epistemic communities and international policy co-ordination', *International Organization*, 46 (1): 1–35.

Habermas, J. (1971) *Towards a Rational Society*. London: Heinemann.

Habermas, J. (1981) 'Modernity versus postmodernity', *New German Critique*, 22: 3–14.

Habermas, J. (1986) *The Theory of Communicative Action* Vol. I: *Reason and the Rationalization of Society*. Cambridge: Polity Press.

Habermas, J. (1987) *The Theory of Communicative Action.* Vol. II: *The Critique of Functionalist Reason.* Cambridge: Polity Press.

Habermas, J. (1989) *The Structural Transformation of the Public Sphere.* Cambridge, MA: MIT Press.

Haimes, E. (1993) 'Theory and method in the analysis of the policy process: a case study of the Warnock Committee on Human Fertilisation and Embryology', in M. Hill (ed.), *New Agendas in the Study of the Policy Process.* London: Harvester Wheatsheaf.

Hamilton, P. (1974) *Knowledge and Social Structure.* London: Routledge.

Harloe, M., Pickvance, C. and Urry, J. (eds) (1990) *Place, Policy and Politics: Do Localities Matter?* London: Unwin Hyman.

Harré, R. (1981) 'Philosophical aspects of the macro–micro problem', in K.C. Knorr-Cetina and A.V. Cicourel (eds), *Advances in Social Theory and Methodology: Towards an Integration of Micro- and Macro-Sociologies.* London: Routledge.

Harré, R. and Bhaskar, R. (2001) 'How to change reality: story vs. structure – a debate between Rom Harré and Roy Bhaskar', in J. Lopez and G. Potter (eds), *After Postmodernism: An Introduction to Critical Realism.* London: Athlone.

Harvey, D. (1989) *The Condition of Postmodernity.* Oxford: Blackwell.

Harvey, D. (1990) 'Between space and time: reflections on the geographical imagination', *Annals of the Association of American Geographers*, 80 (1): 418–34.

Hay, C. (1995) 'Structure and agency', in D. Marsh and G. Stoker (eds), *Theory and Methods in Political Science.* London: Macmillan.

Hay, C. (2002) *Political Analysis: A Critical Introduction.* Basingstoke: Palgrave.

Held, D. (1991) 'Democracy, the nation-state and the global system', *Economy and Society*, 20 (2): 138–72.

Heller, A. (1986) 'The sociology of everyday life', in U. Himmelstrand (ed.), *The Social Reproduction of Organization and Culture.* London: Sage.

Hekman, S. (1990) *Gender and Knowledge: Elements of a Postmodern Feminism.* Cambridge: Polity Press.

Hindess, B. (1981) 'Review', *Sociology*, 15 (4): 636–7.

Hindess, B. (1982) 'Power, interests, and the outcomes of struggles', *Sociology*, 16 (4): 488–511.

Hindess, B. (1983a) *Parliamentary Democracy and Socialist Politics.* London: Routledge.

Hindess, B. (1983b) 'Review', *Sociology*, 17 (1): 125–6.

Hindess, B. (1986a) 'Actors and social relations', in M.L. Wardell and S.P. Turner (eds), *Sociological Theory in Transition.* London: Allen and Unwin.

Hindess, B. (1986b) 'Interests in political analysis', in J. Law (ed.), *Power. Action and Belief: A New Sociology of Knowledge?* London: Routledge.

Hindess, B. (1987a) *Politics and Class Analysis.* Oxford: Blackwell.

Hindess, B. (1987b) *Freedom, Equality and the Market: Arguments in Social Policy.* London: Tavistock.

Hindess, B. (1988) *Choice, Rationality and Social Theory.* London: Unwin Hyman.

Hindess, B. (1989) *Political Choice and Social Structure: An Analysis of Actors, Interests and Rationality.* London: Edward Elgar.

Hindess, B. (1990) 'Liberty and equality' in B. Hindess (ed.), *Reactions of the Right.* London: Routledge.

Hirst, P. and Thompson, G. (1999) *Globalization in Question.* Cambridge: Polity Press.

Holmwood, J.M. (1996) *Founding Sociology? Talcott Parsons and the Idea of General Theory.* London and New York: Longman.

Holmwood, J.M. and Stewart, A. (1983) 'The role of contradictions in modern theories of social stratification', *Sociology*, 17 (2): 234–54.

Holzner, B. (1978) 'The construction of social actors: an essay on social identities', in T. Luckmann (ed.), *Phenomenology and Sociology.* Harmondsworth: Penguin.

Hoppe, R. (1993) 'Political judgement and the policy cycle: the case of ethnicity policy arguments in the Netherlands', in F. Fischer and J. Forester (eds), *The Argumentative Turn in Policy Analysis and Planning.* Duke University Press, NC: UCL Press.

Horowitz, I.L. (ed.) (1964) *The New Sociology: Essays in Social Science and Social Theory in Honour of C. Wright Mills*. Oxford and New York: Oxford University Press.

Hunter, J.D. and Ainlay, S.C. (eds) (1986) *Making Sense of Modern Times: Peter L. Berger and the Vision of Interpretive Sociology*. London: Routledge.

Jackson, N. and Carter, P. (1991) 'In defence of paradigm incommensurability', *Organization Studies*, 12 (1): 109– 27.

Jacobs, S. (1987) 'Scientific community: formulations and critique of a sociological motif', *British Journal of Sociology*, 38 (2): 266–76.

James, S. (1997) *British Government: A Reader in Policy Making*. London: Routledge.

Jameson, F. (1991) *Postmodernism or the Cultural Logic of Late Capitalism*. London: Verso.

Jessop, B. (2000) 'Governance failure', in G. Stoker (ed.), *The New Politics of British Local Governance*. London: Macmillan.

Jewson, N. and Mason, D. (1986) 'The theory and practice of equal opportunities policies: liberal and radical approaches', *The Sociological Review*, 34 (2): 307–34.

Joas, H. (1988) 'Symbolic interactionism', in A. Giddens and J. Turner (eds), *Social Theory Today*. Cambridge: Polity Press.

Jones, M. (1996) 'Posthuman agency: between theoretical traditions', *Sociological Theory*, 14 (3): 290–309.

Judge, D., Earnshaw, D. and Cowan, N. (1994) 'Ripples or waves: the European Parliament in the European Community policy process', *Journal of European Public Policy*, 1 (1): 27–52.

Kalberg, S. (1994a) 'Max Weber's analysis of the rise of monotheism: a reconstruction', *British Journal of Sociology*, 45 (4): 563–83.

Kalberg, S. (1994b) *Max Weber's Comparative-Historical Sociology*. Cambridge: Polity Press.

Kassim, H. (1994) 'Policy networks and European Union policy making: a sceptical view', *West European Politics* 17 (4): 15–27.

Katz, E. (1957) 'The two-step flow of communication', *Public Opinion Quarterly*, 21 (1): 61–78.

Keane, J. and Held, D. (1984) 'Reflections on the welfare state and the future of socialism: an interview', in C. Offe, *Contradictions of the Welfare State*. London: London, pp. 252–99.

Kellner, D. (1990) 'The postmodern turn: positions, problems and prospects', in G. Ritzer (ed.), *Frontiers of Social Theory: The New Syntheses*. New York: Columbia University Press.

Kickert, W. (1993) 'Complexity, governance and dynamics: conceptual explorations of public network management', in J. Kooiman (ed.), *Modern Governance: New Government–Society Interactions*. London: Sage.

Kickert, W.J.M., Klijn, E.-H. and Koppenjan, J.F.M. (eds) (1997a) *Managing Complex Networks: Strategies for the Public Sector*. London: Sage.

Kickert, W.J.M., Klijn, E.-H. and Koppenjan, J.F.M. (1997b) 'Managing networks in the public sector: findings and reflections', in W.J.M. Kickert, E.H. Klijn, and J.F.M. Koppenjan (eds), *Managing Complex Networks: Strategies for the Public Sector*. London: Sage.

Kickert, W.J.M. and van Vught, F.A. (eds) (1995) *Public Policy and Administrative Sciences in the Netherlands*. London and New York: Prentice Hall.

King, A. (1999) 'Against structure: a critique of morphogenetic social theory', *The Sociological Review*, 47 (2): 199–227.

Klijn, E.-H and Teisman, G.R. (1997) 'Strategies and games in networks', in W.J.M. Kickert, E.H. Klijn and J.F.M. Koppenjan (eds), *Managing Complex Networks: Strategies for the Public Sector*. London: Sage.

Knoke, D. and Kulinski, J.H. (1991) 'Network analysis: basic concepts in Thompson, G., Francis, J. and Mitchell, J. (eds), *Markets, Hierarchies and Networks: The Co-ordinal of Social Life*. London: Sage.

Knorr-Cetina, K.D. (1981) 'Introduction: the micro-sociological challenge of macro-sociology: towards a reconstruction of social theory and methodology', in K.D. Knorr-Cetina and A.V. Cicourel (eds), *Advances in Social Theory and Methodology: Towards an Integration of Micro- and Macro-Sociologies*. London: Routledge.

Knorr-Cetina, K.D. and Cicourel, A.V. (1981) (eds) *Advances in Social Theory and Methodology: Towards an Integration of Micro- and Macro-Sociologies.* London: Routledge.

Kooiman, J. (1993) 'Social-political governance: introduction', in J. Kooiman (ed.), *Modern Governance: New Government–Society Interactions.* London: Sage.

Kooiman, J. (1999) 'Social-political governance: overview, reflections, and design', *Public Management,* 1 (1): 67–92.

Kooiman, J. (2003) *Governing as Governance.* London: Sage.

Krokidas, A. (1993) 'Review', *Sociology,* 27 (3): 534–6.

Kumar, K. (1995) *From Post-Industrial to Post-Modern Society: New Theories of the Contemporary World.* Oxford: Blackwell.

Lacan, J. (1977) *Ecrits: A Selection.* London: Tavistock.

Laclau, E. (1990) *New Reflections on the Revolution of Our Time.* London: Verso.

Laclau, E. (ed.) (1994) *The Making of Political Identities.* London and New York: Verso.

Laclau, E. and Mouffe, C. (1985) *Hegemony and Socialist Strategy.* London: Verso.

Laclau, E. and Mouffe, C. (1987) 'Post-Marxism without apologies', *New Left Review,* 166: 79–106.

Larrain, J. (1994) 'The postmodern critique of ideology', *The Sociological Review,* 42 (2): 289–314.

Lash, S. and Friedman, J. (1992) 'Introduction: subjectivity and modernity's Other', in S. Lash and J. Friedman (eds), *Modernity and Identity.* Oxford: Blackwell.

Latour, B. (1986) 'The powers of association', in J. Law (ed.), *Power, Action and Belief: A New Sociology of Knowledge?* London: Routledge.

Latour, B. (1987) *Science in Action: How to Follow Engineers and Scientists Through Society.* Milton Keynes: Open University Press.

Latour, B. (1988) *The Pasteurization of France.* Cambridge, MA: Harvard University Press.

Latour, B. (1991) 'Technology is society made durable', in J. Law (ed.), *A Sociology of Monsters: Essays on Power. Technology and Domination.* London: Routledge.

Lave, J. (1986) 'The values of quantification', in J. Law (ed.), *Power, Action and Belief: A New Sociology of Knowledge?* London: Routledge.

Law, J. (1986a) 'On power and its tactics: a view from the sociology of science', *Sociological Review,* 34 (1): 1–38.

Law, J. (ed.) (1986b) *Power, Action and Belief: A New Sociology of Knowledge?* London: Routledge.

Law, J. (1986c) 'Power/knowledge and the dissolution of the sociology of knowledge', in J. Law (ed.), *Power, Action and Belief: A New Sociology of Knowledge?* London: Routledge.

Law, J. (1986d) 'On the methods of long-distance control: vessels, navigation and the Portuguese route to India', in J. Law (ed.), *Power, Action and Belief: A New Sociology of Knowledge?* London: Routledge.

Law, J. (ed.) (1991a) *A Sociology of Monsters: Essays on Power. Technology and Domination.* London: Routledge.

Law, J. (1991b) 'Power, discretion and strategy', in J. Law (ed.), *A Sociology of Monsters; Essays on Power, Technology and Domination.* London: Routledge.

Law, J. (1994) *Organising Modernity.* Oxford: Blackwell.

Law, J. and Hassard, J. (eds) (1999) *Actor Network Theory and After.* Oxford: Blackwell.

Layder, D. (1984) 'Sources and levels of commitment in actors' careers', *Work and Occupations.* 11 (2): 198–216.

Layder, D. (1986) 'Social reality as figuration: a critique of Elias's conception of sociological analysis', *Sociology,* 20 (3): 367–86.

Layder, D. (1993) *New Strategies in Social Research: An Introduction and Guide.* Oxford: Polity Press.

Layder, D. (1994) *Understanding Social Theory.* London: Sage.

Layder, D. (1997) *Modern Social Theory: Key Debates and New Directions.* London: UCL Press.

Layder, D. (1998a) *Sociological Practice: Linking Theory and Social Research*. London: Sage.

Layder, D. (1998b) 'The reality of social domains: implications for theory and method', in T. May and M. Williams (eds), *Knowing the Social World*. Buckingham: Open University Press.

Lemert, C. (1993) 'After modernity', in C. Lemert (ed.), *Social Theory: The Multicultural and Classical Readings*. San Francisco: Westview Press.

Leonard, P. (1984) *Personality and Ideology: Towards a Materialist Understanding of the Individual*. London: Macmillan.

Levin, P. (1997) *Making Social Policy: The Mechanisms of Government and Politics, and How to Investigate Them*. Buckingham: Open University Press.

Lévi-Strauss, C. (1963) *Structural Anthropology*. New York: Basic Books.

Lévi-Strauss, C. (1974) *The Savage Mind*. London: Weidenfeld and Nicholson.

Levitas, R. (1976) 'The social location of ideas', *The Sociological Review*, 24 (3): 545–57.

Levitas, R. (1977) 'Some problems of aim-centred models of social movements', *Sociology*, 11 (1): 47–63.

Lewis, P. (2002) 'Agency, structure and causality in political science: a comment on Sibeon', *Politics*, 22 (1): 17–23.

Lidz, V. (1981) 'Transformational theory and the internal environment of action systems', in K.D. Knorr-Cetina and A.V. Cicourel (eds), *Advances in Social Theory and Methodology: Towards an Integration of Micro- and Macro-Sociologies*. London: Routledge.

Lockwood, D. (1964) 'Social integration and system integration', in G.K. Zollschan and W. Hirsch (eds), *Explorations in Social Change*. London: Routledge.

Lopez, J. and Scott, J. (2000) *Social Structure*. Buckingham: Open University Press.

Luckmann, T. (ed.) (1978) *Phenomenology and Sociology*. Harmondsworth: Penguin.

Luhmann, N. (1982) *The Differentiation of Society*. New York: Columbia University Press.

Luhmann, N. (1989) *Ecological Communication*. Cambridge: Polity Press.

Lukes, S. (1973) 'Methodological individualism reconsidered', in A. Ryan (ed.), *The Philosophy of Social Explanation*. London: Oxford University Press.

Lukes, S. (1974) *Power: A Radical View*. London: Macmillan.

Lyon, D. (1994) *Postmodernity*. Milton Keynes: Open University Press.

Lyotard, J.F. (1986) *The Postmodern Condition: A Report on Knowledge*, trans. G. Bennington and B. Massumi. Manchester: Manchester University Press.

Lyotard, J.F. and Thebaud, J.L. (1985) *Just Gaming*. Manchester: Manchester University Press.

MacIver, R.M. and Page, C. ([1950] 1964) *Society: An Introductory Analysis*. London: Macmillan.

Mann, M. (1986) *The Sources of Social Power*: Vol. 1. Cambridge: Cambridge University Press.

Mannheim, K. (1950) *Diagnosis of Our Time*. London: Routledge.

Marsh, D. (1995) 'Explaining "Thatcherite" policies: beyond uni-dimensional explanation', *Political Studies*, 43 (4): 595–613.

Marsh, D. (ed.) (1998) *Comparing Policy Networks*. Buckingham: Open University Press.

Marsh, D. and Rhodes, R.A.W. (eds) (1992) *Policy Networks in British Government*. Oxford: Oxford University Press.

Marsh, D. and Smith, M. (2000) 'Understanding policy networks: towards a dialectical approach', *Political Studies*, 48 (1): 4–21.

Marsh, D. and Stoker, G. (eds) (1995a) *Theory and Methods in Political Science*. London: Macmillan.

Marsh, D. and Stoker, G. (1995b) 'Conclusion', in D. Marsh and G. Stoker (eds), *Theory and Methods in Political Science*. London: Macmillan.

Martino, J. (1993) 'Review', *British Journal of Sociology*, 44 (1): 177–9.

Marx, K. (1954) *Capital*, Vol. 1: *A Critical Analysis of Capitalist Production*. London: Lawrence and Wishart.

Marx, K. (1957) *Capital*, Vol. 2: *A Critique of Political Economy*. Moscow: Foreign Languages Publications.

Marx, K. (1964) *The Economic and Philosophical Manuscripts of 1844*. London: Lawrence and Wishart.

Marx, K. (1973) *Grundrisse: Foundations of the Critique of Political Economy*. Harmondsworth: Penguin.

Marx, K. (1984) *Capital*, Vol. 3: *Capitalist Production as a Whole*. Chicago: Charles H. Kerr.

May, C. (1993) 'Review', *Sociology*, 27 (3): 558.

May, T. (1996) *Situating Social Theory*. Buckingham: Open University Press.

Mayntz, R. (1993) 'Governing failures and the problem of governability: some comments on a theoretical paradigm', in J. Kooiman (ed.), *Modern Governance: New Government–Society Interactions*. London: Sage.

McLennan, G. (1995) 'After postmodernism: back to sociological theory?', *Sociology*, 29 (1): 117–32.

McNay, L. (1992) *Foucault and Feminism: Power, Gender and the Self*. Cambridge: Polity Press.

McNay, L. (2000) *Gender and Agency: Reconfiguring the Subject in Feminist and Social Theory*. Cambridge: Polity Press.

Mead, G.H. (1967) *Mind, Self and Society*. Chicago: University of Chicago Press.

Meethan, K. and Thompson, C. (1993) 'Politics, locality and resources: negotiating a community care scheme', *Policy and Politics*, 21 (3): 195–205.

Meltzer, B., Petras, J. and Reynolds, L.T. (1975) *Symbolic Interactionism: Genesis, Varieties and Criticism*. London: Routledge.

Melucci, A. (1984) *Altri Codici: Aree di movimento nella metropoli*. Bologne: II Mulino.

Mennell, S. (1992) *Norbert Elias: An Introduction*. Oxford: Blackwell.

Meny, Y., Muller, P. and Quermonne, J.-L. (1996) 'Introduction', in Y. Meny, P. Muller and J.L. Quermonne (eds), *Adjusting to Europe: The Impact of the European Union on National Institutions and Policies*. London: Routledge.

Merton, R.K. (1968) *Social Theory and Social Structure* (enlarged edition). New York: Free Press.

Merton, R.K. (1973) 'Insiders and outsiders: a chapter in the sociology of knowledge', *American Journal of Sociology*, 78 (4): 9–47.

Miller, P. and Rose, N. (1988) 'The Tavistock programme: the government of subjectivity and social life', *Sociology*, 22 (2): 171–92.

Miller, P. and Rose, N. (1993) 'Governing economic life', in M. Gane and T. Johnson (eds), *Foucault's New Domains*. London: Routledge.

Miller, W.W. (1993) 'Durkheim's Montesquieu', *British Journal of Sociology*, 44 (4): 693–712.

Montesquieu, C. de S. ([1734] 1965) *Considerations on the Greatness of the Romans and their Decline*. New York: Free Press.

Morgan, D. (1975) 'British social theory', *Sociology*, 9 (1): 119–24.

Morgan, D. and Stanley, L. (1993) 'Debates in sociology: contextual and procedural dynamics in the production of a discipline' in D. Morgan and L. Stanley (eds), *Debates in Sociology*. Manchester: Manchester University Press.

Mouzelis, N. (1989) 'Restructuring structuration theory', *The Sociological Review*, 37 (4): 613–35.

Mouzelis, N. (1991) *Back to Sociological Theory; The Construction of Social Order*. London: Macmillan.

Mouzelis, N. (1993a) 'The poverty of sociological theory', *Sociology*, 27 (4): 675–95.

Mouzelis, N. (1993b) 'Comparing the Durkheimian and Marxist traditions', *The Sociological Review*, 41 (3): 572–82.

Mouzelis, N. (1994) 'In defence of "grand" historical sociology', *British Journal of Sociology*, 45 (1): 31–6.

Mouzelis, N. (1995) *Sociological Theory: What Went Wrong? Diagnosis and Remedies*. London: Routledge.

Mouzelis, N. (1997) 'Social and system integration: Lockwood, Habermas, Giddens', *Sociology*, 31 (1): 111–19.

Mouzelis, N. (2000) 'The subjectivist-objectivist divide: against transcendence', *Sociology*, 34 (4): 741–62.

Mullen, E.J. and Dumpson, J.R. (eds) (1972) *Evaluation of Social Intervention*. San Francisco: Jossey-Bass.

Munch, R. and Smelser, N. (1987) 'Relating the micro and macro', in J. Alexander, B. Giesen, R. Munch, and N. Smelser (eds), *The Micro-Macro Link*. Berkeley, CA: University of California Press.

Munck, G. (1995) 'Actor formation, social co-ordination, and political strategy: some conceptual problems in the study of social movements', *Sociology*, 29 (4): 667–85.

Nash, K. (2000) *Contemporary Political Sociology: Globalization, Politics and Power*. Oxford: Blackwell.

Nelson, B. and Stubb, A.C.-G. (eds) (1998) *The European Union: Readings on the Theory and Practice of European Integration*. London: Macmillan.

Nicholson, L. (1992) 'On the postmodern barricades: feminism, politics and theory', in S. Seidman and D. Wagner (eds), *Postmodernism and Social Theory*. Cambridge: Blackwell.

Nicholson, L. and Seidman, S. (1995) 'Introduction', in L. Nicholson and S. Seidman (eds), *Social Postmodernism: Beyond Identity Politics*. Cambridge: Cambridge University Press.

Nugent, N. (1999) *The Government and Politics of the European Union*. London: Macmillan.

Offe, C. (1984) *Contradictions of the Welfare State*. London: Hutchinson.

Offe, C. (1985) *Disorganized Capitalism*. Cambridge: Polity Press.

O'Mally, P., Weir, L. and Shearing, C. (1997) 'Governmentality, criticism, politics', *Economy and Society*, 25 (4): 501–17.

Outhwaite, W. (1983) 'Review', *Network No. 25*. London: British Sociological Association.

Outhwaite, W. (2000a) 'Classical and modern social theory', in H. Andersen, and L.B. Kaspersen (eds), *Classical and Modern Social Theory*. Oxford: Blackwell.

Outhwaite, W. (2000b) 'The philosophy of social science', in B.S. Turner (ed.), *The Blackwell Companion to Social Theory*. Oxford: Blackwell.

Padgett, J.F. and Ansell, C.K. (1989) 'From faction to party in Renaissance Florence', Department of Political Science, University of Chicago, September 1989, p. 33, cited in Harrison White (1992), *Identity and Control: A Structural Theory of Social Action*. Princeton, NJ: Princeton University Press. p. 292.

Pahl, R.E. and Wallace, C.D. (1985) 'Household work strategies in an economic recession', in N. Redclift and E. Mingione (eds), *Beyond Employment: Household, Gender, and Subsistence*. Oxford: Blackwell.

Parker, M. (1992) 'Post-modern organizations or postmodern organization theory?', *Organization Studies*, 13 (1): 1–17.

Parsons, T. (1966) *Societies: Evolutionary and Comparative Perspectives*. Englewood Cliffs, NJ: Prentice Hall.

Parsons, T. (1967) *Sociological Theory and Modern Society*. New York: Free Press.

Parsons, T. (1971) *The System of Modern Societies*. Englewood Cliffs, NJ: Prentice Hall.

Parsons, W. (1995) *Public Policy: An Introduction to the Theory and Practice of Policy Analysis*. Aldershot: Edward Elgar.

Peet, R. (1998) *Modern Geographical Thought*. Oxford: Blackwell.

Peters, G. (1994) 'Agenda-setting in the European Community', *Journal of European Public Policy*, 1 (1): 9–26.

Peterson, J. and Bomberg, E. (1999) *Decision-Making in the European Union*. London: Macmillan.

Pettit, P. (2001) *A Theory of Freedom: From the Psychology to the Politics of Agency*. Cambridge: Polity Press.

Pickering, A. (2001) *The Mangle of Practice: Time, Agency, and Science*. Chicago: University of Chicago Press.

Pierre, J. and Peters, B.G. (2000) *Governance, Politics and the State*. London: Macmillan.

Pierre, J. and Stoker, G. (2000) 'Towards multi-level governance', in P. Dunleavy, A. Gamble, I. Holliday and G. Peele (eds), *Developments in British Politics*. London: Macmillan.

Pierson, C. (1998) 'The path to European integration', in B.F. Nelsen and A.C.-G. Stubb (eds), *The European Union: Readings in the Theory and Practice of European Integration*, London: Macmillan.

Pollack, M.A. (1994) 'Creeping competence: the expanding agenda of the European Community', *Journal of Public Policy*, 14 (2): 95–145.

Popper, K. (1957) *The Poverty of Historicism*. London: Routledge.

Popper, K. (1962) *The Open Society and Its Enemies*. London: Routledge.

Poulantzas, N. (1973) *Political Power and Social Classes*. London: New Left Books.

Reed, M. (1985) *Redirections in Organizational Analysis*. London and New York: Tavistock.

Reed, M. (1992) *The Sociology of Organizations: Themes, Perspectives and Prospects*. Hemel Hempstead: Harvester.

Rex, J. (1988) 'The role of class analysis in the study of race relations', in J. Rex and D. Mason (eds), *Theories of Race and Ethnic Relations*. Cambridge: Cambridge University Press.

Rhodes, R.A.W. (1996) 'The new governance: governing without government', *Political Studies*, 44 (4): 652–67.

Rhodes, R.A.W. (1997) *Understanding Governance: Policy Networks, Governance, Reflexivity and Accountability*. Buckingham: Open University Press.

Richards, D. and Smith, M.J. (2002) *Governance and Public Policy in the UK*. Oxford: Oxford University Press.

Richardson, J. (1996) 'Policy-making in the EU: interests, ideas, and garbage cans of primeval soup', in J. Richardson (ed.), *European Union: Power and Policy Making*. London: Routledge.

Richardson, J. and Lindley, R. (1994) 'Editorial', *Journal of European Public Policy*, 1 (1): 1–7.

Ritzer, G. (1990) 'Micro-macro linkages in sociology; applying a metatheoretical tool', in G. Ritzer (ed.), *Frontiers of Social Theory; The New Syntheses*. New York: Columbia University Press.

Ritzer, G. (1992) 'Metatheorising in sociology: explaining the coming of age', in G. Ritzer (ed.), *Metatheorizing*. London: Sage.

Ritzer, G. (2000) *Modern Sociological Theory*. New York: McGraw-Hill.

Ritzer, G. (2001) *Explorations in Social Theory: From Metatheorizing to Rationalization*. London: Sage.

Rojek, C. and Turner, B. (2000) 'Decorative sociology: towards a critique of the cultural turn', *The Sociological Review*, 48 (4): 629–48.

Rootes, C.A. (1981) 'The dominant ideology thesis and its critics', *Sociology*, 15 (3): 436–44.

Rose, A. (ed.) (1972) *Human Behaviour and Social Processes: An Interactionist Approach*. London: Routledge.

Rose, D. (2001) 'Pass the salt: how language moves matter', in N. Lee and R. Munro (eds), *The Consumption of Mass*. Oxford: Blackwell.

Rose, G. (1988) 'The postmodern complicity', *Theory, Culture and Society*, 5 (2/3): 257–71.

Rose, N. and Miller, P. (1992) 'Political power beyond the state: problematics of government', *British Journal of Sociology*, 43 (2): 173–205.

Rosenthal, N., Fingrutd, M., Ethier, M., Karant, R. and McDonald, D. (1985) 'Social movements and network analysis: a case study of nineteenth-century women's reform in New York State', *American Journal of Sociology*, 90: 1022–54.

Roth, G. and Schluchter, W. (1979) *Max Weber's Vision of History, Ethics and Methods*. Berkeley, CA: University of California Press.

Rubinstein, D. (1986) 'The concept of structure in sociology', in M. Wardell and S. Turner (eds), *Sociological Theory in Transition*. London: Allen and Unwin.

Rumford, C. (2002) *The European Union: A Political Sociology*. Oxford: Blackwell.

Russett, B. and Starr, H. (1996) *World Politics: The Menu for Choice*. New York: Freeman and Company.

Rustin, M. (1993) 'Ethnomethodology', in D. Morgan and L. Stanley (eds), *Debates in Sociology*. Manchester: Manchester University Press.

Ryle, G. and Findlay, J. (1972) 'Use, usage and meaning', in Open University Language and Learning Course Team, *Language in Education*. London: Routledge and Open University Press.

Sanderson, I. (1999) 'Participation and democratic renewal: from "instrumental" to "communicative" rationality', *Policy and Politics*, 27 (3): 325–41.

Saunders, P. (1989) 'Space, urbanism and the created environment', in D. Held and J.B. Thompson (eds), *Social Theories of Modern Societies: Anthony Giddens and his Critics*. Cambridge: Cambridge University Press.

Saussure, F. de ([1916] 1974) *Course in General Linguistics* trans. W. Baskin. London: Collins.

Sayer, A. (1992) *Method in Social Science: A Realist Approach*. London: Routledge.

Sayer, A. (1997) 'Essentialism, social constructivism, and beyond', *The Sociological Review*, 45 (3): 453–87.

Schmidt, S. (1996) 'Sterile debate and dubious generalizations: European integration theory tested by telecommunications and electricity', *Journal of Public Policy*, 16 (3): 233–71.

Scholes, R. (1974) *Structuralism in Literature*. New Haven, CT: Yale University Press.

Scholte, J. (2000) *Globalization*. London: Macmillan.

Schutz, A. (1962) 'Symbol, reality and society', in M. Natanson (ed.), *Collected Papers*. Vol. 1: *The Problem of Social Reality*. The Hague: Martinus Nijhoff.

Schutz, A. (1972) *The Phenomenology of the Social World*. London: Heinemann.

Schwartz, D. (1973) 'The invocation of legal norms; an empirical investigation of Durkheim and Weber', *American Sociological Review*, 38 (2): 340–54.

Scott, A. (1990) *Ideology and the New Social Movements*. London: Unwin Hyman.

Scott, J. (1988) 'Trend report: Social research analysis', *Sociology*, 22 (1): 109–27.

Scott, J. (1995) *Sociological Theory: Contemporary Debates*. Aldershot: Edward Elgar.

Seidman, S. (1992) 'Postmodern social theory as narrative with a moral intent', in S. Seidman and D. Wagner (eds), *Postmodernism and Social Theory*. Oxford: Blackwell.

Seidman, S. (1994) *Contested Knowledge: Social Theory in the Postmodern Era*. Oxford: Blackwell.

Sharp, R. (1980) *Knowledge, Ideology and the Politics of Schooling: Towards a Marxist Analysis of Schooling*. London: Routledge.

Sharrock, W., Hughes, J. and Martin, P. (2003) *Understanding Modern Sociology*. London: Sage.

Shilling, C. (2001) 'Embodiment, experience and theory: in defence of the sociological tradition', *The Sociological Review*, 49 (3): 327–44.

Sibeon, R. (1997) *Sociology and Policy Analysis: The New Sociology of Public Policy*. London: Kogan Page and Tudor.

Sibeon, R. (1999a) 'Anti-reductionist sociology', *Sociology*, 33 (2): 317–34.

Sibeon, R. (1999b) 'Governance and the postnational policy process', in A. Brah, M. Hickman and M. Mac an Ghaill (eds), *Global Futures: Migration, Environment and Globalization*. London: Macmillan.

Sibeon, R. (1999c) 'Power and social action beyond the state', in J. Chriss (ed.), *The Therapeutic State*. New York: Aldine de Gruyter.

Sibeon, R. (2000) 'Governance and the policy process in contemporary Europe', *Public Management: An International Journal of Research and Theory* (special issue on Governance), 2 (3): 307–27.

Sibeon, R. (2001) 'Governance in Europe: concepts, themes and processes', paper presented at the Forli International Conference on Local Development, University of Bologne, Forli, Italy, 29–31 March.

Sica, A. (ed.) (1998) *What Is Social Theory? The Philosophical Debates*. Oxford: Blackwell.

Simmel, G. (1971) *On Individuality and Social Forms: Selected Writings*. Chicago: University of Chicago Press.

Skocpol, T. (1979) *States and Social Revolutions: A Comparative Analysis of France, Russia and China*. Cambridge: Cambridge University Press.

Skocpol, T. (ed.) (1984) *Vision and Method in Historical Sociology*. Cambridge: Cambridge University Press.

Smart, B. (1990) 'On the disorder of things: sociology, postmodernity and the end of the social', *Sociology*, 24 (3): 397–416.

Smart, B. (1991) 'Modernity, postmodernity and the present', in B.S. Turner (ed.), *Theories of Modernity and Postmodernity*. London: Sage.

Smart, B. (1992) *Modern Conditions, Postmodern Controversies*. London: Routledge.

Smith, M. (1993) 'Changing sociological perspectives on chance', *Sociology*, 27 (3): 513–31.

Smith, M.J. (1993) *Pressure, Power and Policy: State Autonomy and Policy Networks in Britain and the United States*. London: Harvester Wheatsheaf.

Smith, M.P. (2001) *Transnational Urbanism: Locating Globalization*. Oxford: Blackwell.

Smith, P. (2001) *Cultural Theory: An Introduction*. Oxford: Blackwell.

Soja, E. (1989) *Postmodern Geographies: The Reassertion of Space in Critical Theory*. London: Verso.

Spillman, L. (ed.) (2002) *Cultural Sociology*. Oxford: Blackwell.

Spivak, G.C. (1990) Remarks taken from an interview, cited in P.T. Clough (1994) *Feminist Thought*. Oxford: Blackwell, p. 116.

Star, S.L. (1991) 'Power, technologies and the phenomenology of conventions: on being allergic to onions', in J. Law (ed.), *A Sociology of Monsters: Essays on Power, Technology and Domination*. London: Routledge.

Star, S.L. (ed.) (1995) *The Cultures of Computing*. Oxford: Blackwell.

Stedman Jones, S. (2001) *Durkheim Reconsidered*. Cambridge: Polity Press.

Stenson, K. (1993) 'Social work discourse and the social work interview', *Economy and Society*, 22 (1): 42–76.

Stewart, M. (1994) 'Between Whitehall and town hall: the realignment of urban regeneration policy in England', *Policy and Politics*, 22 (2): 133–45.

Stoker, G. (ed.) (2000a) *The New Politics of British Local Governance*. London: Macmillan.

Stoker, G. (ed.) (2000b) *The New Management of British Local Governance*. London: Macmillan.

Stones, R. (1996) *Sociological Reasoning: Towards a Past-Modern Sociology*. London: Macmillan.

Stones, R. (1998) 'Tolerence, plurality and creative synthesis in sociological thought', in R. Stones (ed.), *Key Sociological Thinkers*. London: Macmillan.

Strati, A. (2000) *Theory and Method in Organization Studies*. London: Sage.

Strinati, D. (1993) 'Review', *The Sociological Review*, 41 (3): 593–5.

Swingewood, A. (2000) *A Short History of Sociological Thought*. London: Macmillan.

Sztompka, P. (1991) *Society in Action: The Theory of Social Becoming*. Cambridge: Polity Press.

Sztompka, P. (1993) *The Sociology of Social Change*. Oxford: Blackwell.

Thomason, B.C. (1982) *Making Sense of Reification: Alfred Schutz and Constructionist Theory*. London: Macmillan.

Thompson, G., Francis, J. and Mitchell, J. (eds) (1991) *Markets, Hierarchies and Networks: The Co-ordination of Social Life*. London: Sage.

Thompson, J.B. (1995) *The Media and Modernity: A Social Theory of the Media*. Cambridge: Polity Press.

Thompson, N. (2000) *Theory and Practice in Human Services*. Buckingham: Open University Press.

Thrift, N. (1985) 'Bear and mouse or bear and tree? Anthony Giddens's reconstitution of social theory', *Sociology*, 19 (4): 609–23.

Thrift, N. (1994) 'A phantom state? International money, electronic networks and global cities', paper presented at the Centre for Social Theory and Comparative History (June), UCLA, Los Angeles.

Tilley, C. (1984) *Big Structures, Large Processes, Huge Comparisons*. New York: Russell Sage Foundation.

Tilley, C. (1994) 'Social movements as historically specific clusters of political performances', *Berkeley Journal of Sociology*, 38 (38): 1–30.

Torfing, J. (1999) *New Theories of Discourse: Laclau, Mouffe and Žižek*. Oxford: Blackwell.

Touraine, A. (1981) *The Voice and the Eye: An Analysis of Social Movements*. Cambridge: Cambridge University Press.

Touraine, A. (1995) *Critique of Modernity*. Oxford: Blackwell.

Turner, B.S. (1981) *For Weber: Essays on the Sociology of Fate*. London: Routledge.

Turner, B.S. (1990) 'Conclusion: peroration on ideology', in N. Abercrombie, S. Hill and B.S. Turner (eds), *Dominant Ideologies*. London: Unwin Hyman.

Turner, B.S. (1992a) *Max Weber: From History to Modernity*. London: Routledge.

Turner, B.S. (1992b) 'Review', *The British Journal of Sociology*, 43 (1): 141–2.

Turner, B.S. (1994) 'Review', *The Sociological Review*, 42 (4): 786–8.

Turner, B.S. (1999) *Classical Sociology*. London: Sage.

Turner, B.S. (2000a) 'Preface', in B.S. Turner (ed.), *The Blackwell Companion to Social Theory*. Oxford: Blackwell.

Turner, B.S. (2000b) 'Introduction', in B.S. Turner (ed.), *The Blackwell Companion to Social Theory*. Oxford: Blackwell.

Turner, B.S. and O'Neill, J. (2001) 'Introduction: the fragmentation of sociology', *Journal of Classical Theory*, 1 (1): 5–12.

Turner, B.S. and Rojek, C. (2001) *Society and Culture: Principles of Scarcity and Solidarity*. London: Sage.

Turner, J. (1988) *A Theory of Social Interaction*. Cambridge: Polity Press.

Turner, J. (1991) *The Structure of Sociological Theory*, 5th edn. Belmont, CA: Wandsworth.

Ungar, S. (2001) 'Moral panic versus the risk society: the implications of the changing sites of social anxiety', *The British Journal of Sociology*, 52 (2): 271–91.

Unger, R.M. (1987a) *Social Theory: Its Situation and its Task*. Cambridge: Cambridge University Press.

Unger, R.M. (1987b) *False Necessity: Anti-Necessitarian Social Theory in the Service of Radical Democracy*. Cambridge: Cambridge University Press.

Unger, R.M. (1987c) *Plasticity into Power*. Cambridge: Cambridge University Press.

Unger, R.M. (1997) *Politics: The Central Texts* (edited and introduced by Zhiyuan Cui). London: Verso.

Urry, J. (1991) 'Time and space in Giddens's social theory', in C. Bryant and D. Jary (eds), *Giddens's Theory of Structuration: A Critical Appreciation*. London: Routledge.

Urry, J. (1995) *Consuming Places*. London and New York: Routledge.

Urry, J. (2000a) 'A sociology of time and space', in B.S. Turner (ed.), *The Blackwell Companion to Social Theory*. Oxford: Blackwell.

Urry, J. (2000b) 'Mobile sociology', *British Journal of Sociology*, 51 (1): 185–203.

Urry, J. (2000c) *Sociology Beyond Societies: Mobilities for the Twenty-First Century*. London: Routledge.

Vincent, A. (1992) *Modern Political Ideologies*. Oxford: Blackwell.

Wallace, H. and Wallace, W. (eds) (1996) *Policy-Making in the European Union*. Oxford: Oxford University Press.

Wallace, R.E. and Wolf, A. (1999) *Contemporary Sociological Theory: Expanding the Classical Tradition*. Englewood Cliffs, NJ: Prentice Hall.

Wallace, W. (1992) 'Metatheory, conceptual standardization, and the future of sociology', in G. Ritzer (ed.), *Metatheorising*. London: Sage.

Webb, A. (1991) 'Co-ordination: a problem of public sector management', *Policy and Politics*, 19 (4): 229–41.

Weber, M. (1932) *The Protestant Ethic and the Spirit of Capitalism*. London: Allen and Unwin.

Weber, M. (1947) *The Theory of Social and Economic Organization*. New York: Oxford University Press.

Weber, M. (1949) *The Methodology of the Social Sciences*. New York: Free Press.

Weber, M. (1978) *Economy and Society: An Outline of Interpretive Sociology*. New York: Bedminster.

Webster, A. (1993) 'Review', *The Sociological Review*, 41 (1): 156–9.

Weiss, C.H. (1986) 'The many meanings of research utilization', in M. Bulmer, K.G. Banting, S.S. Blume, M. Carley and C.H. Weiss (eds), *Social Science and Social Policy*. London: Allen and Unwin.

Wellman, B. (1983) 'Network analysis: some basic principles', in R. Collins (ed.), *Sociological Theory – 1983*. San Francisco: Jossey-Bass.

Werlen, B. (1993) *Society, Action and Space: An Alternative Human Geography*. London: Routledge.

White, Harrison C. (1992) *Identity and Control: A Structural Theory of Social Action*. Princeton, NJ: Princeton University Press.

Whorf, B.L. (1956) *Language., Thought and Reality*. New York: MIT Press and John Wiley.

Wilsford, D. (1994) 'Path dependency, or why history makes it difficult but not impossible to reform health care systems in a big way', *Journal of Public Policy*, 14 (3): 251–83.

Wuthnow, R., Hunter, J.D., Bergesen, A. and Kurzweil, E. (1984) *Cultural Analysis: The Work of Peter L. Berger, Mary Douglas, Michel Foucault and Jürgen Habermas*. London: Routledge.

Yeatman, A. (1994) *Postmodern Revisionings of the Political*. London: Routledge.

Index

activities-society linkages 24, 48, 62, 63, 64, 68, 75, 88, 114–115, 144
activity-dependence of society 61, 63, 66, 75, 99–100, 114–115, 125
actors/agents 5, 118, 147, 148, 189
  definition of 5, 53, 89, 118, 119, 160
  types of 5, 119
  examples of 5–6, 119
  minimal concept of actor 53, 121
actor network theory 8, 65, 127, 135, 142, 162, 183
agency 8, 18, 35, 118–123, 146
  and reification 4–6, 72, 88, 149–50
  and 'materialization of agency' 149–50
agency–structure vii, 8, 40, 45–49, 75, 98, 153, 169
  as distinct from micro–macro 45, 55, 121, 173
  and social chance 128, 129–31, 178
agency-in-structure 54, 124, 159
Alexander, J. 14, 25, 27, 61, 174
Althusser, L. 3, 36, 84, 127
Archer, M. 8, 15, 26, 46, 47, 53, 63, 75, 78, 86, 97–101, 114, 125, 140–143, 159, 168, 171, 192, 200

Baudrillard, J. 1, 15
Berger, P. 60–64, 66, 68, 75, 82, 84, 87, 93, 94, 115, 182, 190, 191
Bourdieu, P. 41, 53, 155, 182

'cardinal sins' of theoretical and methodological reasoning 1–11, 14, 123, 162, 166, 178, 182, 193, 197–9

causal responsibility 128, 146–47, 148
classical theory 36–38, 202–3
concepts vii, 76, 195
  and social reality 191, 200–03
  re-working of concepts 198–9
conditions-of-action (see social conditions)
conditions of existence (see system needs)
conflation 42, 45, 55, 107
  downwards conflation 42, 64, 97, 181
  upwards conflation 64, 97–98, 180, 181–2
  central conflation 49, 63, 72, 98–99, 115, 181
contingency (see social chance)
co-presence relations 42, 50
critical realism 148
critical social theory 6
cultural sociology 192
cultural studies 120, 192–93
cumulative orientation 26–30, 35, 198, 199

'decentring the subject' 72, 120–21
determinism (see social determinism)
diachronic linkages 78, 87, 130, 178
dialectics 19, 62, 64, 87, 88, 130, 143
  and agency–structure 19, 62, 64, 87, 144
  and the relation of discourses to social contexts 18–19, 25, 32, 81–84
discourses 18, 24, 39, 69, 70, 83, 134, 174, 199
  and society 18–19, 24, 30, 32, 39, 81–84
discourse theory 40, 120
dispositional dimension of social action 101
domains (see social domains)
dualism 26, 48, 64, 98

duality 13, 48, 64, 85
'dualism versus duality' debate 26, 48–50, 72, 73–76, 94, 99, 102–106, 107, 116, 121, 125, 143, 171, 201
Durkheim, E. 7, 9, 29, 36–7, 62, 64, 77, 154, 174, 187, 194

Elias, N. 13, 27, 28, 48, 64–69, 72, 75, 154, 191
emergence 37, 46, 58, 64, 65–66, 68, 76–79, 83, 100, 111, 115, 120, 161, 181, 182
epistemology 18, 25, 26, 31, 69, 188, 200, 202
epistemological pluralism 188
essentialism vii, 3, 9, 54, 138, 178, 197
ethnomethodology 81

false consciousness 139
feminism 10, 14
figurations 29, 65, 68
figurational-institutional distinction 68, 79, 124, 159, 173, 178, 201
forms of thought 76, 83, 140
Foucault, M. 13, 48, 69–73, 75, 132–134, 152, 165, 182, 191
foundations 21–26
functions 10
functionalist analysis 10
functional teleology vii, 6–7, 58, 72, 73, 89, 138, 197

Giddens, A. 13, 23, 28, 45, 47, 50–52, 53, 63, 68, 72, 73–76, 82, 85, 94, 99, 106, 116, 155, 162, 182, 191, 201
globalization 2, 4, 23, 157, 163, 170, 175
governance viii, 52, 67, 118, 154, 162, 165, 167, 177, 182, 196–7
grand theory 3, 9, 14, 67, 69, 70, 71, 106

Habermas, J. 40–41, 53, 80, 151, 160, 182, 201
Hindess, B. 5, 95, 119, 121, 123, 139, 149
hypercontextualism 16, 22, 23

ideal-type 174–175
idealism 32, 36
idiographic knowledge 127
indeterminacy (see social chance)
interests 8, 115, 138–144, 198
    real/objective interests 115, 132, 134, 138–140
    positional interests 115, 140–144
    relational dimension of 142

interdisciplinary orientation viii, 20, 21, 199
intersubjectivity 18, 41, 43, 44
institutions (see social institutions)

language and society 39
Layder, D. 8, 9, 25, 33, 49, 53, 68, 77, 84, 94, 106–111, 155, 171, 173, 176, 184, 187–90, 192, 194, 200, 201
levels of analysis 49, 77, 78, 80, 138, 158, 177
levels of society/of social process 77, 78, 125, 128, 138, 158, 177
Lyotard, J-F 15, 23, 140, 151

macro 35, 36, 41, 42, 53, 54, 110, 173, 178–81
Marxism 14, 15, 36, 84
materials 159, 172
material diffusion 8,159, 162–166, 169, 183, 185, 186, 189, 193–4
materialism 32, 36
metatheory and metaconcepts 8, 12–15, 25, 33, 36, 153, 169, 195, 200
methodology and metatheory 25–26, 31, 195, 200, 202
methodological collectivism 58–59, 64, 65, 125, 161, 165
methodological individualism 38, 58–59, 64, 65, 77, 100, 124, 161, 165, 180, 181
methodological situationalism 114, 124, 174, 180–81, 182
mezo 42, 86, 124, 173, 175–78
micro 35, 42–44, 53, 54, 173, 174–75, 192
micro–macro vii, 8, 13, 45, 46–48, 50–53, 54, 61, 77, 80, 114–115, 153, 169, 172–181, 192
    and methodology 43–44, 49, 54–5, 158, 181–90
    as vertical and lateral dimensions of social reality 155, 158, 171–2, 173, 176, 177, 181–90, 183–4, 185–7
morphogenetic social theory 26, 97
Mouzelis, N. 8, 10, 25, 35, 45, 47, 50–53, 63, 68, 75, 77, 79–81, 83, 86, 99, 101–106, 115, 121, 147, 171, 192, 193, 201

non-actors 121, 148
    definition of 122, 148
    examples of 72, 122–123, 146, 149–50

objective dimension of the social 36, 37, 62, 84, 93–94, 155, 184, 187, 188–9
ontology 13, 30, 46, 188

ontological closure 31, 166, 195–97
ontological depth 37, 77–78, 107, 111,
    171–72, 177, 181
ontological flexibility 3, 14, 23, 31,
    110, 123, 151, 159, 166, 197

paradigmatic dimension of society 102, 116
    paradigmatic dualism 94, 103, 104
    paradigmatic duality 103, 104
Parsons, T. 9, 14, 62–3, 64, 69
path-dependency (see recursion)
perspectivism 168
phenomenology 44, 58, 61, 62, 84, 141
policy analysis vii, 42, 67, 82, 89, 118,
    130, 134, 137, 165, 182, 196–7
policy networks 67, 78, 89, 152, 160,
    161, 168. 176, 177
political science 44, 67, 78, 89, 118,
    127, 176
positional dimension of social action 101
positional interests (see interests)
postmodern politics 151–152
postmodern theory 1, 14, 15–19, 21–23,
    24, 29, 32, 72, 151–152, 157, 178
postmodern society 15, 17, 21, 157
postnational governance 21, 42, 78, 90,
    169, 196–7
poststructuralism 24, 39–40, 72, 82, 120
power 8, 52, 65, 70, 131–138
    agentic 65, 131
    relational 52, 65, 70, 133, 162
    systemic 52, 70, 131, 135–136
    and Foucault 52, 65, 132–134
    as multi-dimensional 136–137, 184

realism 23, 24, 32, 40, 83, 84, 99, 159, 188
recursion 88–90, 125, 160, 161, 199
reductionism vii, 2–3, 39, 138, 161,
    165, 178, 188, 197
    compounded reductionism 3, 165
    deferred reductionism 3, 40
    examples of 3, 40, 58, 165, 188
reflexivity 27
reification vii, 4–6, 9, 28, 39, 41, 72, 79,
    88, 89, 122, 138, 149–50, 160, 197
relationism 133, 142, 152
relative autonomy 25, 36, 110, 129,
    171, 187, 198
relativism 15, 23, 25, 202

sensitizing theory 13–14, 33
situational-interactive dimension of
    social action 102

social chance 29, 36, 38, 67, 126–129,
    151, 153
social conditions (see social structure)
social- and system-integration distinction
    1, 41, 48, 50, 68, 73, 79–81, 124,
    159, 173
social determinism 16, 18, 19, 36, 39, 40, 72
social domains 58, 77
    social domain theory 58, 77, 106–111,
    155, 187–90
'social facts' 36–7, 77, 187, 194
social institutions 36
social networks 41, 65, 74, 88,
    158–162, 168
social ontology (see ontology)
social realism (see realism)
social relations 173, 192
    across time-space 88, 158–162, 192
social structure 35, 42, 53–54, 73–4, 103,
    111, 123–26, 148, 150, 151, 159,
    164, 168
    micro-structure 55–56, 193
    macro-structure 42, 55, 86, 124, 173,
    178, 193, 194
social systems (see social networks)
social theory 20–21, 31, 200
    and social sciences 20–21, 200
sociology as discipline 2, 24, 199
sociological theory 20, 22, 31
spatiality 110, 156–158, 169
strategic essentialism 10, 28, 152
strategic anti-essentialism 32, 152
structuralism 38–9, 71, 72, 74, 82, 120, 174
structural conditioning 98, 115, 140, 141
structural contradictions 84–88, 93, 198
'structural necessities' 86
structuration theory 14, 23, 28, 45, 48,
    73–76, 98, 103, 155
subjectivity 18
subjective dimension of the social 62,
    63, 84, 155, 184, 187, 188–9
substantive theories 12, 25
symbolic interactionism 43, 57, 82, 102
syntagmatic dimension of society 103, 116
    syntagmatic dualism 105
    syntagmatic duality 104
synthesis 8, 26–30, 73, 195
system needs 7, 11, 58, 73, 79

taxonomic collectivities 123, 138, 148
teleology (see also functional teleology)
    58, 72, 79, 141
theoretical contradictions 18, 19, 28

time–space vii, 8, 36, 110, 111, 134,
    155, 162, 173–74, 177, 183, 185
temporality 9, 110, 153–156
time-frames 110, 154, 155, 174, 185
transformation of materials 138, 163, 185
transmission of materials 138, 162–163,
    169, 185
translation sociology 142
transnational dimensions of the social 169

unintended consequences 63, 119, 126, 149

vertical and lateral dimensions of society
    37, 110, 138, 171–2, 173, 176,
    183–4, 185–87
    conceptual aspects 37, 110, 138,
        155, 171–72, 173, 177
    methodological implications 37,
        183–4, 185–7

Weber, M. 37–38, 126, 131, 151, 202